Cover *Jalal listens to the rose* cat.no.14

IMPERIAL IMAGES IN
Persian Painting
A Scottish Arts Council Exhibition

ROBERT HILLENBRAND

A Scottish Arts Council Exhibition

Scottish Arts Council Gallery
19 Charlotte Square, Edinburgh EH2 4DF
13th August-11th September 1977

Catalogue Design and Graphics:
Graham Duffy, Graphic Partners, Edinburgh
Printed by: Pillans and Wilson, Edinburgh
Exhibition Installation: Barry Mazur and Brian Griggs.
Typing; Bernadette Baigrie, Sally Schofield

ISBN 0 902989 42 1
© Scottish Arts Council LG

CONTENTS

COLOUR PLATES

ACKNOWLEDGEMENTS

The Scottish Arts Council would like to thank first of all Robert Hillenbrand for the research and the selection for the exhibition. We are especially grateful to him for the various and detailed aspects of this catalogue, in particular the introduction and catalogue entries, which he has prepared with such care and thoroughness.

The Scottish Arts Council would like to join Robert Hillenbrand in thanking the lenders to the exhibition, all of whom have shown exceptional generosity with both material and advice. Her Majesty the Queen, His Royal Highness the Aga Khan, Professor Brisch of the Museum für Islamische-kunst, Berlin; Boston Museum of Fine Arts, Boston; the British Library, London; the British Museum, London; the Chester Beatty Library and Gallery of Oriental Art, Dublin; Edinburgh University Library, Edinburgh; the Calouste Gulbenkian Foundation Museum, Lisbon; the Metropolitan Museum of Art, New York; the University Library, Uppsala; the Nationalbibliothek, Vienna; and the William Rockhill Nelson Gallery of Art, Kansas City, are among the innumerable individuals and institutions who have shown such generosity towards our exhibition. For their help, and to all those not mentioned here, we are indebted.

ROBERT BREEN
SCOTTISH ARTS COUNCIL

PREFACE

After the interest aroused by the recent Festival of Islam, the unique attractions of Persian art should need little introduction. But major exhibitions of Persian painting have been rather rare in Britain: only the three London exhibitions of 1931, 1951 and 1967 come to mind. It is perhaps salutary, therefore, to draw attention to the extraordinary wealth of material in this field preserved in British collections. Most of the items in the exhibition are in fact drawn from these sources. Many choice items have also come from abroad; the response from American museums has been particularly encouraging; I should like to take this opportunity of thanking most warmly the institutions and private collectors who by their generous loans have made this exhibition possible.

The primary aim of the exhibition is – as its title suggests – to explore the depiction of royalty in Persian book painting. Both the formal and informal aspects of court life are covered, and the central theme has been interpreted generously to include material on aspects of religion, daily life and myth. The secondary aim is to trace the development of the so-called "classical style" in Persian painting. Thus emphasis is laid on material from the Mongol and Timurid periods. A particular feature of the exhibition is the display of nineteen leaves from the celebrated "Demotte" *Shahnama,* arguably the most important illustrated version ever produced of the Persian national epic. A few words about the layout of the catalogue may be in order. The aim of the introduction is two-fold, one purpose is to explain some of the principles and conventions which underlie Persian pictures and which make them so different from Western painting. The other is to sketch, in a relatively connected way, the characteristics of the major schools of Persian painting and thus to clothe in some substance the identifications and attributions given in the catalogue entries. Lack of space in this section has precluded a survey of the political history of Iran between the 14th and 19th centuries, but the chronological table in the exhibition will give at least the essential dates and dynasties.

Similarly it has not proved possible to explore the imperial theme in this section. Instead, each of the eight subdivisions of the catalogue is prefaced by a short introduction which seeks to relate the miniatures of that section to the events and customs of court life. Such prefatory remarks are intended only to convey in general terms some of the flavour of royal life; they cannot of course claim to be equally relevant to both the Mongol court of the fourteenth century and that of the Qajars in the nineteenth.

I have deliberately broken with convention in using the catalogue entries partly to outline the stories which the paintings illustrate. After all, only a few visitors to the exhibition will already know these stories. I crave their indulgence. In the interests of the general public I have also dispensed with the scholarly transliteration of Islamic names.

It is a pleasure to acknowledge the manifold help that I have received in preparing the selection for the exhibition and its catalogue. My thanks go in the first instance to the Scottish Arts Council for inviting me to participate in this exhibition and for giving me every possible facility. I should like to single out Lesley Greene for her indefatigable enthusiasm and for her unstinting efforts to make the exhibition a success.

I owe a special debt of gratitude to Professor Ernst Grube and to Mr B.W. Robinson, not only for their numerous kindnessess but also for their various catalogues, which have been quite simply indispensable. If I do not cite their works in each instance, it is only because I have used them continually. Mr Reza Honari kindly identified the subjects of four of the minatures. I would also like to thank Dr Eleanor Sims most warmly for her extremely valuable comments on the introduction and many of the catalogue entries. How much work owes to my wife she knows better than anyone. My gratitude for her painstaking criticism of the text, and even more for the countless ways in which she has lightened my load over the past year, it is heartfelt.

ROBERT HILLENBRAND

Introduction

General Principles

Persian painting has its own laws. To understand and accept them is the quickest road to enjoyment of this subtle art. Happily, the laws vary surprisingly little over the centuries. They derive from one central fact – that Persian painting is mainly an art of book illustration – even though wall painting, now largely vanished, was also important. In medieval Islam this meant that the painter was doubly subordinate: first to the text itself, and then to the calligrapher who copied it. Calligraphy was the most highly prized of the arts of the book, but specialists in binding, leather tooling, papermaking, illuminating and gilding also pooled their skills with those of the painter to produce a volume. No firm evidence has been found to indicate that his status was higher than theirs. Thus circumstances obliged the painter to function not only as an individual but also as a member of a team. Small wonder, then, that in general a rather conservative approach prevailed. Committees do not encourage innovation.

This association with the luxury book had other implications for Persian painting. Inevitably it reduced the scale of the picture itself. Only a handful of Persian paintings measure more than a foot square. To us, though probably not to the artist, this might seem a restriction, and indeed the action habitually breaks out of the picture space into the margin. Nor is this device used timidly. In the bolder examples the action continues beyond the text itself, thereby forcing the viewer to treat the entire page as part of the picture. Countless ingenious variations were played on this theme.

Other artists accepted this small scale and turned it to their advantage. Rather than simplifying the content of a picture, they crowded it with minute detail and sumptuous colours. Thus was bred the fabled technique of Persian painting, which at its best has an unrivalled command of finish. For the most detailed work, brushes no thicker than a single hair were used, yet even the fine lines tend to be bold and sweeping rather than laborious. No doubt the practice of calligraphy was of decisive importance in this respect. Until the later 16th century deep, intense colours were the rule; these give medieval Persian painting its distinctive purity of tone. The artist's dependence on the written word also limited the range of subject matter available to him. Unlike the practice in western Europe, sacred texts and theological works – with some important exceptions such as histories of the prophets – were not illustrated. In this respect at least painters complied with the iconoclasm inherent in Islamic orthodoxy. Illustrations to poetic works (which, indeed, sometimes had an esoteric religious content) were therefore the staple of the Persian painter. Princely taste tended to poems above histories

or scientific treatises and among poems the *Shahnama* of Firdausi (died c. 1020) and the *Khamsa* of Nizami (died 1207) enjoyed pride of place. Most Persian miniatures illustrate one or the other of these poems. With its elements of heroic myth, its celebration of nature, romance and royal ceremonial, this poetry matched the idealised world of the paintings that illustrated it. But a major controlling factor was that certain incidents from these various works quickly established themselves as the favoured subjects for illustration. Moreover, these subjects developed a set iconography that discouraged further experiment. Thus the artist's field of choice, which was limited at the outset, quickly contracted still further. This is why Persian painting developed so delicate a sense of nuance. If the broad outlines of a composition were immutable, the challenge lay in wresting some new insight of colour, design or even emotion from the familiar components of the picture.

The close association between painting and book production had one final consequence for the Persian artist: it made him dependent on royal patronage. Only royalty, and in exceptional cases a wealthy noble, could afford to maintain the large atelier (*kitabkhana* – "book-house") needed to produce these luxury books. The painter became, in a sense, a civil servant. Textual evidence about the organisation of these ateliers is still sparse. But it is highly unlikely that the artist was free, until the later 16th century, to branch out on his own to choose his own subjects and patrons. His art was in no sense public. It was exercised for the private delectation of the ruler, and the book that his paintings decorated might not leave the royal library for generations. Indeed, the finest books were part of the royal treasury. Being eminently portable, they belonged with the liquid assets of the monarch. Thus to Western eyes Persian painting operated within a daunting set of constraints. These included the unavoidable small size of the pictures, their limited subject matter, almost exclusively royal patronage and the reduction of the painter to one specialist among the many concerned with book production. Yet within these constraints, which continued for centuries, a classic style of painting developed. Clearly Persian artists were not fettered by these various factors. Even in the later Safavid period, when the decline of the illustrated book and the expansion of patronage had emancipated the painter from the royal atelier and had broadened his subject matter, the old tradition lingered. Artists now painted

single leaves which were eagerly collected and bound into albums. Almost to the end they avoided easel painting of European style. Throughout its greatest periods Persian painting was virtually impervious to influences from the west – though influences from the Far East were significant. Bihzad, by common consent the outstanding Persian painter, was a contemporary of Leonardo da Vinci. Yet his masterpieces owe nothing to the ideals or discoveries of the High Renaissance. In judging Persian painting it is therefore imperative to lay aside some of the criteria by which Western painting is often assessed. It seems pointless to criticise the Persian artist for his inaccurate perspective or anatomy, and for his lack of modelling or proportion. Certainly his conventions blandly transgress every canon of Western representational art. But in all probability he would have rejected those canons outright as unfitting for his art, since they might well lead to a laborious and unimaginative approach. Thus praise and criticism must be directed at the Persian artist on his own terms.

What then are the conventions that govern Persian painting, at least until the later Safavid period? It is not are they so outré that it requires an difficult baldly to enumerate them. Nor expert to fathom them. But they can be applied with endless sublety and diversity. The key to the whole style lies in the creation of a dreamlike world delineated in a highly symbolic fashion. One or two plants denote a garden, the index finger in the mouth is the mark of some astonishing feat, a bare torso identifies a slave. Naturalism is deliberately denied by the flatness of handling and the lack of modelling. Indeed, natural forms become ornamental patterns. Little attempt is made to differentiate male and female faces; girls and youths alike display the moon-faced ideal of Persian poetry, with slanting eyes, arched eyebrows and a tiny mouth above a double chin. Single figures are often embedded in a background of one colour. These figures are toylike, and a deliberately unreal colour and lighting further distances the action. Sometimes, to a Western eye, the desire to tell a story conflicts with the perennial aim to make the setting of the scene as choice as possible. Thus convention permits a battle full of realistic, gory detail to be re-enacted against a flat backcloth of green or mauve rocks and a deep blue sky spangled with golden stars. Vegetation is treated with microscopic detail. Clumps of flowers, for example, are greatly enlarged so that their colours can be seen to best advantage, while ornamental trees grow in the most arid terrain. Indeed, in its most lyrical moods Persian painting depicts nature transfigured. A high horizon, ending against a golden sky, allows the artist to dispose a series of figures one above the other, leaving the viewer to understand that the figure nearest the horizon is furthest away.

Finally, convention makes the artist embed panels of script in the midst of his picture, or encourages minor sorties of the action from the picture space into the area beyond.

This, then, is the world of Persian painting in Western imagination. It is undeniably decorative, and for many that constitutes its principal charm. But to dismiss it as "mere" illustration would be seriously to underrate its aims and its achievements. Its great masterpieces, such as the Rashid al-Din codices, the Demotte *Shahnama* or the Gulbenkian *Anthology*, move us by their appeal to the emotions and by their relevance to the human condition. It is only part of their aim to delight the eye. They stimulate the mind and move the heart. These are intensely serious works that deserve to be taken seriously and to be analysed with care. Frequently they reveal that the artist has pondered over the text and has himself tried to express its subtleties and undertones in some symbolic way. But this is only one of several ways in which they challenge our perceptions. Deliberately they strike chords of pathos, rage, joy and tenderness. Often they proceed by understatement rather than hyperbole. Sometimes a detail of iconography borrowed from another scene is inserted for the sake of tragic irony. In the 14th and 15th centuries, the period which is subjected to special scrutiny in this exhibition, it was not yet the custom to explore the emotions through facial expression. But the best artists are adept at marshalling other means for the same purpose. Landscape and colour, pose and gesture all play their part. In later periods especially, these devices were supplemented by an expressive use of line. In short, when the Persian painter handles perennial human situations – which is often – he faces much the same problems as any other artist dealing with these themes. The fact that he is a book illustrator rather than a fresco or easel painter, and that he observes the conventions of his medium, is incidental. It should not tempt the critic to minimise his work as being "purely decorative".

The Major Schools of Persian Painting

13th and 14th Century Painting

In this exhibition a wide if not wholly representative sample of 14th century Persian painting has been assembled in an attempt to shed some light on this crucial formative period. The frontispiece from the *Kitab al-Aghani* (60) illustrates a rare survival of pre-Mongol painting as practised in 'Iraq – and probably also in Iran, to judge by the parallels on Saljuq pottery. It is an early example of the perenially close links between the painting of Iran and that of its neighbours. A few Turkish (94) and Indian (145) paintings have also been included in the exhibition to emphasise the decisive role played by Iran in the formation of these national schools. The surviving evidence indicates that the major school of Islamic painting in the 13th century was centred at Baghdad. The miniatures from the al-Biruni manuscript (129-130) represent a late survival of this style. Their figures display black brows, hook noses and staring eyes, elements that owe nothing to the moon face which was the popular Persian convention of the time. All the action is crammed into the frontal plane and the background is the natural colour of the paper itself. The spatial devices of later Persian painting are conspicuously absent. This Baghdad school produced little after 1258, when Mongol hordes from eastern Asia, having overrun and absorbed Persia, conquered 'Iraq. But elements of the style lingered and fused with Chinese features which entered Persian painting in the wake of the Mongol invasion.

These Chinese elements deserve a brief discussion. They are in the main confined to stylistic tags not keyed into any coherent understanding of the Chinese tradition. The understatement of Chinese painting, its ability to use blank space positively, escaped Persian artists. For them, people are the centre of interest. The sense of action is marked. Persian painting is not a contemplative art.

Given the fundamentally different approach of Persian painters, it is not surprising that the borrowed Chinese elements undergo strange transformations in their hands. In Chinese painting, the conventions used to depict clouds, mountains and water, for example, are in such harmony with the view of nature expressed by the artist that they do not seem artificial. In Persian painting, stripped of this context, they are. The Persian artist valued such elements chiefly for their pattern-making qualities. He sharpened their blurred outlines, adding his own decorative curlicues wherever possible, and substituted clashing colour contrasts for the muted monochrome tones of his original. Clouds which in Chinese painting would blend imperceptibly into the rest of the landscape become a bold, intrusive feature in the hands of Persian artists. The same is true of the symbols for fire, smoke, mountains, trees and water. Persian artists particularly favoured the calligraphic jottings that so readily suggest random clumps of grass. The fact that Persian painting saw fit to borrow these particular elements from the Chinese tradition is an eloquent reminder that the very idea of pure landscape as a fit subject for painting is itself a borrowing from China. Not surprisingly, the creatures that inhabit this landscape are often equally alien to Persia: mandarin ducks, phoenixes and dragons. Even the receding planes in which these varied elements are disposed are of Chinese origin. In view of the impressive scale of these borrowings, it is quite astonishing that they should have been so powerless to effect the essential nature of Persian painting. As the 14th century wore on, these startling innovations were assimilated so thoroughly that they finally all but lost their Chinese character. By the end of the century, in the illustrations to the odes of Khwaju Kirmani, they had entered the natural vocabulary of Persian artists. Never again were they to be used in a Chinese spirit.

The uniquely cosmopolitan character of Tabriz, the Ilkhanid capital in the early 14th century, ensured that the paintings produced there would have a remarkably mixed ancestry. Chinese and Byzantine features mingle with more elusive Uighur elements from Central Asia in two supreme masterpieces of this early Tabriz school – the Edinburgh and London manuscripts of the *Jami' al-Tawarikh* ("Compendium of Histories") written by the vizier Rashid al-Din (131 and 170). The exultant carnage of their battle scenes mirrors the traumatic effect on the Persian psyche of repeated invasions by Mongol hordes. In calmer mood, their depictions of enthroned monarchs exude a massive dignity. Tall, sombre figures are appropriately delineated by muted tones. The subject matter of the manuscripts ranges widely, embracing – besides the Quran and Islamic history – scenes from the Old and New Testaments, the legendary Persian past and Buddhist and Indian legends. Much of the iconography seems to be original. An outstanding feature of both manuscripts is their sheer size, which seems magnified by the oblong format used for most of the paintings. Equally striking is the dominance of line over colour; many of the paintings, indeed, resemble tinted drawings. The pale washes of colour and the close shading used in the draperies were not to recur on this scale in Persian painting.

This hybrid style appears somewhat unexpectedly and it may well have been created in the stimulating atmosphere of the international atelier founded by Rashid al-Din. If it was a forced growth of this kind its disappearance on the downfall of the vizier would call for no comment. At all events, the next major manuscript, the so-called "Demotte" *Shahnama*, appears equally unexpectedly. The confusion caused by its multiple styles has generated wide-ranging theories as to its dating and provenance. Since the manuscript is treated in detail in the catalogue (193) there is no need to expatiate on its characteristics and problems here. It must suffice to draw attention to the dense design and spatial complexity of many of its paintings, their subtle gamut of colours and their wide emotional range, within which a marked predilection for drama and violent action can be discerned. Despite the occasional gaucherie attendant on a style in flux, the Demotte *Shahnama* is perhaps the most ambitious illustrated version of the great epic ever produced. Yet its impact on later painting was surprisingly small.

The stature of the Rashid al-Din codices and of the Demotte *Shahnama* cannot be denied. It seems inexplicable that later artists should on the whole have carried these styles no further. Paradoxical though it sounds, Persian painting only found itself when liberated from the large page and confined to a small one. Thereafter, the principal aim of the artist was how to make a composition effective despite its small scale. But the small scale itself appreciably reduced the scope of miniature painting. The artist had to develop a language of gesture, a kind of visual shorthand. In such an idiom there was little room for realism, or for that sense of high destiny that transfigures the supreme masterpieces of Mongol painting. This alternative manner is well exemplified in the small-scale, comparatively unambitious books produced around the middle years of the 14th century (e.g. **133**, **135** and **196**). Typical of this provincial Mongol work is the series of so-called "Small *Shahnamas*". The many minor local courts of post-Ilkhanid Iran produced patrons who were anxious to arrogate to themselves the trappings of kingship but lacked the money to do so on a large scale. They could not finance the huge, highly organised imperial ateliers which had produced books like the Rashid al-Din codices and the Demotte *Shahnama*. So these small patrons were reduced to ordering small books with small illustrations. The demand for such work was apparently felt earlier in the 14th century too. These small *Shahnamas*, with their very numerous illustrations, did not call for the high degree of talent demanded in more ambitious books. Yet this style had a very much wider distribution than its great predecessors; it answered a need that they did not. In these books, a kind of strip cartoon technique was employed. The entire action has to be crammed into a diminutive rectangular panel. In such a format it was natural for bright, jewelled colours to dominate and for the tiny figures to assert themselves by violent gestures. Often the design becomes patternlike, and in this very tendency can be detected the seeds of later Persian painting at its most typical. The most developed provincial style of this period was that practised under the Inju rulers of Shiraz. It has justly been dubbed a folk art and is notable for its penchant for the dramatic, its boldly daubed colours – especially red and yellow – and its rather coarse draughtsmanship.

15th Century Painting

Neither provincial 14th century work nor a couple of ambitious later *Shahnamas* in Istanbul fully bridge the gap between the Demotte *Shahnama* and the mature Timurid style of the 15th century which was to dominate Persian painting for so long.

Once again there are too many missing links. Certainly with the illustrations to the odes of Khwaju Kirmani, executed in 1396 (British Library, Add. 18113) – if not as early as a *Shahnama* in Istanbul dated 1370 – this style has arrived. Although the 1396 manuscript was not available for exhibition, two volumes of epics (**124** and **159**) and the leaves from the Gulbenkian *Anthology* (e.g. **45**, **95** and **203**) illustrate related styles. In its way the Khwaju Kirmani manuscript was as great a feat as the "Compendium of Histories" by Rashid al-Din, or the Demotte *Shahnama*. Like them, it welded elements from diverse sources into a new, coherent whole, and that so naturally that no trace of strain or awkwardness can be discerned. This master and other late 14th century artists (cf. **124**, **125** and **159**) welcomed the limitations of their styles, which were self-imposed. They established a manner which maintained currency for some 250 years. It is marked by small figures, high horizon, fanciful vegetation and a luxurious palette. Man himself has become smaller, subordinated to his surroundings, and these tend to reflect moods (especially violent moods) less than they did earlier. The picture size decreases, and with it the scale of all elements shrinks; detail may challenge the mastery of the grand design; and the sense of drama evaporates in a dreamlike fantasy-world. The intrusion of script into the picture space becomes more varied and playful. Chinese elements no longer occur in their pristine starkness but have been absorbed into the new idiom.

The seductive grace of these miniatures needs no emphasis but perhaps the imagination which produced them had become confined. Their very beauty may have been a snare to the artist who produced them. The paintings of the 14th century are unpredictable, while those of the 15th century are not; in the earlier century an absolute layman can distinguish the various styles but later it takes and expert to do so. And this is just as it should be, for the best Timurid painting was produced for connoisseurs.

It is generally agreed that early Timurid painting reached its peak in the work of the academy founded at Herat by the celebrated bibliophile prince Baisunghur b. Shah Rukh. Here was perfected a style which fused the Jala'irid and Shiraz schools with other, less clearly defined, strands and, as Professor Grube has persuasively argued (*Classical Style, passim*) became the standard of excellence for all later Persian painting. Its hallmarks are an unflagging attention to detail, a preference for slender, elegant figures and a clear design which gains extra strength from intense purity of colour. Many of these features characterise later Timurid and early Safavid painting, but it could be argued that they were never combined with such

consistent felicity as in this first flowering (**108** and **200**). Such, at any rate, appears to have been the opinion of later Persian artists, for they often went to great lengths to imitate this style. Some remarkable recreations of this Herat manner are found as late as the reign of Shah 'Abbas I. It is an art courtly to its fingertips. It is therefore only to be expected that now apparently lighter subjects should gradually gain popularity – picnics, hunts, banquets, performing musicians and dancers. These scenes may succeed each other in an altogether unreal landscape, but there can be no denying that the atmosphere is authentic.

Always in Persian painting, this fastidious courtly manner co-existed with a less ambitious but quite serviceable style which was well suited to large-scale production. Typical of such latter work are the illustrations to the various manuscripts of the *Majma' al-Tawarikh* ("Collection of Histories") by Hafiz-i Abru, commonly assigned to Herat and dated c. 1425 (**67**, **68** and **115**). Not only the text but also the illustrations and their oblong format closely copy the Rashid al-Din manuscripts, which in all probability were easily available in the royal library to scribes and painters alike. But the copy is drained of the vitality which stamps the original. The inevitably limited range of themes appears at times to have impoverished the imaginations of the artists.

Meanwhile, in Shiraz, a vigorous local school was growing up under the patronage of Ibrahim Sultan, a brother of Baisunghur. Its products, such as the dispersed *Zafar Nama* of 1436, compel admiration for their boldness and frequent originality, qualities which triumph over the rather sketchy drawing (**69** and **141**). Even at their least inspired these miniatures do not stoop to the banal formulae used by the painters of the Hafiz-i Abru manuscript for enthronement scenes and the like. The earliest important manuscript of this school, dated 823/1420-1, is the Berlin *Anthology*, of which several leaves are exhibited here (**194 a-e**), while its *floruit* ends within a generation; almost the last major work in the style is the double-page frontispiece from Cleveland dated 1444 (**96**). Much Shiraz work of this period can be identified by the figures alone. They wear tight-fitting caps above long melancholy faces and their narrow torsoes are as straight as a board. The same stiffness seems to permeate their movements and the design itself, for they are disposed woodenly in tight groups, often observing the action from the horizon in serried ranks. Such figures claim more than their normal share of attention because they are set within a ruthlessly simplified landscape.

Later in the century Shiraz became a major centre of production for one of the most appealing schools in Persian painting, the Turkoman style. "Turkoman" is a collective term for certain tribal confederations (as distinct from "Turkman", which is the name of one particular tribe – cf. R.M. Savory in *The Cambridge History of Islam* I [Cambridge, 1970] 395). For most of the 15th century large tracts of Iran were ruled by rival Turkoman dynasties. Their power was concentrated in the west, and thus the Turkoman style is more commonly associated with western than with eastern Iran. But the Uppsala Asafi manuscript (**14**) was produced at Herat in 1502-4 and is in largely Turkoman style. Hallmarks of this school include an obsession with greenery, a detailed linear rendering of the vegetation and a preference for squat, jowly figures. Rosy cheeks add a delicate charm to many of these figures, but the variety of facial types that characterises contemporary Herat painting is quite absent. Colours are fresh and bright, but usually without that peculiar resonance that is found in the best Timurid work from Herat. With one or two notable exceptions, such as the *Khavar Nama,* (e.g. **187** and **198**). Turkoman painting tended to be small-scale, perhaps because this showed off its distinctive qualities to best advantage. It also meant that the paintings could be completed more quickly; the quantity of Turkoman paintings extant suggests large-scale production for a market rather than manuscripts executed for a specific patron.

For many tastes the climax of 15th century painting, and indeed of Persian painting in general, is reached in the school of Herat from c. 1480-c. 1500, a time when Bihzad was at the height of his powers. These decades usher in the age when the names and achievements of individual painters begin to attract the notice of chroniclers. Signatures and later attributions (a kinder term than forgery) proliferate. As a result, controversy has flourished as scholars attempt to allocate paintings in manuscripts (e.g. **119**) to artists who are known, or thought, to have worked on them. What emerges from these arguments is the likelihood that painters to some extent pooled their talents and that training in a royal atelier – in this case the patron was Sultan Husain Baiqara – encouraged a high degree of uniformity among the pupils. Thus to isolate the works of Bihzad from those of his close rivals is a daunting task and no two scholars have agreed on his oeuvre. It seems, indeed, that, unless some new technique of identification is devised, it would scarcely be profitable to continue the controversy. But if the personality behind the works continues to be elusive, there can be no mistaking the innovations which mark the later Herat style and which have traditionally been associated with Bihzad. This is not to say that "his" style is any sense revolutionary. Indeed, some of its features recreate the triumphs of the Baisunghur academy. They consist *inter alia* of a singular intensity of colour which is heightened by vibrant

contrasts – for example, a Negro set against a pale background – and of that attention to detail which had become a mark of Persian painting in Timurid times. But other elements are new: the delight in devising spatial complexities, and an unexpected interest in various poses and in individual types. In his depictions of the human body in movement, Bihzad (and his school) greatly enlarged the existing repertory (cf. **119**), an achievement that was gratefully plagiarised by generations of later painters. The very awkwardness of some of these postures betrays their novelty. Faces are depicted with more confidence and display considerable variety. This has been dubbed "realism", but the term will scarcely fit. The whole trend of Persian painting over the centuries has been to favour the general at the expense of the particular and neither Bihzad nor his school reversed this tendency. These artists, too, composed pictures out of their heads rather than building them up by patient observation. Certainly the figures in a painting attributable to Bihzad are sharply differentiated. Nevertheless, they have a Theophrastic flavour; the sense of a living, unique personality is generally absent. But it does seem that in this school the essence of a given type is captured more faithfully than hitherto. The same sharp focus combined with idealisation is applied to landscape. The flowers are always in bloom, it never rains and the only clouds in the sky are Chinese.

16th Century Painting

If any later Persian paintings can vie with this Herat school, it must be those produced in Tabriz in the next forty years. Many of the artists were in fact masters from Herat who had been removed by Shah Isma'il to his new capital. Their pupils could not fail to be impregnated with the Herat spirit, for Bihzad himself was placed in charge of the royal atelier. Emulation no doubt sharpened the ambition of this galaxy of gifted artists. The lavish patronage of Shah Tahmasp, still youthful and still an eager amateur of painting, expanded the royal atelier in which they worked. Following tradition, they frequently collaborated in illustrating a book. Here, then, is the culmination of the various styles so carefully elaborated in the previous two centuries. Paintings such as **23** mark that fleeting moment of balance between innovation and decline, when a great style reaches the utmost of that which it is capable. The mastery seems effortless. Here, if anywhere in Persian painting, one may speak of perfection. This Tabriz style owes much to Turkoman painting as well as to the school of Bihzad. But its lissom figures, so many of them eternally youthful and the majority with the red Safavid baton in their turbans, seem to be an original creation. At its best, then, the Tabriz school yields nothing to the work produced at Herat under Baisunghur and Sultan

Husain Baiqara. But in many works of this school, so much detail is crammed into the composition that its fastidious precision fails to make its full effect. Similarly, the colour range may be so kaleidoscopic that the very richness confuses the eye. When the demands of detail and colour conflict within a design which is in itself complex, the result is apt to be surfeit.

The move of the capital from Tabriz to Qazvin in 1548 coincided with the virtual demise of the style represented by **23**. Shah Tahmasp, consumed with religious bigotry, turned his back on painting and his atelier was disbanded. The flow of lavish illustrated books became a trickle. The Qazvin style, with certain outstanding exceptions like **51** and the *Haft Aurang* of Jami in the Freer Gallery, seems strangely coarse beside that of the best Tabriz work. Landscape becomes broader and simpler, with large areas given up to a single colour (**46**). In scenes of violent action especially, figures tend to increase in size and they exhibit a curious stiffness (**155**). Yet in courtly tableaux youths and maidens are rendered with a consistently suave line. The obsession with detail gradually disappears. In the later 16th century the enforced change of patronage led the best artists to produce single leaves, which were eagerly collected by connoisseurs and bound into albums. Figure studies – of pages, prisoners and princes among others – became a popular subject for such leaves (**53** and **74**). The tinted drawing now vied for favour with the traditional painting. Indeed, it could be argued that the forte of the Qazvin school was its series of energetic, virile line drawings – which include many notable portraits – rather than its painting. A taste for genre scenes appears; these were executed with the utmost delicacy and heightened by pale washes of colour (**156**).

Three major centres of provincial work can be identified in the Iranian world during the 16th century and all were highly productive. As in the Timurid period, there are manuscripts which will not fit into the major stylistic categories, but they are too few to be of real consequence. When Herat fell to the Uzbeks in 1506 some of the local artists were taken to Bukhara, the enemy capital, while others moved to Tabriz. Thus in its early phases Bukhara painting was saturated with influences from the Herat school of the previous generation. Early Safavid painting in Tabriz was subjected to much the same influences, but these conflicted with the well-established Turkoman style and therefore did not play the same dominant role as at Bukhara. Over the years this influence waned, for the school of Bukhara was not reinvigorated by new blood. To the end it kept its sense of strong colour and certain other Bihzadian features, but the school declined in importance as the century progressed.

A second important centre was

Shiraz. Here illustrated manuscripts were turned out with remarkable regularity throughout the century. On the whole they display tolerably rich colour and detail, while their compositions are as busy as one could wish. But the recurrence of identical figures, and even of virtually entire compositions (e.g. 166) from one manuscript to the next, does smack of mass production. It is a tribute to the patience and skill of Shiraz painters that they maintained high standards of accomplishment even in the face of such hackneyed models. Clearly the details of execution absorbed more of their attention than the design itself. But like other contemporary provincial work, Shiraz painting makes no major breakthrough in style or content. Even so, its popularity in its own time is beyond dispute; the style was even exported to Turkey and India. No other Persian school of painting produced such a mass of work.

The third major provincial style of Safavid times centred in Khurasan. Its products are far less numerous than those of Shiraz, and also markedly less ambitious. Perhaps its most attractive feature is its unerring use of bright, cheerful colours. Simplified drawing and design allow these colours to make their full effect. The figures owe something to the later style of Qazvin in their elongation and in their peaky, rather vapid faces. The painters of the Khurasan school may not have been ambitious, but they well knew how to exploit the particular advantages of their style.

Painting after 1600

With the accession of Shah 'Abbas and the transfer of the capital to Isfahan a decade later, one of the last great styles of Persian painting announced itself. As in architecture, so in painting the standards of this period have imposed themselves on later generations and laid claim – perhaps falsely – to a classic excellence. Certainly to the popular imagination in the West the term "Persian painting" is liable to connote the languid, sleepily erotic youths and ladies which flowed from the facile brush of Riza-yi 'Abbasi. So thoroughly did the fashions of the court permeate the world of painting at this time that no significant provincial school has been identified in the 17th century. The Isfahan style was ubiquitous. Its forte was the single-leaf drawing, a form of art allowing full expression to that mastery of line which was the birthright of the Persian artist.

But a narrow concentration on a few trite subjects blunted the perceptions of the artists and in time their expressive draughtsmanship declined into rote. An artist of the stature of Riza-yi 'Abbasi shows in his often satirical genre drawings (169) how flexible an instrument this calligraphic line could be. Nevertheless, the tedious succession of cupbearers (saqis), saucy pages and reclining lovers in his work shows clearly enough where the tastes of his

patrons lay. The vogue for single leaves was a potent factor in enhancing the status of the artist. From the late 16th century onwards, dozens of artists are known from signatures, attributions and contemporary texts. Often a leaf will bear a long and detailed inscription giving such information as the name of the artist, the date and the reason why the subject was chosen. Mu'in Musavvir is the outstanding exponent of this practice (e.g. 118).

In their use of colour, later Safavid artists often fell far below the exacting standards set in previous generations. Colours now tended to be mixed rather than pure, and the intrusion of these hybrid shades changed the subtle colour harmonies on which the greatest Persian paintings had been based. Nevertheless, this period produced a few outstanding illustrated manuscripts in which these new colours are used with great verve and assurance (212).

As the 17th century progressed Persian painting was subjected to increasingly strong European influences. The international outlook of the Safavid court was emphasised by the quantity of foreigners living in Isfahan. Embassies trekked back and forth between Persia and Europe proposing political alliances and haggling about trade agreements. A minor vogue for pictures of Persians in European costume (105) was in time followed by an increasing readiness to adapt the conventions of European painting to the artist's own purposes. The obvious parallel is the acceptance of Chinese artistic idioms more than three centuries earlier. But Persian artists, unlike their Mughal colleagues, were not able to preserve their own values intact under this onslaught of alien influences. Late 16th century painting is replete with examples of traditional themes transformed and weakened by such European features as modelling, perspective devices and realistic landscape. 107 is typical of this mésalliance.

The period between the Safavids and the Qajars is virtually unrepresented in the exhibition. But throughout this time a hybrid style which mingled Persian and European elements persisted. Zand painting illustrates this fusion. Under the Qajars one style, perhaps as a reaction against this, resorted to a deliberate primitivism exemplified in the many scenes of the court of Fath 'Ali Shah (88 and 89). These illustrate in acute form a major dichotomy in Qajar art, for this age also produced some of the most searching character studies in Persian painting. The court ensembles therefore cannot be explained away as the result of what was once considered the chronic incompetence of Qajar painters. They carry to its logical conclusion that self-conscious imitation of Sasanian art which can already be detected in later Safavid times. Side by side with this style is found a new and unexpected

blend of European and Persian elements which seems to have been inspired by the vogue for portrait painting at the Qajar court. Its hallmark was a patient concentration on the face and sometimes – as in 86 – on the hands. These were treated with a careful modelling normally denied to costume and background. This manner was adopted by several painters, of whom the best was perhaps Abu'l-Hasan Ghaffari. The activity of this school produced in the middle years of the nineteenth century a gallery of memorable portraits of Qajar courtiers and princes – the first time that this had been done in Persia. Perhaps the spur for this new approach was the visit of Abu'l-Hasan to Italy. A comparison with earlier Qajar oil paintings and frescoes (e.g. 89) proves beyond a doubt that the inspiration did not come from the native tradition alone.

Fascinating and piquant though Qajar painting may be, and although its absorption of foreign elements is typical of Persian painting, its products (with the partial exception of book illustrations) do not fit comfortably into the context of Persian painting as a whole. That tradition remained remarkably consistent and self-contained for at least four centuries. It knew its strengths and was usually successful in avoiding potential weaknesses. In its chosen field of the miniature it has no rival. Fortified by generations of experience, master of techniques so exacting that they can no longer be reproduced, impervious to the blandishments of novelty, the Persian painter laboured to give classic expression to traditional themes. To that end he lavished onto a few square centimetres of paper the full resources of his art: rare and precious colours, hair-fine drawing and an exquisite clarity of design. To appreciate such a painting to the full, it must be visualised in its original context. Its setting is the text itself, handwritten by a professional scribe. Even the writing, whatever the script, is intended to delight. Variations of rhythm and spacing, irregular sweeps and flourishes, all ensure that it is never monotonous. Text and painting are set within gilded and illuminated frames, mounted on polished, specially thin gold-flecked paper and finally enveloped within a supple, choicely tooled leather binding. Such a work is truly a gift for a king. It is our privilege to savour, with the patron – and with the Jew of Malta – "infinite riches in a little room."

Birth, Childhood, Love and Death

کاتب برگرفته شاه و تنابور ... جهان دیده نیک پر نور در بر

جهان کز زیر ابر آید برون ماه ... نهد پای شه در افتاد و آر سپد نهد

عیاران به سر مست آن پری ... جوشه معشوق خود مولای خود بله ... سر خود را بر زیر پای خود بله

گه شه را نانج بر سر به که درپا ... مکان فاش یکی ده بازی کرد ... درآن خدمت که بر پایش نیاز ... ترش رویی بشیرین در اثر کرد

از آن آتش که در خاطر گذرد ... تقاضای پای و من بوسی درآمد ... نهان در گوشش گفت وکو شاپور ... که گرشه شد کرفته نعمت معذور

جیران شد شاد و جون شد بازد ... لنگ ... کنون رسید که مطلب نهد خال خجالت بر رخ ماه ... نهان زرسید که مطلب و بستی

بنام وسنگ پرور داران دلفروز ... اک که خود را با تا امروز ... بسی سوکند خورد و عهدها ست ... که گری کابین نیارد سوی او

شد دانست کان تخم روید ... بدو راخت نیارد جز به پیوند ... بکابین کردنش می در جام ریزد ... که از دست آن زمان این

بکابین کردنش راجع سازم ... ولی باید که می در جام ریزد ... که از دست آن زمان این

Birth, Childhood, Love and Death

This section shows how varied the subject-matter of Persian miniatures can be. It embraces the whole pageant of royal life from the cradle to the grave. Both the births shown here (1 and 2) are prodigious; the births of Muhammad and Jesus are also depicted as extraordinary events. But even here a tenuous link with royal life can be maintained, for the first son of the Mughal emperor Akbar was born by Caesarian section. The school scenes (3-5) may give a slightly misleading picture of royal life, since it was not customary for royal children to be educated without distinction of rank alongside other children. It was common for them to have at least one special tutor.

The prince remained in the women's quarters until he was circumcised at the age of seven, an event marked by a great feast. A grounding in religious studies (especially Quran and *hadith*) and in poetry was essential. From his early days the prince was involved in royal ceremonies (7), and even as a boy he often held high office. He might be sent, for example, to govern a province. His authority, however, was likely to be nominal for in medieval times he was placed under the tutelage of an *atabeg*, a senior army commander who in theory acted as his advisor.

The prince was often married in early adolescence. But while royal polygamy was widely practised in Islamic as in Sasanian times, it is a matter seldom alluded to in Persian painting. The ruler is shown enthroned or communing with one consort, not several (24). In medieval as in more recent times a pompous procession led the bride to her future home (31, 32). Scenes of courtship or illicit love, however, fired the imagination of the painter more than the actual wedding ceremony (17, 28, 29). Persian history is replete with accounts of strong-minded women, including queens who ruled "like men". It need therefore occasion no surprise to see Shirin, neglected by her royal husband, boldly visiting her admirer Farhad (27) or Fitna reinstating herself in the affections of her royal lover by a mixture of brawn and chutzpah (34, 35). Homosexual love was widely thought to complement love between the sexes and it is frequently illustrated (10, 11). In much Persian amatory verse, indeed, it is unclear whether the beloved is male or female. The homosexual theme finds its most explicit expression in later Safavid art but it had been embedded in Persian culture for many centuries. It is perhaps fitting that a royal lover – Sultan Mahmud of Ghazna – should have become the exemplar of this passion (11).

Strangely enough, the ruler was rarely shown as an old man, but death and burial were popular themes (193b). There is no emphasis on death as the great leveller. In death as in life the ruler is a being apart (38). If he is mortally wounded in battle, all action is suspended while he dies (39). Muhammad had condemned extravagant mourning customs, but these continued unabated (41; cf. also several leaves of the Demotte *Shahnama*). Similarly, his injunction against the building of mausolea – for the graves of believers should be level with the ground – was ignored, especially by royalty. In many miniatures the inscriptions over the doors of their tombs contain the royal titles. The coffin was borne to the cemetery in solemn procession (193b) and was often encased within a sarcophagus. Although rulers were often buried together, no record seems to have survived of a Muslim notable being buried with his horse, as Rustam is depicted (193b) and as was the custom among the Huns.

1
The birth of Shakmuni (the Buddha)
Miniature painting
Hafiz-i Abru, *Majma' al-Tawarikh*
Herat, c. 1425
Baltimore, Walters Art Gallery, no. 10.676E
Dimensions: leaf 430 x 335 mm
Published: Yale, *Journal of History of Medicine*, 1960

The traditional biography of the Buddha made its way into the Islamic world via Persian sources and enjoyed a certain popularity in the cosmopolitan society of Baghdad under the 'Abbasids. Here, in the 9th and 10th centuries, this and other Indian works, such as the *Kalila wa Dimna* and the Book of Sindbad, were translated into Arabic. Eventually the work reached the west where the Buddha, under the name of Josaphat, was venerated as a saint. Its popularity was mainly due to the edifying parables and fables woven into the narrative framework.

The inclusion of such material in Rashid al-Din's World History (131 and 170) and in the continuation of that work by Hafiz-i Abru shows how seriously these Muslim historians sought to make their history truly worldwide. The Muslims possessed only rudimentary ideas about Buddhism, but their version of the stories is uncoloured by Islamic doctrine. Miniatures such as this evoke not the limited world of Persia but the international horizons of the 'Abbasid and Mongol empires.

According to the traditional account, the Buddha (whose various names in the non-Indian versions include Shakmin or Shakamuni, from Čakya Muni) was born by miraculous means to Queen Maha Maya, consort of a pagan king who had given himself over to riotous living. When her time was near, she retired to a grove of blossoming *sal*-trees in which flocks of birds were singing. As she approached, a branch of the largest tree bent down and as she held it she was delivered. Her child "left his mother's womb . . . stretching out his hands and feet, unsoiled by any impurities". But two showers nevertheless came from heaven to refresh them. Thus, although the detail of the mother bracing herself against a tree recalls the apocryphal traditions of the Virgin Mary giving birth, the artist has followed the text closely.

2
The birth of Rustam
Miniature painting
Firdausi, *Shahnama* (text: Warner I, 320-22)
Provincial Persian, perhaps western Indian, c. 1450
London, private collection
Dimensions: leaf 260 x 175 mm; painting 135 x 120 mm
Previously exhibited: Zürich and the Hague, 1962; Oxford, 1966; London 1967
Published: Zürich and the Hague, *Catalogue*, no. 993; pl. 84; Robinson, *PD*, p. 139, pl. 78; Robinson, *PMP*, no. 113 (a)

The dominant personality of the *Shahnama* is Rustam, the national hero of Iran. Firdausi describes him as cast in more than mortal mould, and thus it is fitting that his birth should be prodigious. When the mother's time drew near and it became apparent that the birth would be dangerous, his father Zal implored the help of the Simurgh, the mythical bird that had fostered him. Her advice was that Rudaba, the mother, should be drugged into unconsciousness by wine and that a *mubad* or Zoroastrian priest should then cut the child from her side. Curiously enough, the painter has shown Rudaba wide awake and in almost jaunty mood, but other details, such as the blanket modestly draping her lower half, and the priest's rolled-up sleeves, are apt. Equally so is the name "Rustam" bestowed upon the child, for its

iconography of this scene is closely related to that of Laila and Majnun at school, a subject much more frequently encountered (cf. **4**).

The rosy faces of the boys are typical of Turkoman work (cf. **24**); so too is the vegetation of ff. 1b and 2a and the rocks with vestigial humanoid faces or animal forms in that miniature and on f. 13b. The execution of details here is of high standard. A network of minute wrinkles clusters at the joints of the seated figures while the hair of the boys is drawn with the utmost fineness. By keeping the central space empty the artist ensures that his scrupulously accurate rendering of the reed matting will attract due attention. Against this dun background the blue tilework and indigo sky stand out with extra force.

4
Laila and Majun at School

Manuscript; 109 ff. and one double-
   page plus 3 single miniatures
Qasimi, *Laila va Majnun*
Khurasan, c. 1560-70
Copyist, Mulla Mir Bakharzi
London, Victoria and Albert Museum,
   no. 359-1885, ff. 27b and 28a
Dimensions: 27b: painting 143 × 66
   mm; 28a: 98 × 54 mm
Published: Stchoukine, *MS*, no. 197;
   VAM 1965, 16 and pl. 29

Laila and Majnun (see **19-21**) fell in love while they were still at school. Their passion set them apart from their schoolfellows, and the artist has symbolised this by allotting an entire page to the lovers and their teacher, while the other page shows the rest of the class at work. But the division goes deeper than this; the lovers are depicted in the cloistered atmosphere of a mosque whereas the other children are set against the animated, even rowdy, background of a classroom.

---

meaning is "I am delivered" or "I bear fruit". The earliest Islamic depiction of the Caesarian section is on f. 16a of the Edinburgh al-Biruni ms. dated 707/1307-8 (T.W. Arnold, *Browne Festschrift*, 6-7; cf. E. G. Browne, *Arabian Medicine*, 79).

Although this leaf and others from the same manuscript have certain links with the style of Shiraz – e.g. the tall forms and thin waists – certain details of costume and appearance suggest a quite different provenance. Examples are the strange fashion of wimples affected by the attendants of Rudaba, the way their feet are decorously covered and the marks painted on some of their foreheads. Recent scholarship has tended to favour the theory that the manuscript was produced in western India, at the court of the Bahmani Sultans in the Deccan. Islamic painting offers several examples of styles which penetrated into areas remote from their country of origin (cf. Grube, *Classical Style*, 11-16.) and this Indian provenance could easily be explained by the fact that at this time the court culture of eastern Islam, from Anatolia to India, was predominantly Persian in tone.

For other leaves from this manuscript, see **41** and **209**.

3
Mihr and Mushtari at school

Manuscript; 186 ff. and one double
   page plus 6 single miniatures
'Assar, *Mihr u Mushtari*
Turkoman style, Dhu'l-Hijja
   876/May-June 1472
Copyist, Murshid
London, British Library, Add. 6619,
   f.22a
Dimensions: open book 200 x 265 mm;
   painting 87 x 63 mm.
Published: Rieu, *Catalogue* II, 626-7;
   Titley, *Catalogue*, no. 87

For an outline of the story, see **122**. This miniature illustrates a very early stage of the tale, when Mihr and Mushtari are educated together. It seems doubly appropriate that Mihr, whose name means "sun" and who is the child of the king, should have a golden writing tablet. His finger points to the word *dars* (from Arabic *darasa*, 'study'); perhaps this is a deliberate pun. Writing tablets of this kind were standard equipment in medieval schools, as was the ferrule of the teacher (cf. Hayward Gallery *Catalogue*, No. 344). At the back Mushtari holds his tablet so that the spectator can see it though for him the writing is sideways. In general the

The illustrations of this manuscript have a jewelled quality which is due not only to their bright colours but also to their small size. Indeed, they are made to seem even smaller than they really are because the artist deliberately uses only half the page. As in the other paintings of the manuscript, the abundant detail is unusually delicate for the Khurasan school, but a sure sense of grouping ensures that this detail does not encroach on the main design.

5
Garden scene with teachers and pupils

Drawing with wash
Qazvin, late 16th century
Cleveland, Cleveland Museum of Art, no. 39.508
Dimensions: leaf 256 x 231 mm; painting 211 x 133 mm
Previously exhibited: Venice, 1962
Published: Anderson Galleries, Sale Catalogue of V. Everit Macy Collection (New York, 1938), 84, no. 407; *Cleveland Handbook*, no. 727; Grube, *MMP*, no. 91

Lightly coloured drawings had been known in Persian book painting as early as c. 1400 at the Jala'irid court, as the Freer *Divan* shows. There they were relegated to the margin. Here, and repeatedly throughout the later 16th century, their scale expands and they are developed for their own sake. They gave artists of the first rank opportunities for creative experiment which the very perfection of early Safavid painting (e.g. **23**) discouraged. These artists did not have the option of inventing totally new subjects for illustration. But genre scenes of this type are a marked feature of Safavid painting; their immediate origins are in the late Timurid paintings of Herat. They form a kind of sub-plot in courtly scenes. Here the informality which is a natural concomitant of a drawing allows the artist to explore genre subjects in greater depth. In so doing he has created one lively vignette after another.

The frieze-like quality of the lower third of the picture, and the splendid tree which gracefully fills out the emptiest part of the composition, find numerous parallels in Safavid painting (e.g. Robinson, *Keir*, III. 209 and III. 326). The difference lies in the quality of finish: this is a triumph of understatement.

6
Children at play

Manuscript; 52 miniatures
Provincial Timurid school; 843/1439
Nizami, *Khamsa (Makhzan al-Asrar)* (text, tr. Darab, 227)
Uppsala, University Library, O vet. 82, f. 29a
Dimensions: 160 x 125 mm
Previously exhibited: Gothenburg 1928, Copenhagen 1929, London 1931, Stockholm 1957

Published: Tornberg, *Cat.*, no. CLI; *London 1931*, no. 539E; *BWG*, no. 58 and pl. LIV; Stchoukine, *MT*, no. XLIII; Stockholm, *OM*, 9 and pl. 2; Robinson, *Bodleian*, 80

A rarely illustrated tale of the first poem of Nizami's *Khamsa* ("quintet") recounts how the child of a nobleman, while out with his fellows, fell down and broke his backbone. His best friend suggested that they should hide him in a well but the wisest child, who was his enemy, fearful of being blamed, reported the matter to his father, who put it right.

The artist has improved on the bald account given in the text by showing the children playing polo (cf. **47**). The rather schematic setting is typical of exterior scenes in this manuscript – landscape is rendered as a greyish tufted waste. No immediate parallel for the type of shading used on the horizon presents itself, but stranger still is the convention used for clouds. These white bars have nothing in common with the Chinese forms then current; they vaguely recall border designs in architecture and metalwork.

7
A child showered with money

Miniature painting
Unidentified text
Provincial school, early fifteenth cent.
Cambridge, Fogg Art Museum, Harvard University, Cambridge, Mass., Sarah C. Sears collection, no. 1936.26
Dimensions: leaf 296 x 193 mm; painting 130 x 92 mm.
Published: Schroeder, *Fogg*, no. IX

No particular occasion for this ceremony suggests itself, though it was common practice at Islamic courts to scatter gold over people, or to fill their mouths with gold, as a sign of honour. Special robes of honour were also distributed; the attendant on the left may be carrying these. Schroeder notes the tale in the *Shahnama* that when the infant Shapur was elevated to the throne "all the grandees poured jewels on him" but he concedes that the panels of text shown here do not appear in this section of the epic. Moreover, the

6

setting of the scene is rather low-key for such a royal occasion: the costume of the participants does not suggest high rank.

Although difficult to categorise, this painting certainly belongs to a provincial rather than to a metropolitan Timurid school. Decisive pointers in this direction include the simple setting, the big figures in their plain robes, and the avoidance of spatial complexities. The absence of fine detail is further evidence on this score; indeed, outlines are distractingly thick in some places. But the painting has its felicities such as the courtiers conversing in private and the figures unobtrusively staggered to prevent stiffness.

8
A youth and an old man
Manuscript; 16 ff. and 2 tinted drawings
Firdausi: *Shahnama* (extracts)
Qazvin or Isfahan, c. 1590–1600
Cambridge – Kings College Library, no. Pote 135
Dimensions: book 180 x 110 mm
Published: Robinson, *Bodleian*, 159; E. G. Browne, Handlist of Muhammadan Manuscripts in Cambridge Libraries (1922), p. 129

It is typical of the changing nature of patronage in the later 16th century that a slender volume of extracts from the *Shahnama* should be produced in preference to a complete copy. It would be inappropriate for such a book to contain those illustrations which traditionally accompanied the *Shahnama*. Thus the artist has broken with tradition altogether and replaced the mythical scenes by two portrait studies of the kind fashionable at the time. The contrast of youth and age had already been explored by Bihazd earlier in the century. The artist here has ingeniously compensated for the

small scale of his work by setting it within a series of frames. Especially eye-catching are the panels of calligraphy above and below each portrait. These are bordered by dark blue bands with floral scrolls picked out in gold. A narrow vertical frame encloses this ensemble and is itself laid against the buff ground colour of the paper which is heightened by animals, trees and plants in gold. The effect of this varied secondary ornament, which contrives to be rich without becoming obtrusive, is to focus attention all the more directly on the drawings themselves. As Robinson notes, they have something in common with the work of Aqa Rida, as he then signed himself. They epitomise the controlled facility of drawing which marks so much late 16th century work and exploit the decorative potential of discreet touches of blue and gold. Soon after this the Isfahan style became over-ripe in both line and colour.

9
A youth offers a girl wine
Manuscript; 239 ff. and 7 miniatures, all but one on 3 double pages
Amir Khusrau Dihlavi, *Khamsa*
Herat, 978–9/1570–2
The inscription attributes the work to Nadir al-'Asri Farrukh Beg

Cambridge, Kings College Library, no. Pote 153.
Dimensions: 240 x 175 mm
Previously exhibited: London 1967
Published: see bibliography cited in **55**

The painting lacks both margin and text and its execution is indifferent. The cypress in particular is so summarily painted that no detail can be distinguished, yet the artist has found time for an absurdity – the little bird in its branches. Signs of damage can be seen in places.

10
Two youths in a drunken frolic
Miniature painting
Bukhara, late 16th century

London, India Office Library and Records, no. J. 56-12
Dimensions: leaf 245 x 165 mm; painting 185 x 110 mm
Previously exhibited: London 1967
Published: Robinson, *PMP*, no. 168; Robinson, *IOL*, 187, no. 920 (illustrated)

Medieval Persian society found bisexuality no cause for comment; the literature and poetry of the time accepted it as natural. Mahmud of Ghazna sired a numerous family but it was his love for his male slave Ayaz that caught the imagination of later generations and passed into legend. Even in such a formal literary genre as the "Mirrors for Princes", manuals of statecraft and court life, the ruler is soberly advised to alternate his attentions between youths and women. By the later Safavid period pictures such as this certainly embodied the contemporary ideal of male beauty but they contained an extra element of glamour and sexual fantasy that brings them close in spirit to the cover girl of a modern magazine.

Here the impassive faces belie the faintly scabrous subject matter, though the page's feet and hemline suggest the agitation that his face conceals. Even in his flustered state his gestures are the essence of grace, notably the trailing arm with the turban and the sinuously entangled other arm. The artist intensifies the drama of the convoluted pose by bright colour but his detailing remains shoddy, outlines are often needlessly thick and faces schematically painted. In the Isfahan style which takes this fashion further such infelicities vanish.

Although the curling sidelocks of these youths were cultivated as a personal embellishment, they may conceivably also have had a less worldly *raison d'être*, for it was commonly believed that if the believer tottered on the narrow bridge over hell the Imams (descendants of Muhammad's son-in-law 'Ali) would catch him by his locks and save him from falling into the abyss.

11
Sultan Mahmud and Ayaz
Manuscript; 51 ff. and 4 miniatures
Hilai, *Sifat al-'Ashiqin* ("Dispositions of Lovers"), f. 33a
Khurasan school, c. 1580

Private collection
Dimensions: page 285 x 185 mm
Previously exhibited: London 1951; Oxford 1966; London 1967
Published: Robinson, *VAM 1951*, no. 81; B.W. Robinson, "Persian Painting" in *The Concise Encyclopaedia of Antiques V* ed. L.G.G. Ramsay (London 1961), 77 and pl. 54C; B.W. Robinson, in *The Complete*

The romance follows the fluctuating fortunes of the lovers Amir Ahmad and Mahsati. Both are the children of religious dignitaries, but both are given to wine and riotous living. Mahsati, indeed, is a remarkably liberated woman, an accomplished singer and harpist, ever ready with impromptu verses. After many picaresque adventures the couple settle down to a God-fearing life.

Here the artist has chosen to illustrate the moment when Amir Ahmad has chanced upon Mahsati in a tavern and she comes out to perform on the harp. Instead of the throne mentioned in the text she sits on a blue carpet spangled with dots. Cool colour harmonies account for much of the charm of this picture, which is otherwise plain to the point of bareness. The summary treatment of tree and ground indicates that the Turkoman style is still in its infancy.

13
Humay meets Humayun

Miniature painting on silk
Herat, c. 1430

Private collection; formerly in Comtesse de Béhague collection
Dimensions: leaf 320 x 430 mm; painting 190 x 280 mm.
Published: A. U. Pope in *Apollo* XX (1934), 207 and colour plate; Kühnel, *SPA*, 1854-5 and pl. 878 (in colour)

As in **98**, the use of silk as a medium coincides with a style of painting which, if not exactly Chinese, contains a strong element of chinoiserie. In this it is typical of much Timurid work produced in the first half of the 15th century (cf. Grube, *KdO* V/1 (1968), 1-23). These tall, stately figures, standing still as statues swathed in their robes, bring wall hangings to mind rather than book painting (cf. hangings in **194e** and **200**). The colours are as bright as any in contemporary manuscript painting, but the artist has adapted his style to the medium, for outlines are soft and at times disappear altogether. The composition could scarcely be simpler or more symmetrical, but this seems natural in the context of a formal meeting of the lovers with their attendants. Although the faces betray no expression, inconspicuous gestures catch the romantic atmosphere: Humay timidly draws her robe across her cheek, and their heads incline slightly towards each other. Humay's delicately arched eyebrows meet at the bridge of her nose, in conformity with Persian taste. The moon faces also represent a contemporary ideal of beauty, though in this case of Far Eastern origin.

14
Jalal listens to the rose

Manuscript; 110 ff. and 34 miniatures
Asafi, *Dastan-i Jamal u Jalal*
Herat, paintings possibly finished at Tabriz; text completed 908/1502-3. Three miniatures bear dates: two have 909/1503-4 and one has

Encyclopaedia of Antiques, ed. L.G.G. Ramsay (London, 1962), 817 and pl. 297C; Robinson, *PMP*, no. 178

The text accompanying this miniature states that one night Sultan Mahmud of Ghazna, overcome by an access of love for his favourite Ayaz, laid his head under the foot of the sleeping youth. When Ayaz was later chided for having permitted this he replied that he had no right to object to whatever Mahmud wished to do. After his death Mahmud became increasingly celebrated in Persian literature not only as an examplar of the just ruler but also as the ideal lover (cf. C.E. Bosworth in *Iran* IV (1966) 85-92).

In its economy of drawing and design the painting typifies the school of Khurasan. It is composed with mathematical exactness, and colour is used to reinforce the carefully marked divisions of the picture space. Many of these colours, like the flowering tree and the set of undecorated metal objects, recur on f. 17b of the manuscript. Reliance on such stock

properties characterises provincial work of the later 16th century. The paper which frames the painting is speckled with gold and enlivened with trees and flowers, a treatment reserved for the pages with miniatures.

12
Amir Ahmad sees Mahsati for the first time

Manuscript; 111 ff.; 2 double-page and 17 single miniatures
Early Turkoman style, 867/1462-3
Three romances: the book is open at *Amir Ahmad u Mahsati*

London, British Library, Or. 8755, f. 29b; formerly in Baroness Zouche collection
Dimensions: leaf 175 x 250 mm; painting 85 x 62 mm
Published: Robinson, *Bodleian,* 59; Meredith-Owens, *Handlist,* 69; G.M. Meredith-Owens, in *Forschungen zur Kunst Asiens. In Memoriam Kurt Erdmann*, ed. O. Aslanapa and R. Naumann (Istanbul, 1969), 172-81; Titley, *Catalogue,* no. 64

910/1504-5
Copyist: Sultan 'Ali
Patron: probably Mir 'Ali Shir
Uppsala, University Library, O Nova 2,
f. 43a
Dimensions: 270 x 170 mm
Previously exhibited: Gothenburg
1928, Copenhagen 1929, London
1931, Stockholm 1939; Rome 1956;
Stockholm 1957; London 1976
Published: Tornberg, *Catalogue*, IX and
no. CLXXI; *London 1931*, no. 715c,
BWG, no. 119 and pl. LXXXII;
Kühnel, *SPA* 1857 and pls. 883B-
884; K.V. Zettersteen and Lamm,
*The Story of Jamal and Jalal. An
illuminated manuscript in the library of
Uppsala University* (Uppsala, 1948);
Robinson, *AOI* (1954), 106 and fig.
18; Stockholm, *OM,* 10 and pl. 5;
Robinson, *Bodleian,* 54 and 61;
Robinson, *PD,* 140 and pl. 87;
Welch, *KBK,* 43-5, 48 and fig. 7;
Hayward Gallery Catalogue, no. 591

The poem deals with the adventures of
the star-crossed lovers Jalal ("glory")
and Jamal ("beauty"), and is an
allegory of man's desire to be united
with God. In this scene Jalal has
entered an enchanted garden in which
"the flowers speak like parrots" – birds
which were proverbial for their
wisdom. Here the rose discourses to
Jalal on the pangs of love. Behind him
is his vizier, and his clever servant,
appropriately named Failasuf,
("philosopher") holds his horse.

Much of the interest of the manuscript derives from its origin in Herat at
a time when Bihzad was working there
at the height of his powers. Yet these
miniatures illustrate a very different
style, even though points of resemblance to the school of Bihzad may be
noted, such as the avocado-shaped
trees or the way the scene bulges into
the margin (cf. the British Library
Nizami of c. 1490, Add. 25900, f. 161a).
This manuscript marks the final
flowering of the Turkoman style which
spread over so much of Persia in the
later 15th century. Many of its
paintings recall the supreme masterpiece of that style, the Sleeping Rustam
in the British Museum, in their
peculiar sensitivity to vegetation. The
range of green tones used here, for
example, is quite remarkable and is
further heightened by sparse touches of
red. Nature is transfigured in this
idyllic garden.

15
Shirin sees Khusrau's picture
Manuscript; 323 ff. and 17 miniatures
Nizami, *Khamsa (Khusrau u Shirin)*
Tabriz school, 949/1542-3
Copyist: Muhammad Muhsin Tabrizi
Cambridge, Fitzwilliam Museum,
MS. 373, f. 36b
Dimensions: leaf 370 x 265 mm.
Previously exhibited: London 1951,
1967
Published: *Sotheby,* 19. vii. 1935, lot 26;
Robinson, *VAM* 1951, no. 37;
Robinson, *VAM* 1952, 5, 7 and pl.

21; Stchoukine, *MS,* no. 32;
Robinson, *PMP,* no. 44

For the subject matter, see **22**. The
setting is not the meadow mentioned in
the text, but a palace courtyard
complete with a lavish tiled pavement
and an ornamental pond. Shapur is
nevertheless shown eavesdropping on
the scene. The generous three-quarter
page size of the painting is repeated in
the other miniatures of this manuscript.
But the artist avoids monotony by
constantly varying the shape of the
margin and of the text written within it.
Behind Shirin the open door of the
pavilion is completely filled by a prospect of the garden – a familiar device
for enriching man-made with natural
beauty. Safavid garden pavilions
habitually exploited this interpenetra-
tion of interior and exterior space.

16
**The maiden Golandam and a man
in love with her**
Maul ana Muhammad ibn Husam
al-Din: *Khavarnama* – an epic poem
about the exploits of 'Ali and other
Shi'ite saints
Perhaps Herat area, c. 1475.
Geneva, Collection of Prince
Sadruddin Aga Khan, No. Ir. M. 13
Dimensions: leaf 292 x 216 mm
Bibliography: for the work in general,
see Y. Zoka in *Hunar va Mardun* 20
(1343/1963), 17-29; see also nos. 18
and 27 of the same journal
The manuscript was broken up soon
after 1953 and its miniatures are now
in various public and private collections. For individual miniatures
see *CB Catalogue* I, no. 293; Gray,
PP 1961, 104-7; Grube, *MMP,* nos.
46-9; Grube, in *MMAB* N.S. XXI
(1963), 291 and fig. opposite 285;
Robinson, *PMP,* no. 125; M. L.
Swietochowski, in *IAMMA,* 61;
Welch, *Collection* I, 107-8; Welch,
KBK, 44 and fig. 9; Robinson, *PMA,*
no. 13; Hayward Gallery Catalogue,
no. 574a-b

Lush vegetation, stocky diminutive
figures and scintillating colours alike
mark this painting as an example of the
mature Turkoman style. The success of
the picture depends partly on its
strong areas of colour – horse, tree,
tent and sky – boldly juxtaposed, but
also on its clear, simple composition.
Thus the main action is neatly strung
out in the lower section of the picture,
in an almost chronological order.
Spectators are relegated to the upper
tier and their absorption in each other
prevents them from intruding. At the
centre of the scene stand three trees, so
close together that they function as one.
They impose a certain division and
hence symmetry on the picture, and on
a deeper level may be intended as
allusions to the participants – Persian
poets habitually compare a lovely
woman to a cypress.

Much of the interest of the
Khavarnama manuscript lies in the fact
that the artists, bereft of an established

iconography for these scenes, were
thrown on their own resources to
devise suitable images. In this case the
artist seems to have adapted the scene
from Nizami's *Laila u Majnun* where
Majnun is brought to Laila's tent (cf.
21). Perhaps the key feature is the
bare torso of the lover. Slaves were
commonly depicted in this way and the
particular gloss of this image may well
be that the man is enslaved as well as
distracted (*majnun*) by his passion.

Accounts of tents in medieval
Persian texts frequently stress their
links with architecture. The arched
doorway and the collar of the domed
tent offer tangible proof of this, and
even the diaper and floral decoration
echoes the modes of architectural
ornament.

For this miniature, see Welch,
Collection I, 107-8, with colour plate.

17
Zal at the window of Rudaba
Miniature painting
Firdausi, *Shahnama* (text: Warner I,
270-3)
Tabriz, 955/1548-9
Private collection
Dimensions: leaf 230 x 160 mm;
painting 100 x 70 mm
Previously exhibited: Oxford 1966
Bibliography: the body of the
manuscript from which this leaf
comes is in the Chester Beatty
Library, Dublin (cat. no. 214; cf.
CB Catalogue II, pl. 41). For this leaf,
see Robinson, *PMP,* no. 138

The nobleman Zal and Rudaba,
daughter of the king of Kabul, had
heard such reports of each other that
they fell in love even before they met.
Here the artist depicts the scene of their
first meeting, selecting, as usual, the
moment just before Rudaba like
Rapunzel lets down her tresses and
invites Zal to scale the wall with their
help. Purists might complain that they
seem too short for that task, and that
the quantity of retainers not only finds
no warrant in the text but also destroys
all sense of the privacy of this romantic
encounter. But the interlocking glances
of the lovers and the moving, impulsive
gesture of Rudaba, embowered as it
were in gorgeous blossoms, are fully in
the spirit of the text.

Stylistically the painting is a
curiosity. The dumpy almost neckless
figures with bland plump features
mark the Turkoman style, which by
1548 was almost forty years out of
date. It is debatable whether the
painting should be interpreted as an
incongruous survival or – as the
anachronistic turbans suggest – as a
deliberate revival. After all, even in the
early 17th century artists were found
who could work in a pure Timurid
idiom. As the numerous set pieces
depicting conflicts with dragons show,
artists were trained to be sensitive to a
given manner and could reproduce it
accurately even when the common
style was quite different. For all its
acceptance of convention and tradition,

pleasure are on display here – music, wine and dancing; even the servants are all beautiful women. In front of the embracing couple are dishes filled with pomegranates, a fruit with paradisical associations. The artist has contrived to avoid a forced symmetry of design despite the two-tier arrangement and the niches that frame every figure in the upper group. The subtle interaction between the figures and their setting depends on calculated deviations from the regular proportions which govern the picture. Shirazi painters specialised in such underlying geometrical layouts.

The miniature is mounted on blue-green paper speckled with gold – a pleasing and typical combination.

19
Laila and Majnun faint on seeing each other

Manuscript; 346 ff. and 42 miniatures
Nizami, *Khamsa* (*Laila u Majnun*; text, tr. Gelpke, Mattin and Hill, 187)
Turkoman style, 907/1501
Copyist, Na'im al-Din al-katib al-Shirazi

Oxford, Bodleian Library, MS. Elliot 192, f. 150a
Dimensions: book 295 x 175 mm; painting 100 x 98 mm
Previously exhibited: London 1931, 1951, 1967; Oxford 1972
Published: Sachau and Ethé, *Catalogue*, no. 587; Arnold, *PI*, pls. XXVIII and XXXVIIb; Gray, *PP 1930*, 69 and pl. 8; Guest, *Shiraz Painting*, 57; Robinson, *VAM 1951*, No. 21; Stchoukine, *MT*, no. LXIV; Robinson, *Bodleian*, 54-8 and pl. V; Robinson, *PM*, and pl. XIV; Robinson, *PMP*, no. 135; Robinson and Gray, *PAB*, no. 23

Laila and Majnun are the classic star-crossed lovers of Persian literature. While still at school they fell in love so deeply that the boy received the nickname Majnun ("demented"). He left his family to live among wild beasts in the desert and although his friends tried to win Laila for him by force of arms she was eventually married to another man. The lovers nevertheless exchanged letters and poems but when they met were so overcome by emotion that (according to one version of the text) they fainted. Even after Laila's husband had died they were not united; Laila pined away and Majnun expired on her grave.

By the early 16th century it had become customary to treat Majnun's visit to the tent of his beloved as a genre scene. The forlorn passion of the lovers is all the more poignant in these everyday surroundings, and in the more developed versions of this scene Laila and Majnun are scarcely noticeable. In this sharply divided picture only the lower group focusses on Majnun, emaciated by his physical and mental sufferings. But though some of the figures in the upper seem engrossed in their business, a symbolic link with the main scene is made. One

Persian painting was still an art subject to fashion.

18
Bahram Gur in the White Pavilion

Miniature painting
Nizami, *Khamsa* (*Haft Paikar*) (text, tr. Wilson, 234, 250)
Shiraz style, c. 1570

Cambridge, Fitzwilliam Museum, no. PD. 142-1948
Dimensions: leaf 405 x 279 mm; painting 152 x 104 mm
Previously exhibited: London 1967
Published: Robinson, *PMP*, no. 152

Bahram Gur was equally celebrated as huntsman and lover. The *Haft Paikar* tells on one level of how he married the daughters of the Kings of the Seven Climes and of how each told him a story in her pavilion before they retired for the night. Each pavilion is associated with a certain colour, day of the week and planet. But these associations are carefully arranged in an esoteric Sufi sense, as are the stories themselves, to describe the seven stages of the soul on its journey to God. Thus on the holy day of Friday the pavilion and its royal occupants are white – the single colour which is unmixed and here symbolises God Himself.

Numerous trappings of princely

unfortunate grasps desperately at the tent flap as he is borne to the ground by a savage lion – presumably a creature Majnun has befriended. Thus Majnun's evil fortune continues to spread to those around him.

20
Laila and Majnun in the desert
Manuscript; 77 ff. and 8 miniatures, of which 6 are on three double-page openings; all of them are later insertions.
Jami, *Baharistan* ("Spring-land")
Bukhara, completed 954/1547; the miniatures themselves can be dated c. 1525-30
Dedicated to 'Abd al-'Aziz Bahadur, governor of Bukhara 1540-49; the dedication to Sultan Husain Baiqara and the date of 1498 are both spurious.

Lisbon, Calouste Gulbenkian Foundation Museum, no. L.A. 169
Dimensions: leaf 310 x 200 mm
Previously exhibited: Lisbon 1963
Published: for the manuscript in general, see A. Sakisian in *AI* IV (1937), 342-3 and figs. 6-7; Kühnd,

in *SPA*, 1861 and pls. 888A, B; Robinson, *Bodleian*, 68; Gray, *AOI*, no. 122

This is essentially a landscape picture. It was of course common practice in earlier Persian painting to have a decorative landscape setting for exterior scenes. Indeed, it often claimed most of the pictures, thereby subordinating the figures. The difference here lies in the accumulation of generally credible detail such as trees, bushes and flowers. Even the rocks are modelled. Camels browse and ruminate by a stream in the foreground. They are the finishing touch that gives the picture almost the quality of an observed – rather than an imagined – landscape. As novel elements, their effect is to raise familiar features above the level of cliché. This scene is therefore the most original in the manuscript, even though its innovations were to have no immediate posterity. The peaceful timeless landscape is the perfect setting for this idyllic encounter between the embracing lovers, and it is easy to forget that the text never allows this to happen.

The attribution "work of the slave Bihzad" in a cavity of the rock is false, as is the same attribution in **184**. But the figures of the lovers pay tribute to his influence, which in the generation after his death was still the decisive factor in Bukhara painting.

21
Majnun brought before Laila's tent
Manuscript: 356 ff. and 9 miniatures, of which at least six are contemporary with the manuscript, the remainder dating from the 17th century
Nizami, *Khamsa* (*Laila u Majnun*; text, tr. Gelpke, 102-4)
Abarquh, 847-9/1443-5; owner's entry after the colophon is dated 853/1449-50
Copyist, Mahmud b. Muhammad b. Yusuf al-Tustari, known as Kaghidhi
Princeton University Library, no. 77G; formerly in Sambon and Riefstahl collections
Dimensions: page 254 x 160 mm
Previously exhibited: Venice 1962
Published: Sale of Sambon collection, Hotel Drout, 25-28.5.1914, lot 188; Moghadam and Armajani, *Catalog*, no. 7; B. W. Robinson in *AO* I (1954), 109; Robinson, *Bodleian*, 26-7, 59; Grube, *MMP*, no. 44

For the story in general, see **19.** Denied all access to Laila, Majnun resorted to subterfuge and persuaded an old woman to lead him fettered before the tent of his beloved. He is shown with the bare torso of the slave and his tousled hair can perhaps be seen as an apt commentary on his state of mind.
It is generally agreed that the paintings of Timurid date in this manuscript are among the earliest in the Turkoman style. Laila herself is an excellent example of that style. A slightly unexpected tendency towards caricature can be seen in some of the other figures. The tents shown here appear to be versions of the Turkoman yurt, with their characteristic walls of wicker staves overlaid with simple geometric patterns (cf. P. Andrews in *Iran* XI (1973), 93-110). But some of the decoration is conceived in a Chinese spirit for which no parallel can be found today.

22
Shirin sees Khusrau's portrait
Miniature painting
Nizami, Khamsa (*Khusrau u Shirin*)
Turkoman school, c. 1490
Cincinnati Art Museum, no. 1947. 508
Dimensions: leaf 277 x 178 mm; painting 121 x 107 mm.
Previously exhibited: San Francisco 1937; Buffalo 1938; New York 1940; Baltimore 1941.
Published: L. Katz, *The Brooklyn Museum Annual* v/3 (1963-4), 28-9

One day Khusrau, son of King Hurmuzd, dreamed that he would be blessed with the swiftest of horses, the finest of musicians and the loveliest of women, Shirin. Learning from his friend Shapur that an Armenian princess of rare beauty bore that name,

20

he implored him to arrange their betrothal forthwith. Shapur contrived that Shirin should see a portrait of Khusrau, and she instantly fell in love with this image.

At the core of the legend lies the historical fact that the Sasanian monarch Khusrau took one of his many Monophysite Christian subjects to wife. His motives were probably as much political as romantic. But both artist and poet visualised the Armenian Shirin – and for that matter the Chinese princess Humay – as being totally integrated into the Islamic world.

The hairdress of the ladies indicates a date in the later 15th century (cf. **16**). Typically Turkoman features include the somewhat stocky figures, while the generous use of space and the delicate colours suggest a fairly early stage in that style. The blossoming white trees outlined against a royal blue sky are a particularly happy stroke which was imitated to the very end of Turkoman painting (cf. **17**). Streaky golden clouds float above the horizon, a reminder that Chinese conventions could at times be ignored (cf. **6**). In two of the upper panels of script the margins have been ruled so as not to enroach on the pointing of the script. This detail suggests that the very last task of the painter was to complete the multiple margins framing the picture.

23
Khusrau spies Shirin bathing
Manuscript; 396 ff. and 17 miniatures, 14 of which are contemporary with the text
Nizami: *Khamsa (Khusrau u Shirin;* Tabriz, 945-9/1538-43
Copyist: Shah Mahmud Nishapuri al-Shahi
Artist: Sultan Muhammad
Patron: Shah Tahmasp

London, British Library, Or. 2265, f. 53b
Dimensions: leaf 377 x 660 mm.; painting 289 x 187 mm.
Previously exhibited: London 1967, 1971, 1973, 1976, 1977
Published: the most convenient bibliography can be found in Robinson, *PMP,* no. 39, to which may be added Grube, *WI,* pls. 78-9; Kirketerp-Møller, *Bogmaleri,* 130-1, 133; Welch, *KBK,* 63-8 and fig. 15; Rice, *IP,* 142-7, pls. 62-5 and V; Welch, *RPM, passim*; Hayward Gallery Catalogue, no. 600

This manuscript contains some of the supreme masterpieces of Persian painting; it takes its place among the great manuscripts of the world.

This painting is the work of Sultan Muhammad, the premier court painter of Shah Tahmasp. He has signed his name on a boulder by the stream. A rare and absolute certainty of touch has combined lushly fantastic landscape, still purity of colour and an apparently artless composition to produce the classic version of this ancient theme (cf. **194b**). Yet he departs from the

work of his predecessors by no more than nuances. The eyes of the lovers interlock across a diagonally composed picture, as tradition demands. But Sultan Muhammad transfigures this ancient scheme by his bravura use of colour. Shirin's horse Shabdiz, black as night, snorts and paws the ground beside the pool and forces the eye to encompass the space around him. Similarly, the huge and potentially neutral area above Shirin's head is filled by a blossoming tree, graceful as a dancer, to which Shabdiz turns. Compared with the strong tones of gold, midnight blue, black and (originally) silver, the mild pastel tones marking off the varied planes of the landscape soothe rather than excite the eye. These are colours to savour.

24
Khusrau and Shirin wedded
Manuscript; 468 ff. and 48 miniatures
Nizami, *Khamsa* (with *Khamsa* of Amir Khusrau in the margins)
Turkoman style, c. 1505
London, India Office Library, Ethé 976 and Ethé 1200
Dimensions: leaf 275 x 185 mm.; painting 75 x 110 mm
Previously exhibited: London 1951, 1967
Published: Robinson, *VAM 1951,* no. 22; Robinson, *VAM 1952,* pls. 14-17; Stchoukine, *MS,* no. 92, pls. I, III and X; Robinson, *VAM 1965,* pls. 11-12; Robinson, *PM,* pl. XV; Robinson, *PD,* 139 and pl. 85; Stchoukine, *Syria* LI (1974), 295-6; Robinson, *IOL,* 25-42 and no. 100 (illustrated)

The *Khamsa* of Amir Khusrau imitated that of Nizami. Thus, by having the later work inscribed in the margins of the earlier, the discriminating but unknown patron for whom the manuscript was made could compare original and pastiche at his leisure.

The paintings of the manuscript document the passage from the late Turkoman to the early Safavid style, though the new manner is occasionally uncertain. This miniature is without question a mature masterpiece in the Turkoman manner. Content to work on a small scale, the artist has striven to render every detail precious. His colours glow like jewels. At the same time they are components of the design, for each major colour is echoed elsewhere in the painting. Moreover, the major divisions of the picture space are made effective less by line than by strong unblended colour. In this figure drawing the artist foreshadows later Safavid practice, for he reduces the human form to a few expressive shapes, notably ovals. Equally prophetic is the drapery convention whereby each curve of the body is translated into a spray of radiating lines.

The white plaster walls emphasise a recurrent feature of domestic planning. Since people habitually dispensed with furniture and sat, ate, talked and slept

on the floor, a major focus of decoration was the area immediately above the floor. Hence the splendid dado, which finds parallels in roughly contemporary buildings.

The peculiar charm of the painting resides in its restrained language of gesture. The gently inclined heads, the passive modesty of Shirin (her arm half shielding her from Khausrau) and the tentative way in which he takes her arm are details conceived in a deeply romantic spirit. No splendid detail of adornment is spared – even Shirin's hands bear beauty spots and her fingers are bedizened with rings and paint. The calculated asymmetry of the couple ensures that the window into an equally romantic world of trees perpetually in flower and fruit is left clear.

25
Khusrau and Shirin meet during a hunt
Miniature painting
Tabriz style, c. 1530
India Office Library, no. J. 55-5
Dimensions: page 240 x 170 mm; painting 195 x 140 mm
Published: Robinson, *IOL,* no. 138 (colour pl. III)

Although the division of the painting into three major tiers seems crude at first sight, notably in the bands of colour and the symmetrically paired figures, the relative importance of the three tiers is subtly graded. The bisected figures and horses of the top tier do not detain the eye for long. But Khusrau's coal-black stallion draws the eye like a magnet. The microscopic detail of the saddlecloths of the royal pack also invites closer scrutiny, unlike the horse trappings elsewhere in the picture. No doubt the artist deliberately intended the dramatic contrast between the lovers, standing stock still gazing at each other, and the violent action which explodes in the predella beneath them. The direction of movement in this lowest tier runs counter to that above, thereby preventing the composition from becoming monotonous. A curious mannerism prevails in the figure drawing in that the eye further from the viewer is indicated only by a slit, thus imparting a faintly roguish air to the scene. The flurry and variety of the chase is suggested with great economy. An original touch is the detail of the leading rider dismounting, presumably to be in at the kill, for his cheetah – trained to sit on the crupper of his horse – is just bringing down its prey. Robinson notes that the turbans of the figures have been repainted to conform to Ottoman type and that the original manuscript was therefore war booty from Tabriz.

26
Shirin offers Khusrau pomegranates
Miniature painting
Nizami, *Khusrau u Shirin*
Shiraz, later 16th century

Cleveland, Cleveland Museum of Art,
no. 47.500
Dimensions: leaf 307 x 187 mm;
painting 209 x 141 mm

The unfinished state of the painting
explains the unruled margins of the
text panels but not the unduly coarse
outlines of the horizon and the
lutenist. Unusual features include the
spiky rays of sun and stars and the floral
decoration within the royal tent.
Amongst certain tribes, incidentally,
white tents to this day connote marriage. In earlier Islamic art the ruler is
frequently offered pomegranates. The
fruit was associated with paradise and
was thought to strengthen the faith of
those who ate it.

27
Shirin visits Farhad

Miniature painting
Nizami, *Khamsa (Khusrau u Shirin)*
Probably Shiraz, c. 1480
Private collection
Dimensions: leaf 260 x 155 mm;
painting 155 x 105 mm
Previously exhibited: Oxford 1966;
London 1967
Published: *Sotheby*, 18.v.i 1962, lot 57;
Robinson, *PMP*, no. 134

Farhad, a renowned artificer, fell
distractedly in love with Shirin even
though she was the wife of his king. As
proof of his devotion he made a
channel through the mountain so that
she could be supplied with fresh milk
daily. This conduit can be seen at the
base of the picture. Shirin's husband
Khusrau heard of this feat, and in a
jealous rage promised Shirin to
Farhad if he would perform the
impossible – namely to cut a road
through Mount Bisutun. Farhad set to
work, first carving an image of Shirin
in the rock to encourage himself. Here
Shirin is shown visiting him at his
labours.

This painting follows the traditional
iconography for the scene; its most
unusual feature is the arrangement of
rocks, script and tree to form an arched
frame for Shirin. The bas-reliefs reveal
an acquaintance with the Sasanian
reliefs at Taq-i Bustan, though at
several removes. While the horseman
is quite an accurate rendering of the
Sasanian original, the upper panel is a
fantasy of the artist and is conceived
as a typical Timurid court scene. In
their choice of scenes for these panels,
artists allowed themselves a
remarkable licence. Clearly there was
more room for experiment in such
details than in the depiction of Farhad
and Shirin (for discussion of these
reliefs, see P.P. Soucek in *Studies in Art
and Literature of the Near East in Honor
of Richard Ettinghausen*, ed. P.J.
Chelkowski [New York, 1974], 45-52).

28
Tahmina visits Rustam

Manuscript; 31 miniatures including a
double-page composition Firdausi,
Shahnama (text, tr. Warner II, 123)

Herat school, c. 1440
The name of Prince Muhammad Juki,
son of Shah Rukh, occurs on a banner
on f. 296

London, Royal Asiatic Society of
Great Britain and Ireland, Codrington 239, f. 56b
Dimensions: open book 350 x 510 mm;
painting 155 x 127 mm
Previously exhibited: London 1931,
1967, 1976
Published: for the most convenient
bibliography see Robinson, *PMP*,
no. 18, to which may be added
Schroeder, *Fogg*, 52-6; Rice, *IP*, 118-9
and pl. 60; Hayward Gallery
Catalogue, no. 562

According to the *Shahnama*, Rustam
lived to the ripe old age of 550 or so,
but only once in these centuries did he
find time for love. Even then it was not
of his own choosing. While he was

staying with the King of Samangan his
host's daughter Tahmina heard of his
martial exploits and fell passionately in
love with him. She boldly visited him at
dead of night and duly conceived their
luckless son Suhrab, whom Rustam
later killed in error.

An established iconography for this
scene was already current in the early
Timurid period and its classic form is
the leaf in the Fogg Art Museum,
datable c. 1410. The miniature
exhibited here is a reduced version of
the Fogg leaf, but it does not fully
deserve the punishing comparison it
receives at the hands of Eric Schroeder.
With the smaller scale comes an
intimate quality more in harmony with
a love scene. The contrast between the
relaxed appraising paladin and his
demure seductress is admirable. As in
certain other paintings in this
manuscript, however, a partiality for

detail undermines the human interest of the scene. In this page, for example, the wall is treated almost like a page of manuscript illumination.

This *Shahnama* was formerly in the Mughal royal library and it bears the seals of the emperors from Babur to Aurangzib.

29
Absal seduces Salaman
Miniature painting
Jami, *Haft Aurang* ("Seven Thrones"; the leaf is from *Salaman and Absal*; text, tr. A. J. Arberry: "Fitzgerald's *Salaman and Absal*" (Cambridge 1956), 176)
Provincial school, mid 16th century
Private Collection
Dimensions: 165 x 101 mm

A king was grieved at his childlessness and his vizier contrived that a son should be born to him without the agency of a woman. The boy was named Salaman and a beautiful nurse, Absal, was engaged to look after him. In due course she seduced him, but the king eventually managed to destroy her. The story ends with the vizier conjuring up an image of Venus with which Salaman falls in love. In a lengthy envoi Jami expounds the allegorical significance of this story.

The iconography for this scene is patterned on that which was current for Khusrau and Shirin consummating their marriage. Typical borrowings are such details as the sleeping servant, the half-drawn curtains and the full dress of the lovers. The miniatures detached from this manuscript are notable for their audacious use of white, which sets off the other colours admirably. A distinctive stepped frame with rudimentary architectural features and patterned brickwork is found in all three of them (cf. **163** and **192**). These characteristics set the miniatures slightly apart from most 16th century work. But they seem to be products of a provincial school rather than Qazvin, as is suggested in the Maggs Bros. catalogue.

30
Bilqis, Queen of Sheba, with the hoopoe which carried her love letters to Solomon
Tinted drawing   Qazvin, c.1590
London, British Museum, no. 1948 12-11 08; formerly in Anet and Eckstein collections
Dimensions: leaf 161 x 227 mm; painting 99 x 194 mm
Previously exhibited: Paris 1912, London 1931, 1949 and 1959
Bibliography: Martin, *MP*, 7 and pl. 119; Marteau-Vever, *MP* II, no. 208; Anet, *BM* XXII (1912), 105-17 and pl. 1A; Kühnel, *MIO*, pl. 99; BWG, no. 156; *Souvenir*, pl. 45; B. Gray, in *BMQ* XVII (1952), 17-19, pl. VIa; Stchoukine, *SA*, 77, 190 and pl. XXVII; Titley, *Catalogue*, no 395 (223)

It would be difficult to imagine a more discreet allusion to the love affair between Solomon and the Queen of Sheba than the hoopoe, itself almost lost amid the branches of the willow but holding a tiny scroll in its beak. Yet the atmosphere of the painting is unmistakably sensual: the chubby feet and ankles, the errant trailing love-locks, the great sweep of the lady's haunch and her generous if boneless contours. Something of the entwining rhythm proclaimed by her clothing is echoed in the trees on either side and in the flowers; lines continually cross to form graceful ovals. The brook takes up a similar theme and even un-supported drapery does not hang down but defies gravity to remain horizontal, thereby obeying the grain of the whole design. Reclining beauties of this type were fashionable in later Safavid times and in Turkey Ottoman painters such as Levni were developing the theme with notable success in the 18th century.

Although this is a tinted drawing in ink on paper rather than a painting, its special distinction lies in its use of colour. The buff ground is subtly heightened by carefully spaced flowers, trees and rocks, each contributing a new shade, while the texture of gold tooling and embroidered gold thread is conveyed with notable success.

Islamic tradition states that Solomon was given authority over all creation, and so it is perhaps fitting that his beloved should recline in a landscape that is emphatically alive – faces peer out from rocks, trees, flowers and from her very clothes. This device had become popular more than a century earlier in Turkoman painting but by the late 16th century it was a rather stale convention.

The attribution to Bihzad in the top right-hand corner is of course false; Stchoukine suggests that the drawing may be the work of Sadiqi.

31
Wedding procession of Siyavush
Manuscript; 441 ff. and 72 miniatures
Firdausi, *Shahnama* (text, tr. Warner, II, 274-6)

Perhaps Astarabad, c.1600
Birmingham, Selly Oak Colleges
    Library, Mingana Pers. MS. 9, f.86b
Dimensions: page 330 x 230 mm;
    written surface 250 x 145 mm
Previously exhibited: London 1967
Published: Robinson, *PMP*, no. 183

Firdausi's text makes it clear that
neither Siyavush nor his bride took
part in their wedding procession. The
lady Farangis – daughter of the
Turanian King Afrasiyab – is in fact not
depicted here, but Siyavush is, as the
inscription beside him states.
Otherwise the artist has closely
followed the text and entered into its
festive mood. According to Firdausi
servants carried golden cups, camel-
loads of carpets, gold and silver,
jewel-studded cloth and Chinese
textiles. Kinsmen of the monarch
brought trays of saffron and musk
among other gifts. Largesse was
scattered freely over the crowd. The
venerable old man behind Siyavush is
Piran, the Turanian general whose
daughter Siyavush had already married.
By a peccadillo of drawing his arm is
caught in the jaws of a vermilion camel.
    Two painters worked on this
manuscript. The better of them favours
loud, unexpected colours and delights
in embroidered surfaces. His drawing
is feeble and repetitive, as the tilted
faces or the legs of the animals reveal.
    B. W. Robinson, in a typewritten
note appended to this *Shahnama*, lists
the following manuscripts which can
be associated with this distinctive
provincial school of Safavid painting.
Only the first of these manuscripts,
incidentally, is explicitly stated to have
been produced "at Astarabad", though
the third was copied by an Astarabadi
scribe. But in default of evidence to the
contrary, "the Astarabad style" is a
convenient label for paintings of this
type.
    1 *Shahnama* of 972/-565 (British
    Library, Or. 12084-12086)
    2 *Shahnama* of 1040/1630 (Fitzwilliam
    Museum, Cambridge, MS 311-
    see **32**).
    3 *Shahnama* of 971/1564 (Teheran,
    Alam collection)
    4 *Shahnama* of 973/1566 (Istanbul,
    Topkapi Sarayi H.1493)
    5 *Shahnama* of about the early 17th
    century (London, India Office
    Library, Ethé 874)
    6 *Asar al-Muzaffar* (Rampur State
    Library, MS 4187)

32
Wedding procession of Farangis and Siyavush

Manuscript; 440 ff. and 67 miniatures
Firdausi, *Shahnama* (text, tr. Warner,
    II, 274-6)
Perhaps Astarabad, 1040/1630-31
Cambridge, Fitzwilliam Museum, MS.
    311, f. 93a (formerly in Morris and
    Blunt collections)
Dimensions: leaf 370 x 245 mm
Previously exhibited: London 1967
Published: Robinson, *PMP*, no. 184

For the subject matter, see **31**. The
waving banners and striding camels
irresistibly recall "the pilgrim caravan"
of al-Wasiti in the *Maqamat* of al-
Hariri in the Bibliothèque Nationale,
Paris (ms. arabe 5847). The joyful crush
of the wedding procession is well
captured in this undisciplined surging
crowd. Not only do the camels sprawl
into the margin, but the division
between text and picture is erratic. Thus
the last hemistich (*bait*) of the upper
panel breaks off in the middle, to be
completed much lower down at the
top left-hand corner of the main text
panel. By this device the artist seems to
suggest that the bustle of the crowd
has spilled over into the body of the
text and has necessitated a revised
arrangement of the written surface.
Even such a trivial detail as this
encroachment testifies to the
perennial concern of the artist to mesh
text and painting as closely as possible,
and even to try, wherever he could, to
reflect the sense of the text by the
layout of the page.

33
Personage with a parrot

Miniature painting
Tabriz, early 16th century

Cambridge, Fogg Art Museum,
Harvard University, Cambridge,
    Mass., Sarah C. Sears collection
    no. 1936. 25;
Dimensions: leaf 186 x 106 mm;
    painting 70 x 55 mm
Published: Schroeder, *Fogg*, no. XIV

In default of an accompanying text any
interpretation of this scene can only
be speculative. Of the various literary
sources reviewed by Schroeder the
most likely candidate is a tale from
Sa 'di's *Gulistan*. This features an old
man who celebrates his union to a
young girl by quoting the verse:
    "*If, like the parrot's, your food is sugar
    My sweet life is a sacrifice to your
    nourishment*".
Hence the corpse in the cage. But his
gallantry avails him nothing and his
wife rejects him in favour of a younger
man. Whether this is the subject or
not, the picture does show that parrots
were kept as pets, although they have
a wider significance in Iran from their
prominence in books of edifying fables
(such as the *Tuti Nama*, the Book of the
Parrot). They were held to symbolise
worldly wisdom.
The painting typifies the court style of
Tabriz in its essentially decorative
quality. The stereotyped poses and
gestures show that the artist devoted
less care to the figures than to their

surroundings. Indeed, colour and setting are emphasised at the expense of content.

34
Fitna carries the ox

Manuscript; 346 ff. and 12 miniatures

Nizami, *Khamsa* (*Haft Paikar*; text, tr. Wilson,)

Tabriz style, 927/1520-1

London, Royal Asiatic Society, Codrington 246A

Dimensions: 290 x 175 mm

Bahram Gur went out hunting one day with his slave girl Fitna. At her request he performed an unheard-of feat of archery by pinning the hoof of an onager to its ear with a single arrow. She withheld her praise, saying in effect "practice makes perfect". Enraged, he ordered her put to death – but the order was disobeyed. Fitna thereupon set herself the daily task of carrying a new-born calf up sixty steps to a belvedere. Eventually she arranged that the King should see her performing this feat – the calf having grown to a full-sized ox in the meantime. She then reminded the astonished King that "practice makes perfect" and they were reconciled.

Amidst the hyperbole of the story, a picture emerges of the personality and accomplishments expected of the king's favourites. Fitna was, the poet says, "not only beautiful, but skilled in song, lutenist and a nimble-footed dancer too". It is her wit rather than her weightlifting that commends her to the king.

In Safavid architecture the belvedere (*balakhana*) was both an integral part of a palace and a separate kiosk. Its upper part was intentionally of open plan and well ventilated by breezes. In the poem, as in actual architecture, the top is reached by steps but the artist – true to long-established inconography – shows Fitna climbing up a ladder.

Some of the faces slightly resemble Turkish work, notably that of the central courtier in the corner group.

35
Fitna carries the cow

Manuscript; 203 ff. and 14 miniatures, of which 4 – two of the earlier Shiraz school and two of the later Isfahan school – are later insertions at both ends of the book.

Nizami, *Khamsa* (*Haft Paikar*; text, tr. Wilson,)

Qazvin style, Ramadan 969/May-June 1562 (this is the date given in the colophon on f. 202a; a marginal note in French erroneously gives the date 979).

Copyist, Baba Shah Isfahani

Cambridge, Fitzwilliam Museum, MS. 18-1948, f. 67b

Dimensions: leaf 260 x 170 mm

Previously exhibited: London 1951, Abu Dhabi 1976

Published: *Sotheby*, 19 vii, 1938, lot 27 (one miniature reproduced);

Robinson, *VAM 1951*, no. 78; Stchoukine, *MS*, no. 108 and pls. XX-XXI (illustrations of the two paintings of the Shiraz school)

For the subject matter, see 33. The device of enclosing the picture within a multi-ruled margin and then placing several figures outside that margin recurs on f. 54a. It is rather unusual. In this case the figures have been added largely for visual effect, since the text of the poem does not call for them, and the composition within the margins makes good sense without them. The architecture of the pavilion displays a kaleidoscopic range of patterned surfaces and their bright colours make an ideal foil for this light-hearted fable.

36
The ladies of Egypt see Joseph

Manuscript; 176 ff. and 4 miniatures

Jami, *Yusuf u Zulaikha*

Shiraz style, 954/1547-8

Copyist, Muhammad Qavam

The Syndics of Cambridge University Library, MS. Mm. 6. 3, f. 118a

Dimensions: 194 x 119 mm

Previously exhibited: London 1951

Published: Brown, *Catalogue*, no. CCLXVIII; Guest, *Shiraz Painting* Appendix, no. 22 and pl. 35 A, B; Robinson, *VAM 1951*, no. 46; Stchoukine, *MS*, no. 109; I. Stchoukine in *Syria* LI (1974), 297

This miniature typifies the Shiraz style at its most detailed. Virtually every surface is covered with small-scale and rather finicky patterning. This technique successfully evokes the ostentation of a palace. It is therefore appropriate for the carved stucco windows or the splendid balustraded dais on which Zulaikha reclines. But the curtain drawn aside reveals that the world of nature is subject to the same laws of ornamental display. Moreover, the artist, far from using plain walls as a foil for lavish ornament elsewhere, has made them share in the general extravagance. No accent is sufficiently strong to dominate these conflicting colours and patterns, with the result that the eye is quickly surfeited. For the subject see 37.

37
The ladies of Egypt overcome by the beauty of Yusuf

Manuscript; 156 ff. and 26 miniatures

Jami: *Yusu u Zulaikha*

School uncertain; c. 1560

Artist (given on fol. 136b) – al 'Abd Sayyid Shams al-Din

London, British Library, Or. 4535, f. 104a

Dimensions: page 285 x 385 mm.; painting 205 x 147 mm.

Published: Rieu, *Supplement*, 190; Arnold *ONT*, pl. X; Blochet, *MP*, pl. CXXXVI, Stochoukine, *MS*, no. 192 and pl. LXXII; Robinson, *PMP*, no. 181; Titley, *Catalogue*, no. 216

Yusuf, who corresponds to the Biblical Joseph, is a key figure in

Islam – an entire chapter of the Qur'an (Sura 12) is devoted to him. The episode illustrated here recounts how Potiphar's wife, Zulaikha, was reproached for her love of Yusuf by the ladies of Egypt. She determined to let them see his beauty for themselves and invited them to a feast where oranges were served with knives. When Yusuf appeared they were one and all so overcome by love for him that they cut their hands severely. The flame-like halo given to Yusuf is of Buddhist origin. The execution is fastidious with pastel colours (note the presence of a Negress for contrast, almost in the manner of Bihzad) and a characteristic facial type with protuberant eyes, used for men and women alike. But the real distinction of the painting lies in its organisation of space. The whole picture is composed in blocks and numerous linking figures draw the eye from one group to the next. The very theme of refreshments being served helps to link high and low life, while the stairs and the lower inscription panel ensure that the servants are placed physically below the Court ladies.

38
Iskandar on his death-bed

Miniature painting; parent manuscript Anthology, including the *Khamsa* of Nizami, Probably Isfahan, 838-40/1435-6

Copyists, 'Ali Pagir al-Ashtarjani and Zain al-Isfahani

Dublin, Chester Beatty Library and Gallery of Oriental Art, Pers. Ms. 124, I, f. 297b

Dimensions: leaf 270 x 170 mm

Previously exhibited: London 1931; Cairo 1935; London 1967

Published: *London 1931*, No. 470; *BWG*, no. 54; Wiet, *Exposition*, 93 and pl. 69; *CB Catalogue* I, no. 124| and pls. 29-31; B. W. Robinson in *Apollo* (May 1963), 381-2 and fig. 2; Robinson, *PMP*, no. 110

In the Persian tradition Alexander (Iskandar) was poisoned by one of his governors. Earlier painters had made his death the occasion for great set pieces of frantic mourning, but no such emotion can be detected in this phlegmatic scene. All eyes are on him, but he returns their gaze unwinkingly; as Robinson notes, the tableau is comic rather than tragic. The reason is clear – the artist has borrowed the figure of Iskandar from the traditional iconography of Rustam being visited by Tahmina (28). The appraising glance and pose of that half-drunken cavalier is scarcely compatible with this scene of imminent death. This manuscript is one of the rare examples of a distinctive provincial school of Timurid painting associated with Isfahan. The painters, perhaps as a result of illustrating an unusually wide range of subjects, produced many strikingly original features of iconography and even style. An example here is the economical and effective drapery technique.

39
Iskandar comforts the dying Dara
Miniature painting
Firdausi, *Shahnama* (text, tr. Warner, oo, ooo)
Shiraz, Rabi'I, 846 July-August 1442
Private collection
Dimensions: 381 x 215 mm
Published: I. Stchoukine in *A A* XIX (1969), 7 and 11, fig. 2

In the national epic Iskandar (Alexander) does follow history in that he honours the family of his fallen foe Dara (Darius III) and orders the execution of his murderers. But the very human touch he displays in comforting Dara is apparently pure legend. Here the malefactors, prepared for execution, watch impassively.

Numerous vaguely grotesque faces can be distinguished in the rocky landscape; in the course of the century they were to appear in much sharper focus as

a favoured motif of Turkoman painting. The rocky outcrop on which the kings rest acts as a secondary horizon and the motif of the man peeping out above it is a typical feature of the Timurid Shiraz style. The massed bodies at the right-hand edge of the picture are an equally characteristic motif of this school.

40
Crows pecking at corpses
Manuscript; 185 ff. and 20 miniatures
Amir Khusrau Dihlavi, *Divan* ("Poetical works")
Qazvin style, late 16th century
London, British Library, Or. 11326, f. 68a
Dimensions: open book 272 x 425 mm; painting 135 x 73 mm
Published: Stchoukine, *S A,* 137 and pl. XVIIIa; Meredith-Owens. *Handlist,* 72; Titley, *Catalogue,* no. 55

It is typical of Persian painting from the Timurid period onwards that the necessary adjunct for any scene should be a background of landscape or

architecture conceived in terms of stage properties. Here the landscape has a tranquil beauty oddly at variance with the gruesome scene enacted within it.

The bearded gesticulating man dressed in scarlet and the sinister coal-black carrion birds stooping over their prey illustrate the use of colour alone as the vehicle for drama. The triangular projection in the margin points to the central figure and the slanting lines of calligraphy echo this sense of direction.

41
Faridun learns of the death of Iraj
Miniature painting
Firdausi, *Shahnama* (text, tr. Warner, I, 200-203)
Western Indian (?), c. 1450

Oxford, Ashmolean Museum, no. 1962, 153
Dimensions: leaf 260 x 165 mm; painting 125 x 121 mm

King Faridun decided to divide his kingdom and granted the choicest portion, Iran itself, to his youngest son Iraj. Salm and Tur, the two elder sons, then conspired to murder Iraj.

According to Firdausi's text, a messenger on a dromedary brought the head of Iraj to Faridun, who fell off his horse from shock while the troops rent their clothes. The artist tells the story in continuous narrative, a device not often used by Persian painters. Normally the murder of Iraj is a self-contained scene. Here Iraj is still pleading for his life while the mourners wail outside as if the murder had already taken place. Meanwhile Faridun gestures despairingly from the horizon. He is the secondary focus of interest and various compositional devices draw attention to him. Customs such as loud wailing, scratching the face, making the hair dishevelled and rending the clothes were characteristic practices of mourning in the Islamic world, although orthodoxy frowned on them. In this case the gestures remain wooden, far below the highly charged atmosphere of similar scenes in the Demotte *Shahnama* (**193b**).

Despite the stray survivals of the early Timurid Shiraz school in such details as waists and hats, the style is notably distinct from such models. In this painting the fussy, repetitive drapery lines, the brown vegetation and the extremely slant-eyed faces are not easily paralleled in other Timurid work. Decoration, too, is unusually pervasive for provincial work. The use of six columns of text instead of the usual four is perhaps an archaism. Red has a prominent role as often occurs in contemporary painting in Western India, and a strong case has recently been made by Fraad and Ettinghausen for placing pictures such as this within the orbit of the Persianised courts of Gujerat and the Deccan. For other paintings from this school see **2, 145** and **209**.

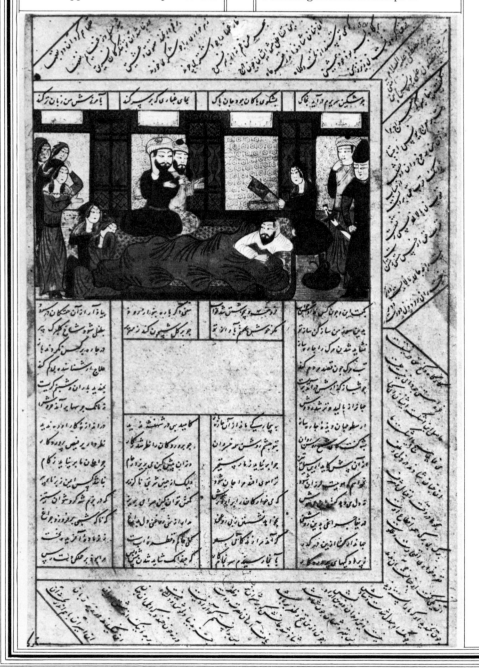

Sports

Hunting was the royal pastime *par excellence* in Islamic Iran. It was a form of conspicuous consumption, since only the richest could afford the great expense of training cheetahs and falcons, the creatures so often used in royal hunts. Cheetahs in particular had to be looked after by teams of experts and became status symbols. They were even displayed in royal processions. On the other hand, while princes were expected to master the art of hunting with hawk and cheetah – the latter seated pillion-wise on the rump of the horse – these creatures were not a prerogative of the ruler alone.

The prey most commonly depicted in Persian art is the gazelle and the onager or wild ass (**193i**). Images of this kind – e.g. Bahram Gur transfixing the ear and hoof of a deer with a single arrow – sometimes have their origins in the pre-Islamic period. But other favoured pre-Islamic stereotypes did not find favour with Persian painters – e.g. the image of the standing ruler stabbing a rearing beast. Perhaps this was regarded as too formal and symbolic an image. Hunting scenes in Persian painting tend to favour a middle way between a naturalistic and a symbolic rendering. The ruler is always shown to advantage, displaying some feat of archery of swordsmanship. He is surrounded by courtiers admiring his prowess. But in fact, many hunts were battues, vast affairs which involved the great princes and nobles of the realm and which lasted as long as three months. They were conducted, according to nomad custom, under the supervision of the Master of the Hunt who owed much of his prestige to his training responsibilities – for these battues were the occasion for the annual cavalry manoeuvres. Beaters herded the game into a vast enclosure and the animals were then systematically slaughtered. The Mongols particularly favoured such "hunts", which functioned as initiation ceremonies for youths of the tribe, and also served to replenish food supplies.

Just as the bloody mêlée of a battue was useful experience for war, so too the horsemanship which was needed for polo served as cavalry training. The pell-mell pace of the game and scores of jostling players were also in some sense a foretaste of battle conditions. Sir Anthony Sherley, writing in the 16th century, compares Persian polo to the rough football played in England at that time. Polo was known in Persia at least as early as c. 500 B.C. Princes were trained in the sport and **47** suggests that they learned the rudiments of the game by first playing it on foot.

The third sport illustrated in this section is wrestling. From Umayyad times onwards, as the 8th century frescoes of Qusair 'Amra show, this was a popular sport in the Islamic world. The form it took in Persia owed much to the influence of the Turkish slave troops imported from Central Asia by the 'Abbasid caliphs from the late 8th century onwards. These men excelled in wrestling and even the clothes they wore in their bouts – the long tight leather trousers shown in **48** – have remained traditional in Iran and Turkey to this day. With the Mongol conquest, royal patronage was extended to wrestling, for this was and is the Mongol national sport. The aim of the Iranian style of wrestling is to force an opponent briefly onto his back; the body is oiled but the opponent is gripped by the top of his trousers.

Among sedentary games chess enjoyed special prestige. It was a proper part of a princely education; in 'Assar's poem *Mihr u Mushtari* (**3, 43**) the prince Mihr demonstrates his skill by defeating ignominiously the best players at chess and draughts in the kingdom of Khwarizm. The great Timur himself enjoyed playing chess and a possibly apocryphal story relates how his son Shah Rukh received that name because Timur was executing a move in chess when he heard the news of the boy's birth. Images taken from the game are a favourite resource of Persian poets.

42
A game of polo
Manuscript; 325 ff. and 13 miniatures
Sa'di, *Gulistan* and *Bustan*
Shiraz, 943/1536-7
Copyist, Murshid al-katib al-Shirazi
Illuminator, Ghiyath al-Din Mahmud Shirazi
Previously exhibited: Lisbon 1963, London 1976
Lisbon, Calouste Gulbenkian Foundation Museum, no. L.A. 180, f. 217a
Dimensions: book 295 x 190 mm
Published: Gray, *AOI*, no. 125; Hayward Gallery. Catalogue, no. 599

Shiraz work of the early 16th century is heavily dependent on the metropolitan style of Tabriz. Yet while the artists of Shiraz were much taken with the elegant, lissom figures of this style and its richly peopled compositions, they found it difficult to reproduce these features. A certain gaucherie marks their imitations. Here, for example, the figures are too numerous and too large to be contained comfortably within the picture space. The result is a rather clumsy overcrowding. The busy atmosphere of the scene and the farrago of colours (e.g. the polychrome goal-posts) are typical of this school, as is the frontal depiction of the youth gaping at the game from the horizon.

The old man and his companion resemble the stock types depicting Naufal and Majnun except that the younger man is bearded. Their presence at this polo match is difficult to explain.

43
Mihr playing polo with King Kaivan
Manuscript
'Assar, *Mihr u Mushtari*;
Turkoman style, c. 1480
London, Royal Asiatic Society of Great Britain & Ireland Codrington 304
Dimensions: 197 x 114 mm
Published: Morley, *Catalogue*, no. 304; Robinson, *Bodleian*, no. 60

For details of this romantic poem, which enjoyed a particular vogue in the later 15th century, see **3** and **127**. Mihr, after suffering shipwreck like his friend Mushtari, makes his way to Khwarizm, where his personality captivates all hearts. The King of Khwarizm, Kaivan, believes him to be of royal blood and devises various trials to test this surmise. One is a game of polo, intended as a test of horsemanship and courage as much as of skill. Polo as usually described in the *Shahnama* was a game for the nobility involving four players a side. But much larger games were popular in later medieval times, with scores of players per side. Such matches served as training for cavalry; indeed the *jukandar* ("mallet-holder" or polo-master) functioned in this military sense too. Children and court ladies also played the game. By the Safavid period strict rules had evolved; it was symptomatic that the size of the pitch was now regulated (about 300 x 170 metres). The spirally fluted purple goal-posts with miniature onion domes shown here are known only from paintings.

This miniature has the simplified, vigorous drawing and bright colour typical of Turkoman painting. A characteristic Turkoman detail is the purple shading of the horizon. On all four sides the painting has curiously ragged edges, which suggests that it was never finished; the margins may have been added later. It is hard to believe that a conscientious artist would have left such a startling pentimento as the double silhouette of the royal horse's head.

44
Amir Khusrau grapples with a boar
Manuscript; 240 ff. and 8 miniatures, of which several have been removed
Shiraz school, c. 1570
Sultan Husain Mirza, *Majalis al-'Ushshaq*
Birmingham, Selly Oak Colleges Library, Mingana Pers. Ms. 12.
Dimensions: page 300 x 190 mm.
Previously exhibited: London 1967
Published: Robinson, *PMP*, no. 151

For the text of this manuscript, see

190; the order of the assemblies differs from the usual arrangement. The 34th assembly deals with the poet Amir Khusrau Dihlavi and shows him grappling single-handed and weaponless with a boar while four of his companions flee in panic. Details like the begging bowl, the staves and the half-naked state of these figures indicate that they are dervishes. Their discomfiture is well caricatured by gaping mouths and flailing arms. On the horizon, hunched neckless figures gesture in astonishment. This violent action takes place against a purple meadow bestrewn with enamelled clumps of blossoms spread out like starfish. The boar trying to escape into the reeds recalls the most famous representation of a boar hunt in Persian art – the Sasanian relief in the grotto at Taq-i Bustan.

45
Gushtasp and Caesar at polo

Miniature painting; parent manuscript has 440 ff. and 38 miniatures
Anthology; this leaf illustrates the Gushtasp Nama, an extract from the *Shahnama* of Firdausi (text, tr. Warner, IV, 350)
Shiraz, 813/1410-11
Probably copyists, Mahmud b. Murtaza b. Ahmad al-Hafiz al-Hasaini and Hasan al-Hafiz
Dedicated to Iskandar Sultan
Lisbon, Calouste Gulbenkian Foundation Museum L.A. 1617 f. 118a; formerly in Yates Thompson and Rothschild Collections
Dimensions: 273 x 180 mm
Previously exhibited: Lisbon 1963; London 1976
Published: To the bibliography

assembled by Stchoukine, *MT*, no. XIV, may be added Gray, *PP 1961*, 69-72, pls. 74-77 and 79; Grube, *WI*, pls. 53-4; Ettinghausen, *Persian Art, Calouste Gulbenkian Collection* (Lisbon, 1972), pl. 15; E. J. Grube, communication to VIth International Congress of Iranian Art and Archaeology, (oxford, 1972, 29-30); Kirketerp-Moller, *Bogmaleri*, 108-10; E. G. Sims, in *aarp* 6 (1974), 56-67; Hayward Gallery Catalogue, no. 551

For the subject matter, see **46**. In later iconography Gushtasp is customarily shown taking part in the game, which is the entire point of the text; here, like Caesar himself, he watches from the horizon.

Much of the interest of this *Anthology*, a key monument of early Timurid painting, lies in the varying responses of its painters to the pictorial conventions which had only recently evolved. A favourite reaction to the high horizon is illustrated here: the device of dividing the figures into three superposed horizontal groups. This arrangement recurs frequently in the manuscript (e.g. f. 166, apparently by the same master). The topmost group is often partly obscured by the horizon. But here the painter has enlivened this potentially sterile formula by depicting various degrees of involvement in the scene. Caesar and Gushtasp both look away from the game, the umpire fixes his eye on the ball, while a lone horseman rides up to collect a mallet from a servant. All these figures serve to frame the central mêlée, which is treated like a cavalry charge. The audacious poses of the horses are perhaps the most striking and original feature of the painting. Caesar's steed is successfully depicted head-on, a trick of drawing that had eluded the Rashid al-Din master and was to elude Bihzad, while the umpire's horse, seen from behind, is a laudable feat of imagination if not observation.

For other leaves from this manuscript, see **65, 95, 174, 197**, and **203**. The miniatures of this *Anthology* have been heavily restored in recent years as a result of damage sustained in a flood.

46
Gushtasp displays his prowess before Caesar

Miniature painting
Firdausi, *Shahnama* (text, tr. Warner, IV, 350)
Qazvin, probably 1576-7
Upper left margin bears attribution to, or signature of, Siyavush
Private collection
Previously exhibited: Paris 1912 (the parent manuscript)
Published: for the manuscript in general, see **155**. For this leaf, see Robinson, *Iran* XIV (1976), 5

Gushtasp, neglected by his father King Luhrasp, had left Iran in anger and gone incognito to the court of the

45

Caesar of Rum (the Byzantine emperor). Caesar's daughter chose him as her husband and her father reluctantly agreed. Eventually he gained the royal favour by putting the local cavaliers to shame at polo and archery.

This episode is rendered rather freely here, for the setting in the text is the exercise ground in front of the royal belvedere. The obvious Safavid equivalent would have been the Ali Qapu on the *maidan* at Isfahan. But Siyavush, true to his preference for large undifferentiated areas of colour, rejects an architectural setting – which would have required much detailed work – in favour of a rocky wilderness in rusty red. This colour dominates the whole painting. Other colours, like blue and black – used for the horses – are chosen simply to act as a foil for it. This large setting accommodates his large figures with ease. The looming crags are typical of Siyavush alike in their sense of drama and in their rather simplified form. Robinson has attempted to identify at least eight painters who worked on this manuscript, which was probably produced for Isma'il II and ranks as a critical document of later 16th century painting. Siyavush is credited with easily the largest share of illustration – some 19 pictures.

Music-making was an integral part of polo at court; hence the trumpeter and drummer accompanying Caesar.

47
Ardashir recognises his son Shapur playing polo

Manuscript; 538 ff, and 23 miniatures
Firdausi, *Shahnama* (text: Warner VI, 263-4)
Dated 18 Dhu'l-Qa'da 967/10 August 1560 "at Shiraz"
Copyist, Hasan b. Muhammad Ahsan

London, India Office Library, Ethé 863
Dimensions: leaf 380 x 225 mm.; painting 225 x 200 mm.
Previously exhibited: London 1931, 1951, 1967
Published: *BWG*, no. 202; Guest, *Shiraz Painting*, Appendix no. 35, pls. 45, 46a; Robinson, *VAM* 1951, no. 50; Robinson, *VAM* 1952, pl. 20; Stchoukine, *MS*, no. 121, pls. XLIV-XLVIII; Robinson, *PD*, 140 and pl. 89; Robinson, *PMP*, no. 148 and pl. 49; Robinson, *IOL*, 89-97, and no. 286

Ardashir, enraged because his wife had tried to poison him, ordered that she should be killed even though she was pregnant. The order was disobeyed and seven years later the king, whose childlessness weighed heavily on him, was told of this. To identify his son he ordered a hundred boys dressed similarly to be set to play polo. He recognised his son because Shapur alone had the courage to carry off the ball right in front of the king. Time and again the *Shahnama* stresses that the ruler must be legitimate if the country

is to thrive. The rightful king could be recognised by the royal splendour (*farr*) which radiates from him, but feats of bravery (cf. **208**) also serve to identify him.

Much of the splendour of the painting is due to its bright, fresh colours. These triumph over the stereotyped mannerisms of dress, gesture, vegetation and even grouping – thus the king and his vizier plagiarise the traditional arrangement used in scenes of Nushirvan and the birds. That the game being played here is indeed polo (*guy*) is indicated by the text, the posts (compare those which still survive in the great square at Isfahan) and the implements. Presumably children learned the rudiments of the game on foot before progressing to mounts (cf. **6**).

48
A wrestling match

Manuscript; 128 ff. and 13 miniatures, six of them contemporary with the text
Sa'di, *Gulistan* (text, tr. J. Ross [London, n.d.], 113-5)
Bukhara 957/1567-8
Copyist, Mir 'Ali al-Husaini al-Katib al-Sultani
Signed "work of Shahm the gilder"

Patron: probably 'Abdallah b. Iskandar of Bukhara
London, British Library, Or. 5302, f. 30a
Dimensions: open book 350 x 500 mm.; painting 280 x 170 mm.
Previously exhibited: London 1967, 1976
Published: Martin *MP*, 54 and pls. 146-7; Blochet, *MP*, pl. CXVIII; Pinder Wilson, *Muslim Courts*, no. 3; Titley, *Catalogue*, No. 348

A master wrestler, who knew a hold for each of the 360 days of the Muslim year, took a liking to one of his pupils and taught him all he knew, reserving one hold only. The youth grew arrogant and boasted that he was better than his master, whereupon the King ordered an exhibition match. Knowing the youth to be stronger, the master at once threw him by using the one hold which he had not divulged, and quipped "As the wise have told us, put it not so much into a friend's power that, if hostilely disposed, he can do you an injury".

Robinson has suggested that this manuscript was produced for presentation to the emperor Akbar by the Shaibanid ruler 'Abdallah b. Iskandar, ruler of Bukhara from 1557-1578. He also draws attention to the Mughal costume worn by the courtiers. This supposition is very probable. Seven of the thirteen miniatures are Mughal work of c. 1605, while the ruler's baldachin bears an **Arabic inscription reading "in the days of the dominion of the mighty** *Khaqan*, Jalal al-Din Muhammad Akbar Padishah . . . may God cause his kingdom and his happiness and his Sultanate to endure". Appropriately enough, the ruler seated beneath appears to be Akbar himself. Perhaps this subject was deliberately chosen for illustration, since wrestling was a popular sport among the Mughal nobility and even the king himself took part. Akbar had first displayed his prowess at the sport when not yet

three (see the *Akbarnama* in the Bodleian Library, MS. Ouseley Add. 171, fol. 13b).

If, then, the work was intended for export, it must represent the best of which the Bukhara school was capable at the time. The artist, Shahm *mudhahhib* ("the gilder"; not a rare title for Persian painters – cf. **195c** and **d**) blends clarity of design with a meticulous attention to detail remarkable in so large and crowded a painting.

49
Youth with his falcon

Miniature painting from the Album of the Amir of Bukhara; 21 ff. and 18 miniatures Isfahan, early 17th century

New York, Pierpont Morgan Library, no. M.386-4
Dimensions: leaf 378 x 241 mm.; painting including borders 238 x 128 mm.; painting excluding borders 140 x 90 mm.
Previously exhibited: San Francisco 1937; Venice 1962; New York 1968
Published: Sarre and Martin, *Meisterwerke* I, pl. 34; Martin, *MP*, 151; Kühnel, *MIO*, 35, 61 and pl. 75; H. Glück and E. Diez, *Die Kunst des Islam* (Berlin, 1925), pl. 515; M. H. de Young Memorial Museum, *Exhibition of Islamic Art*, 32 and pl. 68; Grube, *MMP*, no. 101; Grube, *Classical Style*, no. 88; Asia House Gallery, *Masterpieces of Asian Art in American Collections* (New York, 1970), 36-7

From the later 16th century onwards, patrons gradually began to commission single leaves instead of entire illustrated manuscripts. The painting itself was only one element in a splendid ensemble. Separate specialists executed the panels of calligraphy, painted the meticulous detail of the illumination and prepared the highly polished paper speckled with gold. Finally the binder would assemble many such leaves within tooled leather covers embellished with sunken painted medallions of the floral type found on a larger scale in contemporary carpets. Encased like a relic in its rich multiple frames, such a painting distils, in a supremely formal way, the essence of court life. Small wonder that this leaf found its way into the Album of the Amir of Bukhara.

The young exquisite drawing on a glove with apparently artless grace, one slipper casually discarded, may seem the embodiment of careless relaxation. But his pose obeys the formal conventions established in the previous few decades. The characteristic inclined head is one such convention, but it also allows the artist unobtrusively to utilise the entire height of the picture space. Similarly, tradition requires an undulating silhouette for the youth, and the artist has profited from this to create a twisting pose which expands laterally as well as vertically. The swelling breast of the falcon dovetails with the incurving silhouette of the youth's side. It is only fitting that not even the unsheathed claws of the bird should ruffle his relaxed poise.

50
A mounted prince hawking
Miniature painting
Bukhara style, third quarter of 16th century
India Office Library, no. J. 28-2
Dimensions: page 370 x 235 mm.; painting 140 x 85 mm.
Published: Robinson, *IOL*, no. 894 (illustrated)

Typical hallmarks of the Bukhara style here are the bright but not intense colours, the floral decoration in gold

(which is extraordinarily coarse) and the multi-lobed pointed arch which forms the frame. Such leaves, commonly produced for connoisseurs who lacked the means to commission full-scale illuminated manuscripts, found their way into albums (*muraqqa'at*) consisting solely of such work. This access to a wider range of patrons emancipated the artist from total dependence on the favour of a single prince and made it possible for several of the bolder spirits (such as Riza-i 'Abbasi) to leave the court at least temporarily.

In this picture an uncertain command of detail is apparent in the summary black dabs which render the arrows, in the muddy plumage of the bird and in the simplified patterns of the saddle cloth. The composition derives much of its éclat from its accessories – the carefully spaced accents of deep blue illumination and of calligraphy. These features can attain prominence precisely because the artist is unconstrained by the demands of narrative. It is a display piece, in which, by a paradox, the apparently central theme is the least successfully treated.

The bird on the prince's wrist is a reminder that in Safavid as in earlier times the Persians were keen exponents of falconry. Indeed, a Safavid mews still survived in Isfahan in the 1930s, and this same period saw the composition of a major treatise on the subject. As in the west, the sport was the preserve of the nobility. The groom preceding the prince is the *shutur* or running footman, a fixture in Safavid court life. Despite his jester's cap and pointed slippers, his task was in dead earnest – literally to run in front of his master, clearing a passage where necessary – a job so punishing that deaths in service were not rare.

51
A hawking party in the mountains
Miniature painting
Right half of frontispiece to an unidentified manuscript
Qazvin style, c. 1580

Boston, Museum of Fine Arts, no. 14.624
Dimensions: page 473 x 324 mm.; painting 375 x 248 mm.
Previously exhibited: Venice 1962; New York 1968
Published Coomaraswamy, *Goloubew*, 43-4 and pl. XXXVI; Stchoukine, *MS*, no. 62; Gray, *PP 1951*, 158-9 (colour plate); Grube, *MMP*, no. 92B; Grube, *Classical Style*, no. 77.2; Welch, *KBK*, 73, 76 and fig. 17

Falconry was a favourite sport in Persia and involved training many types of birds. At the Safavid court it was a major institution employing large numbers of people. These men were arranged not only according to their function – e.g. snaring, training, hunting and so on – but also according to species of birds. Thus the Head

Falconer, (*qush-khana-aqasi*) was an official of some standing who flew birds in earnest only at the hunt.

The high standing of the sport, and the range of expertise available about it, helps to explain the care with which the artist has depicted the equipment and the varieties of birds themselves in this leaf and its companion piece in the Metropolitan Museum (no. 12. 223-1). He blends this precise observation with a happy vein of fantasy exemplified by the twisted hollow tree and the rocks cascading into the outer margin. This imaginative treatment of nature, which also governs the marginal decoration, is a fit setting for this exquisite evocation of courtly pleasures. The painting is a supreme example of the Qazvin style. Rural outings of this kind enjoyed a distinct vogue in later 16th century painting, but the use of such scenes for a double frontispiece is unusual. Formal enthronement or hunting scenes are the norm. Below the prince, a youth broils a bird over a fire; Muslim theologians were not agreed as to the legality of eating birds caught by falconry for it was not always possible to slaughter it according to the prescribed rites.

52
The fowler and the pigeons
Manuscript; 150 ff. and 64 miniatures
Nasrallah b. al-Ma'ali, Persian translation of the Fables of Bidpai (*Kalila wa Dimna*)
Turkoman style, 895/1489-90
Copyist, Murshid b. Sadr al-Din
Birmingham, Selly Oak Colleges Library, Mingana Persian Ms. 10, f. 77a
Dimensions: page 265 x 160 mm.
Previously exhibited: London 1967
Published: Robinson, *PMP*, no. 131

For the text, see V. Kubickova, *Persian Fables*, tr. G. Theiner [London, 1960], 124. A raven had watched a fowler scattering grain as a bait beneath his net and warned a flock of pigeons accordingly. They ignored these words and were caught, but saved themselves by following the raven's advice and flying up all at once, thereby taking the net with them. In the classic illustration of this fable (see *SPA*, pl. 865) the raven watches the discomfiture of the fowler. Here the raven has been omitted, perhaps for reasons of space; the illustrations in this manuscript are tiny. They are liable to occur anywhere on the page and rarely take up more than one-third of it. Their execution is usually rather hurried, and margins which do not coincide with those of the page itself are left unruled. The animal paintings in particular are full of spirit. Sometimes there are as many as three pictures per opening, while two are common.

The manuscript has undergone certain vicissitudes over the years; all the pages have been remounted and many have been carelessly trimmed.

More than one scribe worked on the manuscript, for the handwriting changes at f. 78.

53
Horseman attacked by lion
Tinted drawing
Qazvin, c. 1578
Signed Siyavush, in red ink
Baltimore, Walters Art Gallery, no. W.747 (formerly in Kelekian collection)
Dimensions: leaf 323 x 215 mm.; drawing 135 x 102 mm.
Published: Catalogue of Kelekian Estate, no. 23 (1952); Robinson, *PD* 135 and pl. 42 (colour); Welch, *Artists*, 30-33 and figs. 5 and 6

The work and personality of Siyavush the Georgian, one of the major artists of this period, has recently been explored in impressive detail by Anthony Welch (*Artists*, 17-40). This is one of his three signed drawings.

Drawings depicting dragons in a style which mingled fantasy with drama were part of the stock-in-trade of the Persian artist. Sometimes, as here, this tradition bore unexpected fruit. The brutal exaggeration of the lion's mouth and claws owes much to conventions established in such drawings. So too does his fearfully lithe striding form. Even the detail of the horse biting the lion is not original, for in *Shahnama* illustrations Rustam's horse Rakhsh is shown in similar style coping with a marauding lion while Rustam sleeps nearby.

Some of the vigour and intense drama which animate this brush drawing evaporate in paintings by the same artist (e.g. **46** and **155**). There use of colour lends even a plain background an undue importance, while detail obtrudes. But in this drawing only the lion is coloured in full, for the action focusses on him. Siyavush tends to soften the silhouettes of the rocks and the lion, which are executed in reddish tones; he employs a crisp linear style for the rest of the design.

54
A game of chess
Manuscript; 89 ff. and 9 miniatures
Anthology of poetry; the book is open at the poems of Maulana Ashraf Shirvan, 873/1468-9
Copyist: Sharaf al-Din Husain Sultani. According to Miss N. M. Titley, the patron may have been Farrukh Yasar

British Library, Add. 1651, f. 36b
Dimensions: page 233 x 280 mm.;
    painting 120 x 78 mm.
Previously exhibited: London 1967,
    1976
Published: Rieu, *Catalogue 2*, 734;
    Arnold, *PI*, pl. III; Stchoukine, *MT*,
    no. L, pl. XLV; Robinson, *PM*, pls.
    8-10 (this miniature illustrated in
    colour on pl. 8); Robinson, *OA* IV
    (1958), 114 and fig. 13; Kühnel,
    PM, pl. 23; Robinson, *PMP*, no.
    109; Hayward Gallery Catalogue,
    no. 570; Titley, *Catalogue*, no. 97

The *Shahnama* recounts (text, tr.
Warner, VII, 385-8) how chess reached
Persia from India in the time of
Khusrau Anushirvan (531-79). The
consensus of modern opinion, too,
accepts that the game was invented in
India, even though some scholars have
canvassed Persia as the country of
origin. Chess took several forms in the
medieval period. This miniature shows
a board with 64 squares, but Firdausi
describes a game played on a board
with 100 squares (text, tr. Warner, VII,
421-3). The quantities and types of
pieces also varied from one game to
another. They included the king, the
vizier, elephants, dromedaries, knights,
foot-soldiers and *rukhs* (the latter was
the fabulous bird which carried off
Sinbad; the western term "rook"
derives from it). The scale of the
painting is too small to identify any of
these pieces. To judge by his smug
gesture of triumph, the prince has just
won; the youth opposite is already
conducting a post-mortem on the
game. Numerous detailed touches
mark out the lofty rank of the prince.
They include his striped turban, a
fashion which lasted to the end of
Safavid times (**80** and **107**), his larger
stature and the flowered mat on which
he sits. His cross-legged position
conforms to a traditional kingly image
and contrasts with the deferential
kneeling posture of his companions.

Robinson has noted that the painting
is scarcely à propos the love poem it
illustrates, for it fixes on a single line
in that poem ("to the effect that 'the
onlooker sees most of the game'")
and takes it out of context. It is a reminder
that Persian artists were by no means
wedded to the texts which they
illustrated. In its diminutive figures and
love for surface display in rich colours
the miniature seems close to such
mature examples of the Turkoman style
as the India Office Nizami of c. 1505 (**24**)

55
A game of backgammon
Manuscript; 239 ff. and 7 miniatures,
    all but one on 3 double pages
    Amir Khusrau Dihlavi, *Khamsa*.
Herat, 978-9/1570-2
The inscription attributes the work to
Nadir al-'Asri Farrukh Beg

Cambridge, Kings College Library, no.
    Pote 153
Dimensions: 240 x 175 mm.
Previously exhibited: London 1967

Published: Palmer, *Catalogue*, ,
    R. W. Skelton, *AO* II (1957),
    395-6 and fig. 4; Robinson, *PMP*,
    no. 170

The interest of this miniature lies less
in its quality than in its subject matter.
Firdausi describes in the *Shahnama*
(text, tr. Warner, VII, 389-93)
how Buzurgmihr, the vizier of
Khusrau Anushirvan, invented the
military game of *nard* (backgammon)
and challenged the ruler of India to
discover how it was played. The
monarch's advisers were baffled and he
therefore had to pay a year's tribute to
the Shah. In fact a form of backgammon
seems to have been known in Ur c. 3000
B.C. and thence to have travelled to
ancient Egypt. The Romans knew a
similar game. Backgammon has
retained its popularity in the Near East
to this day.

Like its companion piece on the
opposite page, this painting is
unfinished, as its lack of margination
indicates. The dark blue board with its
gold divisions is typical of the whole
painting in its delight in simple
contrasting colours. Such colours, like
the rudimentary drawing and the
bland expressions of the youths, are
hallmarks of the Khurasan style. The
device of a double page with unrelated
compositions recurs in another
manuscript from Khurasan exhibited
here (**104**).

56
Iskandar shooting wild duck from a ship
Miniature painting
Probably from Mir 'Ali Shir Nawa'i,
    Sadd-i Iskandar ("The Rampart of
    Alexander", an imitation of the
    Iskandar Nama of Nizami)
Perhaps Bukhara, later 16th century

London, British Museum, no. 1937
    7-10 0323; formerly in Shannon
    collection
Dimensions: leaf 408 x 285 mm.;
    painting 233 x 132 mm.
Previously exhibited: London 1949,
    1959, 1965
Published: Titley, *Catalogue*, no. 300

It is a measure of the pomp and
circumstance surrounding the ruler in
Persian tradition that he cannot even
go duck-shooting without bringing an
army of retainers. This is no simple
hunting expedition. Iskandar adopts a
pose more in keeping with a convivial
scene, musicians strum lutes and harps,
wine flows freely. One of the courtiers
has partaken not wisely but too well
and has to be supported while his head
lolls slackly. The awning or sail of the
princely boat and the gilded bird's-
head prow make it clear that this is a
pleasure craft. Perhaps the regattas in
Safavid Isfahan had something of this
quality. The Taq-i Bustan reliefs
indicate that such scenes were a
feature of royal iconography as early
as Sasanian times.

But for all the courtly and exotic

flavour of the scene – the ducks, for
example, follow Chinese models – the
treatment of detail is informed by
lively observation. In the foreground
two bare-legged fishermen draw up
their nets, oblivious of the royal party.
Such contrasts of high and low life are
frequent in 16th-century painting. The
courtiers are individuals, not types. In
this, as in their frequently hunched
poses – heads are set askew directly on
the shoulders with no necks – they
derive from Herati models; cf. Rice,
IP, 134 and pl. 60.

Duck shooting would be most
readily available in the marshes of the
Caspian, and it is interesting that a folk
memory of Alexander survives to this
day in the nearly Turkoman steppe. For
the ruined wall which can still be seen
there and was probably erected by the
Sasanians against the Hephthalite
Huns is called Sadd-i Iskandar.

57
Forest conflict
Early 15th century

Geneva, collection of Prince
    Sadruddin Aga Khan, no. Ir. M. 7;
    formerly in Kirkor Minassian
    collection
Dimensions: leaf 190 x 89 mm.
Previously exhibited: New York 1940
Bibliography: Ackerman, *Guide*,
    203; Welch *Collection* I, 93, 95

Hunting scenes in Persian miniatures
tend to have a fixed, frozen quality
which is oddly at variance with the lifelike rendering of the animals depicted.
So carefully composed are they that the
excitement of the chase seems remote.
This tableau may help to explain the
origin of such scenes. Though datable
to the early Timurid period, it
represents a manner which maintained
its currency into late Safavid times, and
is well documented in a series of albums
in Istanbul. This more or less unvarying
style brings serious dating problems in
its train; dates ranging between the
14th and 17th century have been
proposed for a drawing of this type in
the British Museum (no. 1948 12-11
024). The key to the meaning of the
drawing is that it is an exercise. It is
intended to develop and test qualities
of draughtsmanship and composition.
Hence the stylised execution; hence,
too, the lack of emotional rapport one
can sense between the artist and the
violently dramatic scene he has
conjured into being. The picture
divides itself quite naturally into a
series of individual vignettes, unrelated
even though they are crammed close
together. The sense of excited, panicky
activity transmits itself even to leaves,
branches and clouds, elements which
interest the artist just as much as living
creatures and which form an intrusive,
dominant backcloth for the action. The
picture resolves itself into a closely
woven tapestry that denies depth in
favour of line – the leaves betray a hint
of modelling but are all tinted alike.
Yet the eddying curves of the design

are marshalled with the sure hand of a virtuoso.

This linear emphasis weakens an otherwise savage vision of nature red in tooth and claw, and the disproportion of the various creatures, as well as the fanciful Chinese nature of some of them, contrive to distance reality still further. We are left with no more than a reminder of the hunt.

58
Bahram Gur Hunting

Miniature painting
Nizami, *Khamsa* (this leaf is from the *Haft Paikar*; text, tr. Wilson, 50-1)
Probably Shiraz, c. 1490

London, Victoria and Albert Museum, no. E. 1589-1953
Dimensions: page 245 x 140 mm.

painting 185 x 82 mm.
Published: Robinson, *VAM* 1965, 11 and pl. 10

The painting illustrates how Bahram – the Sasanian King Varahran V, 420-38 – came by his title of Bahram Gur. While out hunting one day he saw a lion rending an onager (gur). Drawing his bow, he shot an arrow with such force that, as the text shown here says, "the sharp point struck the shoulders of the two, (and) having pierced (them) passed through both the holes" and buried itself in the ground up to its feathers. Bahram rarely lacks an admiring audience for this and similar feats of the chase (**195f**).

Its colour harmonies make the Turkoman school perhaps the most attractive of the standardised "utility"

styles which perennially flourished beside the more ambitious productions of the metropolitan centres. Landscape in particular is simplified. The horizon lacks the fanciful rocky profile so dear to earlier 15th century artists and has become a straight line. Vegetation is only sparsely detailed, whereas in the finest works of this school (e.g. **14**) the exploration of nature becomes a fit subject in its own right. Here nature is primarily a backdrop for the ostentatious display of the ruler's prowess. But its fresh colour redeems this landscape from monotony; Turkoman work rarely fails to be decorative. The bulky turbans with a trailing end-piece are characteristic of the school.

It is a pity that the manuscript to which this leaf belonged is not known, for if the text was written in its accepted order and without repetitions, this leaf would illustrate in striking fashion how carefully text and illustration were sometimes dovetailed. The distich written in the picture represents precisely the two lines that best describe the king's feat. Since the iconography of this scene was fixed, the credit for this exact reciprocity must go to the scribe.

59
A prince hunting deer and seated with his consort

Miniature paintings; leaves are ff. 1 and 2 of a manuscript temporarily unbound, which has 322 ff. and 93 miniatures plus one double-page miniature exhibited here
Firdausi, *Shahnama*
Shiraz school; *ex-libris* dated 740/1339-40

Private collection
Dimensions: page 291 x 210 mm, painting 265 x 180 mm
Previously exhibited: London 1931, New York 1940 (leaf only)
Published: *London 1931*, no. 532; *BWG*, no. 22 and pl. XIIIa; Ackerman, *Guide*, 194; Schroeder, *Fogg*, 28; Grube, *Kraus*, no. 33; *Sotheby*, 12.4 1976, lot 190

This manuscript, the so-called "Stephens *Shahnama*", despite its damaged state and the disorder of its leaves, is one of the few surviving complete books executed in the Inju style which flourished in Shiraz around 1340. Many more single leaves in this style are of course known. Their distinguishing features are quickly recognisable – red or yellow backgrounds, a symbolic notation for trees, mountains and other elements of landscape, and a preference for chubby red-cheeked faces. Animals are treated with an instinctive grace which is not extended to the human form. This manuscript well illustrates the range of Inju painting, for while battles predominate there are numerous episodes of enthronements and other peaceful scenes which show the painter varying his formulae with considerable success.

the Court and Ceremonies

بمرد و زد ست خوش و دست
که شاه آن شفاعت در پذیرفت
چو خورشید و نتح نزبر در ا
چو پیش او بند نائبد عنان کس

وز ان غم سائی از پای پشت
کنائی را که شد بر وی نکبر
جو شمع انکنت پر آن پسر رفتی
شفیع آنکینت پر آن شه گفت

گنزد دست به آن سر و دنیا
برانذر شاه اده چون اسیر ان
جهان دنیا دد بستا خیر ذا
به چشم جهان بر غلیلت به خاک

کشا با پیش از نیم رخ منای
منوزم بوی شیرپ اید زیاما
که جم ست انک تیغ و کردن
بکنای این و کرده به سنگ خاک
و ان زاری که گفته به سربه انفا
نه خوذی که دولت بند نخواه
و به نیک و به مشو در بند فرزند
بجان فرز لکی اسهست رای
و ان حضرت جو پرون فرزخسرو
جو امد ز ان شب زبرده سهسار بی
بدرون امد ز پرده سحسار بی

بزرگی کن خو خوره ان جبشای
مشو در خون جون میخوار ان
به کشتن زمن نسلیک بدون
بکم بر پسر شاهد ان کو نیک
کبریه های ی به نما انا
جوان اقبال پذیر ربا خو نخواه
نیابت خوکند فرز زدفرز
بدافت او که اذ آن فرخت ا
خرش سپای عدل ز او دور

بن یوسف بمین که کالا دکر
غنایت که این سکه نوبر
که بک معنی دارم زر رنج ا
و و گفته نذری که کرده آن نبرد
که خفی خورد با این ناز بینی
جه ساز د با تو فرز دمنت
جو مره دیکان دشعت ستی
سرکش یوسید دشعت مسی
خرش سپای عدل ز او دور

که بس خوذت اگر جرخ بینش رست
نه ذار د طاقت غنم جد او نند
نه دارم بک خشرنوذی شاه
نه کنند پشداد الحق منذری
کند درکار دارد نیمان خودمنی
همان سپند بر فرز نه از بس خوش
مداوای روان و میوه دل
و لی عهد سپاه خوش خوش گرش
جهان داری ز رد و بیش نغ رمید
نبار کلی خوشذ دوست شنای
شش اذ اذار ی خجای بازری

Enthroned monarchs are one of the crucial themes of Persian painting. It is therefore important to discover why the theme maintained its popularity throughout the whole period covered by this exhibition. The prime function of this image was to act as a symbol of power. In the early 14th century this symbolic intent found corresponding expression in designs of arresting simplicity (61): the enthroned monarch would be flanked by a courtier on each side and the background would be almost entirely plain. Soon these empty spaces were filled by accessory detail, whether this consisted of trees and flowers or of rich artefacts and furnishings. Figures shrank in size to make way for this extra material.

But the aim of the representation had in no way changed; it was still intended to exalt the ruler. Inscriptions above the doors and windows of his palace sang his praises. Sometimes quite crude distinctions of size emphasised royal power; thus King Hurmuzd towers over his undersized and guilty son (100). Even when the monarch is not identified by his crown he still occupies the throne, which itself becomes a potent imperial symbol. His courtiers must stand or squat on the floor and if they are seated their stools are far below the level of the throne. Sometimes they offer gifts in submissive poses, following a custom older than Persepolis. On festal days the King himself will distribute largesse (107). Around the king stands his bodyguard (97), the reminder of his armed might, while close to the steps of the throne is often stationed the vizier. His position was precarious – for the first half-century of Ilkhanid rule not one vizier died in his bed – but the rewards were correspondingly great; when Arghun ascended the throne he ordered enough gold poured over his vizier's head to cover him completely. Of lesser importance was the chamberlain, who is often shown standing guard at the door (100) ready to expel uninvited bystanders (96). Graceful youths bearing covered dishes and ewers with iced beverages ply to and fro. Musicians play and dancing girls perform. Despite such "informal" touches, however, these enthronement scenes show the king on parade. His wealth must be apparent for all to see: patterned silk costumes, Chinese ceramics, inlaid metalwork. Most exotic of all, perhaps, are the carpets – for centuries the gift of kings, often woven of silk and studded with jewels. Even nowadays, when carpets are widely available, their inexhaustibly varied designs, hallowed by extreme antiquity and often of unguessed meaning, stir eddies in the mind as surely as any quatrain of Omar Khayyam. In the sumptuous context of these court scenes, where glazed tilework and tents of embroidered satin also seduce the eye, they help to conjure up images of untold wealth. It is one task of the painter to present this propaganda as convincingly as possible.

Even the leisured air of the gathering emphasises that the kind does not need to labour for his living, unlike the gardener outside his palace (77). On the other hand, these audiences imposed their own strain, since they could continue for hours at a time. Many of these public enthronement scenes take place in the open air; this could perhaps be interpreted as an atavistic hankering after the free life of the nomad. A noteworthy omission from these scenes is any representative of religious orthodoxy – this courtly world was concerned to present itself in purely secular terms.

Enough has been said to indicate how stereotyped the image of the enthroned monarch had become by the 15th century. Even minor details were laid down. It was therefore simple for minor princes with small courts to take over this iconography and give it much wider currency. The painter, like the poet, was a trapping of royal life and a necessity for those ambitious to usurp the royal prerogative. Since book illustration in pre-Safavid times could only flourish at a court, the numerous provincial schools of painting reflect the fissiparous state of the Iranian polity in the post-Ilkhanid period.

60
Mounted prince
Manuscript; 240 ff. and a frontispiece miniature
Abu'l-Faraj al-Isfahani, *Kitab al-Aghani* ("Book of Songs")
Probably 'Iraq, 1219
Copyist, Muhammad b. Abi Talib al-Badri

Copenhagen, Royal Library, Cod. arab. CLXVIII, f. 1a
Dimensions: 286 x 215 mm
Previously exhibited: London 1976
Published: *Codices Orientales Bibliothecae Refiae Hafniensis* Copenhagen, (1851) II, 106–7; S.M. Stern in *AO* II (1957;, 501–3 figs. 1–2; Ettinghausen, *AP*, 62; A.S. Melikian Chirvani, *AA* XVI (1967), 19; Kirketerp-Møller, *Bogmaleri*, 80 and colour plate opposite 82; Hayward Gallery Catalogue, no. 517

Very little survives of Persian book painting before the Mongol invasion. Its characteristics must therefore be reconstructed on the basis of evidence provided by related schools of painting and other art forms, principally pottery. Saljuq pottery in Persia, especially the wares produced after c. 1150, establishes beyond dispute the popularity of courtly themes, among which the mounted prince – often, as here, huge in relation to his horse – was prominent. The facial type then current had much in common with the image here – slanting eyes and a flat face with heavy jowls. This standard depiction of facial features won acceptance in parts of the Arab world too, as the image here, probably painted in 'Iraq, shows. Even the use of the margin to cut off the figures is a typically Persian feature. Other details of the picture reflect quite different traditions. The angels poised in homage over the ruler perpetuate the concept of the classical victory figure, perhaps through the intermediary of Byzantine angels. A similar classical and Byzantine ancestry can be traced for the semi-circular

drapery which frames the royal halo. This was originally an attribute of the personification for Night, and is so used in Byzantine art, but there too (e.g. in the Kahrie Cami) it was finally shorn of meaning and reduced to an ornamental flourish. Byzantine enamelwork seems to have inspired the borders and perhaps the treatment of the water too. Even the distinctive Mesopotamian drapery convention, an angular version of the "scrollfolds" of 129, is executed in gold. It thus recalls the celebrated Byzantine chrysography, the technique of rendering drapery folds in gold. Once again a parallel with enamelwork seems justified.

The armbands carry the name of Badr al-Din Lu'lu', regent of Mosul at this time. Presumably this image is to be regarded as a formal official representation of him.

61
Afrasiyab enthroned
Miniature painting
Firdausi, *Shahnama* (text, tr. Warner)
Tabriz school, early 14th century

Private collection

This miniature and its companion piece (62) are of exceptional interest as hitherto unknown examples of the metropolitan style of Tabriz in the early 14th century. Dr. Melikian-Chirvani is preparing a detailed study of these leaves and it will therefore suffice to draw attention here to one or two unusual features in them. Although they seem to represent the earliest book illustrations to the *Shahnama* yet known (earlier examples paradoxically exist in ceramics) they nonetheless postdate the completion of the epic by some 300 years or so. The reasons for this long hiatus are still not fully clear but the most likely explanation is that such illustrated copies of the epics did exist, only to perish, along with most other Persian book painting, in the course of the Mongol invasions. Rather austere and abbreviated en-

thronement scenes of the kind shown here are commoner in the fifteenth century *Jami' al-Tawarikh* or *Majma' al-Tawarikh* manuscripts (e.g. **56**) than in the Rashid al-Din codices of the early 14th century, but **170** has numerous illustrations of Chinese emperors shown without any accessory details at all. The scene depicted here therefore conforms with the spirit at least of one of the Ilkhanid fashions for portraying royalty. The face of the ruler perhaps evokes 15th century rather than 14th century parallels; it may conceivably have suffered overpainting. The facial types are markedly different from those of the companion leaf; they are rendered in linear fashion with much less shading.

The landscape conventions – comprising principally a jagged stump and a pair of slender blossoming flowers – are recognisably Chinese. Those of the companion leaf, while also Chinese, are quite different and are limited to clumps of grass growing close together, rather like porcupine quills. A further unexpected difference between the two paintings is that the hands of the figures here lack the eloquence which animates those in the other leaf. With the seated lady the drapery conventions used for the back and haunch have a rather Byzantine quality. She wears the same hat as her counterpart in the other leaf, while the courtier has a hat which recurs frequently in the 15th century (cf. **115**). The form of the throne, with zoomorphic extensions, rather like acroteria, in its upper part, is rather different from the many thrones depicted in the Rashid al-Din codices and would repay detailed study.

62
Manizha before Rustam
Miniature painting
Firdausi, *Shahnama* (text, tr. Warner)
Tabriz school, early 14th century
Private collection

The image of the enthroned ruler leaning forward and gesturing vigorously recurs frequently in early 14th century painting. Here it is slightly adapted for the seated paladin. Equally characteristic of that period is the discreet shading used in the draperies, which serves to emphasise the monochrome tonality and linear emphasis of the rest of the work. Nevertheless, the mellow greens and ochres, sharply set off by the black boots, make a felicitous ensemble. The format of the picture departs from the norm of the Rashid al-Din codices and related paintings, for it approximates more closely to a square than to the full oblong of that school.

An outstanding feature of the painting, which seems to place it firmly in the orbit of the Rashid al-Din codices, is the subtle means whereby the artist enhances the drama of the confrontation. He exploits to the utmost the expressive power of the hands and the stances of the protagonists. The shrinking Manizha being urged forward and tentatively extending her hands towards Rustam, her eyes modestly downcast, is a delicate character study. The eager curiosity of the figures opposite her is mirrored in the inclination of their bodies.

63
Enthroned ruler with attendants
Miniature painting
Unidentified historical text
Shiraz school, c. 1340
Princeton University Library, no. 91 G
Dimensions: leaf 106 x 78 mm; painting 62 x 44 mm
Previously exhibited: New York 1940, Venice 1962
Published: Moghadam and Armajani, *Catalog*, no. 195; H. Buchthal, O. Kurz and R. Ettinghausen, *AI* VII (1940), 164, no. 16 of addenda; R. Ettinghausen, *AI* VII (1940), 111 and 121; Ackerman, *Guide*, 194; Grube, *MMP*, no. 27

It is difficult to cite close parallels in Inju manuscripts for the generous, almost sprawling, layout of the text interspersed with small and vertically orientated miniatures. Both text and picture forgo an elegant complexity in favour of simple clarity of word and image. Noteworthy details here include the form of the throne and the polka-dot robe of the King. As in the companion leaf exhibited here (**171**), the condensed nature of the image leaves no room for background detail. Other folios from this manuscript are discussed in B.W. Robinson, *The Kevorkian Collection: Islamic and Indian Manuscripts, Miniature Paintings and Drawings* (the Kevorkian Foundation, New York, 1953), typescript, XIIa, and in Welch, *Collection* I, 62.

64
"Rustam made a paladin"
Miniature painting
Firdausi, *Shahnama*
Probably Shiraz, perhaps late 14th century
London, British Museum, no. 1925 2-20 01
Dimensions: leaf 357 x 286 mm.; painting 120 (max.) x 240 (max.) mm.
Previously exhibited: London BM. 1931, 1933, 1959
Published: Titley, *Catalogue*, no. 136

Although the caption identifies the scene as Zal making Rustam a paladin, no such specific incident seems to occur in the *Shahnama*. Moreover, Zal had white hair from birth and was not a king; he therefore cannot be the royal figure depicted here. Nor can Rustam be recognised in the picture. Inconsistencies between text and picture occur often enough in illustrated 14th century *Shahnama* manuscripts, but this is an extreme case.

The subject is apparently the king addressing his consort. He is easily the most arresting figure in glance, gesture, colour and posture. Numerous devices exalt his status: the stepped frame, which may suggest hierarchy among those depicted, centres on him and his royal attributes of crown, throne and golden robe are predominantly displayed. He alone is bearded. Almost every glance is bent on him, and the artist further fosters a sense of occasion not only by the close grouping of the courtiers but also by using a curious convention of drawing. In this technique the pupils are placed at the corner of eye, which itself is elongated by a line so long that it often disappears into the headdress.

The deep rich colours, large figures with broad faces, and the summary draughtsmanship all suggest that the painting is of Shirazi origin, though it is not of typically Inju style.

65
Enthroned ruler with his consort
Miniature painting; parent manuscript has 440 ff. and 38 miniatures
Anthology; this leaf is taken from Hamdallah Mustaufi al-Qazvini, *Tarikh-i Guzida*
Probably Shiraz, 813/1410-11
Copyists, Mahmud b. Murtaza b. Ahmad al-Hafiz al-Husaini and Hasan al-Hafiz
Dedicated to Iskandar Sultan
Lisbon, Calouste Gulbenkian Foundation Museum, f. 260b.
Dimensions: 273 x 180 mm.
Previously exhibited: Lisbon 1963, London 1976
Published: for a bibliography of this manuscript in general, see **45**

Although this painting goes under the title of "Marriage of the Prophet to Khadija", it is hard to credit this identification. The enthroned figure displays none of the habitual attributes of Muhammad such as the halo or veil - indeed, the enthroned couple exude a carefree laxity which would be entirely unfitting for the Prophet and his wife. Nor was it customary to depict Muhammad in the guise of a ruler.

In some respects the miniature is a passable recreation of one of the several Ilkhanid styles. The bizarre, flamboyant head-dresses for example, find parallels in certain paintings of the period in Istanbul (in addition to unpublished examples, see Grube, *MI*, fig. 4). The costume of the ladies too, especially in such details as the hands tucked into long sleeves, has a Chinese flavour typical of the first half of the 14th century.

This affinity with a style which had disappeared several generations previously is remarkable enough. But a feature of crucial importance is the relationship between this painting and others in the same manuscript. Seen as a whole, these paintings document the transition to the fully-fledged Timurid court style in Shiraz. Clearly the progress towards this classic style was uneven, for the transition seems already to be complete in the Khwaju Kirmani manuscript in the British Museum, which is dated as early as 798/1396. The painting illustrated here

emphasises the range of styles employed side by side and suggests that some of the artists employed on this manuscript were still unfamiliar with the new idiom. This painter confidently manipulates such fairly novel conventions as the high horizon and the deceptively casual grouping in pairs and trios at intervals all over the design. His generous sense of spacing echoes the manner of the master Junaid in the 1396 manuscript. But he prefers a much discreeter use of colour than some of his other colleagues (compare pages 47, 125, 215 and 646) and in this too he declares his allegiance to much early 14th century painting. In place of strong, vibrant colours he prefers delicate outlines which recall the marginal paintings of the *Divan* of Sultan Ahmad in the Freer Gallery of Art, datable c. 1405.

66
Sultan Sanjar enthroned
Miniature painting
Hafiz-i-Abru, *Majma' al-Tawarikh* ("Collection of Histories")
Herat school, c. 1425
Baltimore, Walters Art Gallery, no. W.676F
Dimensions: leaf 430 x 335 mm.
Previously exhibited: Philadelphia 1926
Published: Ettinghausen, *KdO* II (1955), 41-2 and fig. 11

The utility style evolved by artists illustrating copies of this historical work for Shah Rukh is well exemplified here. The oblong format, rather forced symmetry and details of throne, crown and costume are all reduced and simplified reworkings of the pictures in the codices of Rashid al-Din produced a century before. The open-air setting, however, is not paralleled in such scenes in these manuscripts. Such features as the landscape convention, bright colouring and even the folding stool recur in other miniatures of the series. Sultan Sanjar, whose titles and lineage are given in the heading, ruled the Saljuq empire from 1118 to 1157.

67
King Ardashir enthroned
Miniature painting
Hafiz i Arbru, *Majma' al-Tawarikh* ("Collection of Histories")
Herat school c. 1425
Cambridge, Mass., Fogg Art Museum, no. 1960. 187
Dimensions: page 424 x 331 mm.; painting 153 x 230 mm.
Published: for a bibliography of the leaves from this dispersed manuscript, see Grube, *MMP*, 52-3 and Robinson, *PMP*, no. 15. Several other illustrated copies of this text are known; they also date from the early 15th century

This is one of the many miniatures in this manuscript which reproduces scenes from the *Jami' al-Tawarikh* and (**131 170**) in simplified form. The work of Hafiz-i Abru depends heavily on that of Rashid al-Din and it is natural that the Timurid artists should have manifested the same dependence. As in the *Jami' al-Tawarikh* illustrations, the task of producing formal portraits of a line of long-dead kings taxed the inventive powers of the artists to the limit. The brief entries allotted to each reign in the text generally gave them little inspiration. In such scenes the format is still oblong, an archaic feature in view of the popularity of vertical compositions in early Timurid times. Frequently, as here, the setting is in the open air, rather than an interior as in the portotype. But this change has scarcely affected the *modus operandi* of the artist; he declines, for example, to use the high horizon as a means for arranging his figures at various levels.

68
An amir offering a whip to a caliph

Miniature painting
Hafiz-i-Abru, *Majma' al-Tawarikh* ("Collection of Histories")
Herat school, c. 1425

Kansas, William Rockhill Nelson Gallery of Art, no. 47-44/3
Dimensions: leaf 347 x 247 mm.;

painting 148 x 222 mm.

A brief comparison with **67**. from the same manuscript, will suffice to show that this artist, unlike at least one of his colleagues, was not concerned to recreate the Tabriz style associated with the scriptorium of Rashid al-Din. The most noticeable difference is in the facial type – broad, full-cheeked and jowly. Trees, rock, high horizon and grass-tufted background conform to conventions established in the later 14th century and destined to mould later Persian painting.

69
Timur's festivities in Delhi

Miniature painting
Sharaf al-Din 'Ali Yazdi, *Zafar Nama* ("Book of Victory")
Shiraz, 839/1435-6
Copyist, Ya'qub b. Hasan, called Siraj al-Husaini al-Sultani
Patron: possibly 'Abdallah b. Ibrahim Sultan, Governor of Shiraz
Cambridge, Mass., Fogg Art Museum, no. 1960. 198
Dimensions: 257 x 160 mm.
Published: for a comprehensive bibliography of the dispersed leaves from this manuscript, see E. G. Sims,

The Garrett manuscript of the Zafar Name: a study in 15th century Timurid patronage (Ph.D. dissertation, New York University, 1973). For these leaves see also E. Schroeder, in *The Connoisseur* 148 (1951), 74 and pl. 8; R. N. Frye, *The Heritage of Persia* (repr. London 1965), pl. 117

Seated in lonely state, drinking wine in the shade of a tree by a stream, surrounded – at a respectful distance – by courtiers and servants ministering to his needs, this figure distils the essence of kingship as Persian artists conceived it.

The miniatures of this manuscript display a remarkable feeling for size. This sense of scale lends dignity to even the most stereotyped images of courtly pastimes. The capacity to organise a large space with a few carefully disposed figures is more characteristic of the 14th than of the 15th century, but it was never common in Persian painting. Here, for example, as in other miniatures from this manuscript (cf. Ettinghausen, *Berenson,* pl. VII), empty space is used positively to exalt the royal dignity. Perhaps the memory of Timur was still vivid enough for him to merit this heroic stature. The rather free draughtsmanship may be a natural by-product of this large conception. It has no place in the early Timurid court style of Shiraz or Herat with its meticulous attention to detail. It is tempting to suggest that these *Zafar Nama* miniatures are related to the numerous wall paintings with which Timur decorated his palaces.

70
Guyuk, the Great Khan, with courtiers and attendants

Miniature painting
Juvaini, *Tarikh-i Jahan Gushay* ("History of the World Conqueror")
Copyist: Abu Ishaq b. Ahmad al-Sufi al-Samarqandi
Probably Shiraz; completed 16 Shawwal 841/12 April 1438

London, British Museum, no. 1948 12-1105; formerly Huart, Anet and Eckstein collections
Dimensions: leaf 288 x 174 mm.; painting 190 x 115 mm.
Previously exhibited: London 1931, 1949, 1959, 1963, 1967
Published: for this manuscript and its dispersed leaves, see Blochet, *Inventaire*, 38; C. Huart, *Les Calligraphes et les miniaturistes de l'Orient musulman* (Paris, 1908), pls. 2-4; Blochet, *Peintures,* 159, 166, 168; Blochet, *Enluminures*, 89 and pl. XLI; Blochet, *MP*, pl. XCIV; *London 1931*, no. 455; *BWG*, no. 55c, Blochet, *Catalogue,* no. 444; E. Pauty, in *Bulletin de l'Institut d'Egypte* XVII (1935), 39; de Lorey, *Les Arts de l'Iran,* 150; Kühnel, *SPA*, 1843; Gray, in *BMQ* XVII (1952), 18; Robinson *AOI* (1954), 112 and fig. g; Robinson, *PD*, 138 and pl. 74; Robinson, *PMP,* no. 121; E. G. Sims

in *Sanat Tarih Yilligi* VI (1976), 380;
Titley, *Catalogue,* nos. 224-5

The painting displays a growing
interest in vegetation which was to
lead to the distinctive treatment of this
feature in the Turkoman school. Dark
green scales dividing up the surface of
the yellow-green meadow provide an
example of this. The impressionistic
rendering of the tree trunk and its
leaves follows quite different canons.

Bright colours set the tone of this
relaxed and festive scene – everyone
kneels or sits crosslegged at his ease –
and the rich textiles, metalwork and
blue and white ceramics evoke the
luxury of court life. A very similar leaf
from the same manuscript in the
Worcester Art Museum (Grube, *MMP*
no. 35, with additional bibliography)
betrays the large measure of
convention in this picture. The
imperfectly supported awning under
which the ruler sits may embody a
memory of the *chatr* or royal parasol
held above the king's head in the
pre-Islamic Persia.

71
Faridun spurns the envoys of Salm and Tur

Miniature painting
Firdausi, *Shahnama* (text, tr. Warner I,
   192-5)
Northern Iran 899/1493-4; the patron
   was Sultan Mirza ʿAli, probably the
   ruler of Gilan
Copyist, Salik b. Saʿid
Geneva, collection of Prince Sadruddin
   Aga Khan, no. Ir. M. 17
Dimensions: leaf 292 x 165 mm.
Previously exhibited: New York 1934
Bibliography: for this leaf, see
   Riefstahl, *Demotte Catalogue,* no. 16;
   Survey, pl. 851; Welch, *Collection* I,
   127-9. For a general bibliography of
   paintings of this school, see Grube,
   Kraus, 102-5 and Robinson, *Keir,*
   159-62

Faridun, Shah of Iran, had divided his
empire between his three sons and
given the marches to the two elder
sons, Salm and Tur, while reserving
Iran itself for the youngest, Iraj. Salm
and Tur sent an ambassador to
threaten war if he did not disinherit
Iraj. The aged Faridun refused,
covering them with reproaches, and as
a result Tur murdered Iraj, thereby
inaugurating that long enmity between
Iran and Turan which is a leitmotif of
the poem. The artist here has simplified
the panoply described in the text, no
doubt for reasons of space. But he has
also diverged from it in several
important respects. Thus he depicts not
one ambassador but two; he shows
them kneeling in postures of
submission rather than seated; Faridun
is enthroned, not standing; and behind
him on the same massive gold throne
sits the symbolically tiny figure of Iraj.
These changes all serve to enhance the
dignity of the monarch, a theme
emphasised also by the grouping of the
other figures. As is often the case,

however, the king is dressed with
little greater splendour than some of
his courtiers, such as the mace-bearing
chamberlain. The Shah's crown bears
the repeated lobed device known as the
ju-i, a Chinese symbol of prosperity.

This miniature and its companion
piece (**146**) illustrate an unusual
variation on the Turkoman style. They
come from a *Shahnama* with an
unusually lavish number of illustrations
probably produced in Gilan, an area
intimately associated with the rise of
the Safavids.

72
Portrait of Hulegu Khan

Qazvin, mid-16th century (?)

London, British Museum, no. 1920
   9-17 0130 (transferred from
   Department of Oriental Manuscripts
   and Printed Books, Album Add.
   18803, Or. 57a, f. 19)
Dimensions: leaf 247 x 360 mm.;
   painting 87 x 144 mm.
Previously exhibited: London, British
   Museum 1931, 1949, 1959
Bibliography: E. G. Browne, *A
   Literary History of Persia III* (repr.
   Cambridge, 1969), frontispiece;
   Titley, *Catalogue,* no. 395 (96)

The inscribed borders, like the
asymmetrical lobed spandrels and the
outer marginal caption *taswir Hulegu
Khan* ("portrait of Hūlegū Khan"),
postdate the drawing itself. The
identification of the figure as Hūlegū
the sacker of Baghdad and the first
Mongol Ilkhan, remains uncertain.
Nevertheless, the bow and arrow was
the Turco-Mongol symbol of royal
power, as distinct from the sword of
Arab tradition. The goblet too
functioned as an attribute of the ruler.
Bow, dagger and mace fitting are all
picked out in gold – a discreet
heightening of the dominant monochrome tonality. Indeed, the whole
surface of the paper is dusted with tiny
specks of gold.

A remarkable sureness of line is a
constant of Persian painting. But even
within that distinguished tradition this

drawing stands out. Lines thicken, or
become almost imperceptibly thinner,
at will. The clustering of folds at the
joints is not yet a mannerism, though in
this respect, as in the sinuous line, the
drawing is an early version of a
technique later to be debased in the
Safavid style of Isfahan. The discarded
turban betrays the same fascination
with line – it is as much an experiment
in abstract pattern as a fine still life. But
while the broad outlines of the design
exude confidence, the artist can also
render convincingly details seen at
extreme close range – hence the
accurate detail of eyebrows and
sideboards and the delicate modelling
used sparingly around the eyes and
chin. All in all, the drawing is a triumph
of relaxed calligraphic grace, every line
in place even to the casually outstretched boot with its upturned toe.
The pose is deliberately informal – the
prince has even removed his turban –
and the setting echoes this mood, with
willow branches inclining gracefully to
fill the voids in the composition. This is
far from an idealised portrait – the
squat, brutalised features and the
shaven skull, not entirely clean, suit the
Mongol Khan well.

73
Enthroned monarch with courtiers and musicians

Manuscript; 123 ff. and 4 miniatures,
   plus one double-page frontispiece
Amir Khusrau Dihlavi, *Intikhab-i
   Divan.* Probably Tabriz, completed
   943/1536-7 Vienna, National-
   bibliothek, Cod.
Mixt. 356, ff. 1b. and 2a
Dimensions: page 281 x 172 mm.
Previously exhibited: Vienna 1901,
   1916, 1935, 1953
Published: Flügel, *Handschriften* 1, 542,
   no. 559; *Katalog* 1901 no. 345;
   Katalog der Buchkunst-Ausstellung
   (Vienna, 1916), 86, no. 271; Holter,
   Les principaux manuscrits, 100-01,
   no. 7 and pl. XIXa; Holter, *PM,*
   38-9 and pls. I-V; *BDM,* no. 105;
   Robinson, *Bodleian,* 86; Stchoukine,
   MS, no. 173, p. 198 and pl. XVIII

Scenes of enthroned monarchs appear in the earliest major group of Islamic illustrated books and their history stretches back into the classical world. Only rarely does the possibility of portraiture arise. Almost every detail of the iconography has a long pedigree. This applies for example, to the seated pose of the ruler, the cup he holds, his flanking attendants and the symbolic dome under which he sits. The whole scene is, in fact, an archetype, (cf. the very similar scene on f. 50 of this ms.) and therefore any marked originality would be out of place. Even the rich illuminated border is characteristic of such frontispieces. It is the task of the painter to reassemble the familiar elements into as pleasing a pattern as possible.

Typical of the early Safavid period is the turban with its red baton. This, the so-called Taj-i Haidari, consisted of twelve seams, a reference to the Twelve 'mams venerated by the Shi'ites. For the early Safavids this emblem was at once political and religious, and in granting their followers the right to wear it they employed a special ceremonial. The inscription over the door reads "He is the Conqueror"; this probably refers to God rather than to the king.

74
Portrait of a Safavid prince, possibly Shah Tahmasp
Miniature painting
Tabriz style, c. 1540
School of Sultan Muhammad

Boston, Museum of Fine Arts, no. 14.590
Dimensions: 310 x 128 mm.
Published: Sarre and Martin,
  Meisterwerke, pl. 28; c. Anet, *BM*
  XXII (1912), 111-2 and pl. II;
  Marteau and Vever, *MP*, pl. CXIX;
  Schulz, *PIM* II, pl. 141b; Kühnel,
  MIO, 59 and Abb. 62;
  Coomaraswamy, *Goloubew*, 29-30
  and pl. XXI; Sakisian, *LMP*, 112
  and fig. 137; Kühnel, in *SPA*, 1877
  and pl. 901B; Stchoukine, *MS*,
  no. 23

Shah Tahmasp, a contemporary of Queen Elizabeth I, shared with her, in his carefree youth, a considerable personal vanity. He too – if this picture can be taken as a portrait – seems to have relished being pictured with a wasp waist. His arched eyebrows meet at the bridge of his nose, thus obeying the Persian canon of beauty. Such a detail, like the stray lock escaping his turban or the slanting eyes and miniscule mouth, confirms the idealised nature of this image. Until the late Safavid period, contemporary portraits of any Persian ruler were a rarity.

Clearly this type of image foreshadows the youths of the later Isfahan style. But the differences are instructive. This artist maintains the primacy of colour, with a correspondingly simple line – the face is a mask, innocent of expression. Despite the broad handling he employs, he is at heart a miniaturist. He allows his love of detail free play in his treatment of the jewelled belt (which is of a type already standard in Timurid times) and its accessories. Two generations later such detail was out of place. The colours, too, had lost their purity, curves had become suggestive and faces were often stamped with a knowing simper.

Perhaps a training in book illustration explains the artist's curious choice of frame and his eagerness for the figure to make contact with it wherever possible.

75
Seated man
Drawing
Qazvin style, c. 1580
Inscription – probably an attribution –
  states "work of Sadiq"

Boston, Museum of Fine Arts, no.
14.636
Dimensions: 175 x 105 mm
Published: the earlier literature is
resumed in Stchoukine, *SA*, 78. See
also Grube, *WI*, 144 and pl. 85;
Welch, *Artists*, 94, 101, 104 and
figs. 24-6

Seldom is the virtuosity of the Persian
draughtsman more casually displayed
than in these few telling strokes. They
suffice to create an idiosyncatic
personality. The main outlines of the
pose are familiar enough – kings,
dervishes, prisoners are often depicted
sitting cross-legged. But with the
possible exception of the turban and
sash, which are made the vehicles for
rhetorical flourishes of drapery (cf. **158**)
the drawing lacks that sense of
mechanical assurance which mars so
many Safavid figure studies. No line
continues for long. Energetic
spluttering strokes suggest crumpled
patches of drapery. Above all the
unpredictable rhythm of broad and
fine strokes, though a mannerism,
contrives to imbue the figure with life.
Sometimes the lines do not even meet,
leaving the viewer to complete them in
his own mind – another device to
ensure immediacy. The prehensile
index fingers are a stock convention of
Persian drawing, but certain key
details of the pose seem to be original.
The drooping, heavy-lidded eyes
suggest a pensive and lacklustre mood.
In his absorption the man absently
toys with one of his buttons. He gazes
unseeingly into the distance. These
details, trivial though they might be,
are nevertheless enough to distinguish
this work from many superficially
similar contemporary drawings.

76
Khan Uzbek II eating melons
Miniature painting
Bukhara, c. 1580
London, British Museum, no. 1948
12-11 010; formerly Anet and
Eckstein collections
Dimensions: leaf 327 x 198 mm;
painting 141 x 115 mm
Previously exhibited: Paris 1912,
London 1949, 1959
Published: Marteau and Vever, *MP*,
pl. CLXXI; Martin, *MP*, pl. 149;
Gray, *BMQ* XVII (1952), 18; Titley,
Catalogue, no. 395 (224)

The pleasing and unusual pastel
tonality of magenta and pale green, set
off by other accents like the white
turban, coal black boots and the
curiously oily tan of the prince's face,
marks that love of colour contrasts
which Bukharan artists inherited
some seventy years earlier from Bihzad
and his atelier. But this is also a notable
portrait, minutely detailed where need
be – as in the beard and moustache –
but elsewhere relying almost entirely
on broad sweeping lines loosely
indicated. The sagging paunch,
straining against the loosely knotted
girdle, is drawn with satirical accuracy.

So too is the prince's absorption in the
food which is his downfall as a
physical specimen. With sly humour, no
attendants are shown; he is off duty,
alone with his hobby. The melons are of
the *kharbuza* type long associated
with Transoxiana. Indeed, the melons
of that area were sufficiently prized in
the 10th century to be packed in snow
in lead containers and transported
overland some two thousand miles to
the caliphal court at Baghdad.

77
Enthronement scene
Manuscript; 345 ff. and 13 minatures
Nizami, *Khamsa* (*Iskandar Nama* –
"Book of Alexander")
Tabriz style, 932/1525-6
London, Royal Asiatic Society of
Great Britain & Ireland
P. Codrington 249a, f. 69a
Dimensions: open book 265 x 380 mm
painting 223 x 150 mm
Previously exhibited: London 1967
Published: Morley, *Catalogue*, no.
249A; Robinson, *PMP*, no. 34

This scene of an enthroned king has a
pendant in the immediately preceding
miniature which shows a queen in a
nearly identical setting, and also seated
on a frail gilded dais. The artist has
made much of the contrast between the
freely growing, unconstrained atmosphere of the exterior and the
regimented interior. In this respect the
gardener shouldering his spade and
about to stride into the palace is a
pivotal figure. He is the only bare-
footed person to be seen. Gardeners
are something of a stock motif in
Tabriz painting – their use as a
reference to everyday life, and thus as a
foil to the hothouse atmosphere of the
court, seems indisputable.

Most of the miniature has been
treated as an architectural elevation
articulated by arches, niches, spandrels
and rectangular panels – but people as
well as decoration occupy these spaces.
The text is in the vertical compart-
ments of the building, beneath the
crenellated pediment, as if it were a
building inscription. Even the net

77

vaulting in the niche behind the king is a typical feature of Safavid architecture. Such architectural compositions are found in some of the best early Safavid work (cf. Robinson, *Keir*, III. 209).

78
Iskandar in council with his seven sages

Miniature painting
Nizami, *Khamsa* (*Iqbal Nama*; see the
translation by S. Robinson of W.
Bacher's paraphrase and translation,
in *Persian Poetry* (Glasgow, 1883),
201)
Khurasan style (?), c. 1590
Cambridge, Fitzwilliam Museum no.
P.D. 144-1948 (formerly in Manuk
collection)
Dimensions: leaf 558 × 407 mm;
painting 215 × 162 mm
Previously exhibited: London 1967
Published: Robinson, *PMP*, no. 179

Alexander legends proliferated in the medieval literature of both East and West. A common feature of these legends is to exalt his status as sage and philosopher in addition to his role as a conquerer. In Muslim tradition yet another element enters: he is venerated as a prophet. Here he is shown as the seeker after knowledge surrounded by his seven sages—Aristotle (his vizier), Apollonius of Tyana, Socrates, Plato, Thales, Porphyrius, and Hermes. The use of the number seven is certainly not accidental. In Islam, as in other cultures, it is associated (*inter alia*) with concepts of completeness and with the cosmos itself—Nizami repeatedly uses it in the *Khamsa* with such connotations (cf. *18*).

Although the summary, even crude, landscape and the bright rather than intense colours accord with the Khurasan style, certain details cast doubt on this attribution. They include the careful distinctions between the various facial types and the love of detail. This finds expression in the tiled floor whose mauve stars and hexagons have no echo in extant buildings, in the varied headgear and in the tooled gold decoration of one of the pieces of metalwork. The slack-jowled faces seen here are common throughout later sixteenth century painting and do not suggest a particular school.

79
Isma'il declares himself Shah

Manuscript; 307 ff. and one double
page plus 19 single miniatures
Anonymous history of Shah Isma'il
Isfahan style, later 17th century
Copyist; Miss N.M. Titley tentatively
suggests Muhammad 'Ali b. Nura
Artist, Mu'in Musavvir
London, British Library, Or. 3248,
f. 74a
Dimensions: open book 258 x 373 mm;
painting 170 x 120 mm
Published: Rieu, *Supplement*, 34–5;
Titley, *Catalogue*, no. 82

Although Persian painters were pre-

occupied with the affairs of royalty and never tired of depicting the ruler at war, hunting or enthroned, they tended to avoid illustrating precise, unique events. Perhaps the reason was simply that there were no models. This history of Shah Isma'il does have a visual model in the histories of Timur, but the illustrations of these manuscripts are again usually unspecific. Much credit must therefore go to the artist for scenes such as this or f. 43 b. which shows Isma'il led before an *imam* as a youth.

The text adjacent to this folio deals with the triumphal entry of Isma'il into Tabriz and his accession in 907/1502. He is depicted wearing white as is customary in this manuscript – possibly to stress his sanctity. Above him, a divine validates this impromptu assumption of power. Isma'il waves a sword, presumably a reference to the

well-known incident in which he threatened with death those citizens of Tabriz who would not accept his rule. His followers, the *qizilbash* ("red-heads") cluster round. Their headgear is a mark of loyalty to his regime. Presumably the same propagandist intention accounts for the use of red ink for the name of Isma'il in the text.

The hand of Mu'in Musavvir is patent in the mauves and cool blues which predominate in the manuscript. The handlebar moustaches were a durable fashion of later Safavid times.

80
A prince, possibly Shah Sulayman (1667-94), with attendants

c. 1680

London, British Museum, no. 1948
12-11 019; formerly Anet and
Eckstein collections
Dimensions: leaf 267 x 395 mm.;

painting 143 x 226 mm.
Previously exhibited: London
1931, 1949 and 1959
Bibliography: *BWG*, no. 382 and pl.
CXII-B; Gray, in *BMQ*, XVII
(1952), 18; Gray, *PP 1961*, 170;
Titley, *Catalogue*, no. 395 (226)

The inscription here – *Ya sahib al-zaman*, "O Lord of the Age" – is usually taken as a punning reference to Muhammad Zaman, the most celebrated of the westernising Persian artists of the later 17th century. The new European manner makes itself felt in the overlapping planes or coulisses of the grassy landscape, which blot out the forelegs of the second horse, in the treatment of the blue breeches of the foremost page, in the changing play of light on the coat of the mounted courtier and in the virtuoso (but quite unrealistic) way in which the manes of the horses shade off into their coats. These partial concessions to naturalism only serve to highlight the painter's undeviating fidelity to more ancient traditions. Thus he depicts the horses in virtually identical fashion. Above all, he uses time-honoured conventions to exalt the Shah. The ruler is centrally placed and is the largest figure of all; courtiers on foot offer him homage, while his mounted companion discreetly effaces himself. The royal horse is caparisoned with marked richness, and even wears a coronet. The Shah himself is most gorgeously dressed and his massive turban, a standard fashion of the time, lends him extra grandeur – the effect brings to mind the royal Sasanian crown. His bow and quiver carry associations of royal rank. Courtiers, one of them in Mughal dress, do him honour. Motives of propaganda, perhaps related to the decline of Safavid power, thus predominate. They help to explain the unrelieved formality of this scene, so much at variance with the animated activity of a typical frontispiece showing the enthroned ruler. Its quality of frozen ceremony shows how tenacious was the mystique surrounding the Persian ruler.

81
Portrait of the Nawab Mirza Muhammad Baqir and his young son Mirza Husain
Miniature painting
Signed Mu'in Musavvir and dated
1085/1674-5

Geneva, collection of Prince Sadruddin Aga Khan, no. Ir. M. 48. Formerly in Goldschmidt collection and in the Olsen Foundation at Bridgeport.
Dimensions: page 420 x 290 mm.,
leaf 136 x 242 mm.
Previously exhibited: Venice 1962
Published: H. Goetz in *Eastern Art* II (1930), 143-66; E. Kühnel in *Pantheon* 29(1942), 108-14; Grube, *MMP*, no. 119; Stchoukine, *SA*, 68; Welch, *Collection* I, 223 and colour plate on 225

Restraint is the key to this picture. Its understatement is masterly. It has outgrown the showy virtuosity which mars some of the work of the previous two generations. At the same time it is profoundly traditional. It uses conventional props – sprays, rocks, flowers, clouds – but they are incidental and the pale gold in which they are rendered, the antithesis of naturalism, underlines the fact. The real interest of the painting is psychological. It lies in the interaction of father and son. Here too restraint is the dominant feature. Their glances do not meet; only the expressive outstretched hands mark the contact between them. The portly impassive figure of the nawab, toying absently with his beads as he glances past his son, has a remarkable sense of dignity and contained power; the eye cannot stay away from him for long. His size has something to do with it, for it is a function of his importance. Thus perspective is not sufficient to account for the slightness of his son. The physical distance between them, and the deferential gesture of the youth, are further means towards the same end.
In his manipulation of form and colour Mu'in Musavvir displays the same sure control. Much of the airy quality of the painting derives from the bright flowered fabric, possibly chintz, of the nawab's robe (hence earlier theories that the painting is of Indian origin), while the ample curves of bodies and cushions are set off by the rectangular carpets and the multiple frames. Such is the sense of open space that the eye only gradually takes in the writing materials by the youth and the five substantial but microscopic inscriptions. The longest ones trail behind the scudding clouds and blend into their wake; the others are tucked away near the border of the red carpet. All in all, the painting is remarkably free from that European influence which disturbed the equilibrium of so many contemporary Iranian painters.

82
Karim Khan-i Zand
Miniature painting from album with
27ff.
Probably Shiraz, third quarter of
18th century

London, British Library, Or. 4938,
f. 1; formerly in Churchill collection
Dimensions: leaf 380 x 250 mm.;
painting 228 x 165 mm.
Previously exhibited: London 1967
Published: Rieu, *Supplement*, 262;
Browne, *Literary History* IV, pl. V;
Robinson, *PMP*, no. 102; Titley,
Catalogue, no. 42

Inscribed on the back of the leaf in a nineteenth century hand are the words 19th century hand are the words "Contemporary portrait said to be of Kerim Khan Zand". The attribution, though tentative, is convincing. Although he controlled southern Persia from 1750 until his death in 1779,

he never took the title of Shah and was content to be called *wakil* ("regent"). The painting is executed in washes of brown and yellow; the technique, though not the colours, prefigures that of Qajar portraits. This likeness agrees in striking fashion with a more formal portrait in the British Library (Add. 24904, inside cover – see Browne, *Literary History* IV, pl. IV) and shows that he abstained from the trappings of royalty. He is not enthroned but kneels at his ease. His background was tribal. Indeed, the tribe to which he belonged was part of the Lur confederation, and the Lurs have traditionally been notorious for their unruliness and banditry. The aggressive pose and expression of the sitter are therefore not entirely out of place. But in fact Karim Khan was noted as a benevolent ruler and patron of scholars, and he embellished Shiraz with many magnificent buildings.

83
Portrait of Prince 'Ali Quli Mirza
Miniature painting from album with
27 ff.
London, British Library, Or. 4938,
f.6; formerly in Churchill collection
Dimensions: framed leaf
380 x 250 mm.; painting
320 x 214 mm.
Previously exhibited: London 1967
Published: Rieu, *Supplement*, 262;
Robinson, *PD*, 141 and pl. 100
(in colour); Robinson, *PMP*,
no. 102; Titley, *Catalogue*, no. 42

Possibly owing to the influence of photography, realistic portraits of Qajar notables were a favoured genre of 19th century Persian painting. This typical example serves also as an epitome of Iran at this time, caught between time-honoured traditions and new-fangled European ways. The courtier sits on a European chair with Persian bolsters stacked behind it. His high black hat (*kulah*) and his western trousers make an incongruous combination. Carved plaster and decorative mirror-work, a Qajar speciality, cover the wall behind him and bear a bold artist's signature. The artist has caught to a nicety the expression which hovers on the faces of so many courtiers of the time, at once wary and lugubrious. The sitter held the post of Minister of Education, Commerce and Industry under Nasruddin Shah (ruled 1848-1896).

84
Khusrau Khan Kirmani
Miniature painting from album with
27ff.
Probably Tehran, c. 1850-60
Artist: Abu'l-Hasan Ghaffari, Sani' al-Mulk
London, British Library, Or. 4938, f. 6;
formerly in Churchill collection
Dimensions: leaf 380 x 250 mm.;
painting 320 x 214 mm.
Previously exhibited: London 1967
Published: Rieu, *Supplement*, 262;
Robinson, *PD*, 141 and pl. 97

(in colour); Robinson, *PMP*, no. 102; Titley, *Catalogue*, no. 42

The English, French and Persian inscriptions on the reverse of this leaf identify it as the work of Sani'al-Mulk, the honorific of Abu'l-Hasan Ghaffari. He was the foremost painter of his time and his wide range is proved by his two major achievements: a set of life-size oil paintings of Nasruddin Shah and his court, and the set of several thousand illustrations produced under his supervision for a manuscript of the Arabian Nights. In this painting he shows another side of his talent. No one could doubt that this is indeed a "ressemblance frappante" as the French inscription states. He has pushed daring to an extreme in giving only the head. Once again the tall fur hat of the well-to-do Persian provides an excellent foil for the face. The artist does not squander his capacity for detail on the fripperies of clothing, furnishings and bric-à-brac which so laboriously amplify, and thus disfigure, other Qajar portraits in this album (e.g. ff. 2-4, 7 and 9-11).

85
Portrait of Hajji Mirza Aghasi, vizier of Muhammad Shah

Miniature painting
About 1840

London, British Museum, no. 1931,
11-27 01; presented by Keith Abbot
in 1931 from the collection of his
father, Keith E. Abbott, British
Consul-General at Tabriz in 1848
Dimensions: 235 x 165 mm.
Previously exhibited: London 1936,
1939, 1949, 1959
Published: Titley, *Catalogue*, no 395 (166)

This painting typifies the Qajar portrait style, with its hallucinatory directness. The life of the painting is concentrated into the face. The alertness of that face belies the slumped posture of this notorious and unpopular politician. Seamed as it is by countless wrinkles, ravaged by time, with sagging pouches under the eyes, it might at first appear to belong to a dotard. But the watchful heavy-lidded eyes and the full red mouth tell a different story. It is a face not easily forgotten. Even the hands are those of a courtier – plump, well-tended, garnished with red fingernails, while the slippers are fastidiously fine. Elsewhere in the portrait the artist displays a fine indifference to detail and is content with washes of a single colour or mottled combinations of tones. Thus he has overcome that delight in minutiae which marks so much of earlier Persian painting. At the same time he has retained a sense of the power of single strong colours, as in the black *kulah*, which focusses attention on the vizier's face. The greatly lengthened ear shows that the artist is in no sense a slave to realism in the European manner, while even the folds and wrinkles of the face obey laws of abstract pattern.

Hajji Mirza Aghasi was chief servant to the Crown from 1835 to 1848. In that year of revolutions he too was unseated and had to flee for his life to take sanctuary in the shrine of 'Abd al-'Azim. He was rightly suspicious of foreign governments but incapable of withstanding their inroads, and his extravagance was a byword.

86
A Qajar prince

Miniature painting
Presumably Teheran, c. 1845
Private collection
Dimensions: 530 x 395 mm
Previously exhibited: Zurich and the
Hague, 1962; London 1967.
Published: *Kunstschatze aus Iran*,
no. 1008; Robinson, *PMP*, no. 99

This portrait shares with many court paintings of the time a distinctive presence. This can in part be attributed to the loss of its original background but it is also due to the dramatic contrast between the lush detail of the coat and pale countenance which emerges from it. The clothing proclaims a pomp strikingly at variance with the melancholy and shrinking personality on whom it sits so uneasily. Perhaps even deliberate irony is intended. Such psychological insight is the major achievement of Qajar painting; it is a quality all the more unexpected in that it is not generally found in the other arts of the period. The combination of western and oriental dress is characteristically Qajar and may have been echoed in the background (cf. **83**). But comparison with related works suggests that, in view of the detail lavished on the coat, the setting would have been simple.

87
Portrait of Fath Ali Shah

Manuscript: 2 miniatures
Khaqan (pen-name of Fath 'Ali Shah),
Divan
Tehran, Shawwal 1216/February 1802
Copyist, Muhammad Mahdi
Portraits signed by Mirza Baba
The Royal Library, Windsor Castle,
MS. A/4
Dimensions: 418 x 287 mm.
Previously exhibited: London 1931,
1951, 1967
Published: Holmes, *Specimens*, 16 and
pl. 152; *London 1931*, no. 726A;

BWG, no. 390; B. W. Robinson, in *The Connoisseur* (December 1951), 181, fig. XII; Robinson, *VAM 1951*, no. 145; B. W. Robinson, in *Eretz Israel* VII (1963), 95* and 104*; Robinson, *VAM 1965*, 18 and pl. 36; Robinson, *PD*, 31 and fig. 5; Robinson, *PMP*, no. 95

Individualised royal portraits of this scale and formal nature are virtually unprecedented before Qajar times. Later Safavid painters certainly show an inclination towards portraiture but the flavour of the official photograph which clings to this picture was not in their style. They preferred to show the ruler accompanied by courtiers. But here the face of the monarch stares out at us directly, the only human element in the frozen splendour which envelopes him.

Most of the reign of Fath 'Ali Shah, self-styled Asylum of the Universe and progenitor of some five hundred children, took place in the 19th century.

European conventions for rendering landscape and perspective are indeed observed in half-hearted fashion. Yet the closest parallels for the portrait of this contemporary of Napoleon are the images of the pre-Islamic Sasanian kings. Like them, he had himself depicted in bas-reliefs representing ceremonial or hunting scenes. Like them, he seems to have regarded the trappings of royalty as an integral part of the imperial image, with obvious propaganda functions. It would be hard to cite a previous Islamic ruler of Iran who was portrayed in such panoply. The very bolster against which he reclines is a mosaic of seed-pearls and pearls decorate the carpet – a Sasanian fashion. Altogether, there is something medieval – even barbaric – in this cult figure loaded with jewels, a substantial, portable share of his country's wealth displayed on and around him. Many of the insignia shown here are on public view in the National Bank at Teheran.

88
The Court of Fath 'Ali Shah
Chromolithograph
Undated; early 19th century
By Robert Havell
London, Royal Asiatic Society
Dimensions: 1138 x 250 mm.

This version may be compared with the water-colour copy of the same scene (89). It is in a very damaged state, and the copyist has inevitably changed certain features. He has, for example, imparted a rakish angle to the eyebrows of the Shah, making him at once fierce and quizzical. Nevertheless, the compact form of this chromolithograph does give a more immediate impression of the Qajar court than do the larger water-colour copies. It is possible thereby to enjoy on a grand scale the contrast between the illusionistic perspective of the red carpet and the wooden gestures of the courtiers, or between the varied headgear and the identical feet.

The inscription reads:

' From a painting in the possession of Thos. Alcock Esq., of Kingswood. Copied from the wall of the Palace of Nugaristan. The picture on paper varnished, bears the following description by the Artist who presented it :-

"The Court of Persia is one of the most magnificent and splendid in the world and the greatest ceremony is used in the presentation of a person of rank to His Majesty Fettah Ali Shah, Shadow of God upon Earth. In the picture the King covered with jewels of a costly description, wearing on his head the Taj or crown and with a Caleoon or water pipe in his right hand, is represented sitting on a throne richly carved and studded with precious stones and his back supported by an embroidered pillow. His beard, the admiration and delight of his people, descends to his girdle, on his arms he wears two large diamonds called "The Mountain of Light" and "The Sea of Splendour", and when the sun's rays fall upon him it is impossible to look on "The Threshold of the World's Glory!" with any steadiness. When the King is seated in public his sons, ministers and courtiers stand erect with their hands crossed and in the exact place of their rank. The Princes wear a cap resembling the royal diadem, the greater number of the ministers and courtiers wear shawl head-dresses and the Ghoolam-i-Shahi or bodyguard including the Shield, Sword and Quiver bearers have the usual Kolah or black sheepskin cap.

The six figures in the European dress are Sir Gore Ouseley, Sir Harford Jones and Sir John Malcolm on the right, General Gardani (*sic*) Monsieur Jouannier and Monsieur Jaubert on the left of His Majesty. There are also Turkish, Arab and Indian Envoys distinguished by their

peculiar costumes. The Military Officers wear a dagger in their girdles, the Civilian a pen-case or roll of papers, and all have long robes or kubas and cloth boots in the Royal Presence, the slippers being left outside the Hall of Audience &c.

Dedicated by permission to the Royal Asiatic Society. By their Obedient Humble Servant, Robt. Havell.

All the figures in the picture are portraits.''

89
The court of Fath 'Ali Shah
Watercolours on varnished Whatman paper
The watermark bears the date 1816
Reduced copy of a mural painted in Teheran by 'Abdallah Khan in 1812/13

India Office Library, Add. Or. 1239-42; formerly in Elphinstone Collection
Dimensions: central group (Add. Or. 1239): 350 x 530 mm.; court group (Add. Or. 1240): 250 x 520 mm.; left hand group (Add. Or. 1241): 340 x 1320 mm.; right hand group (Add. Or. 1242): 330 x 1350 mm.
Published: J. Dieulafoy, *La Perse, la Chaldée et la Susiane* (Paris, 1881), 126; S. G. W. Benjamin, *Persia and the Persians* (London, 1887), 319; G. N. Curzon, *Persia and the Persian Question* (London, 1892) I, 338; Schulz, *PM* I, 196; E. G. Browne, *A Year amongst the Persians* (London, 1926, ed.) 105; B. W. Robinson, *Eretz Israel* VII (1963), 102-3 and pl. XXXIII; Robinson, *IOL*, nos. 1280-3; Sir Denis Wright, *The English Amongst the Persians* (London, 1977), cover and frontispiece (in colour)

Even allowing for the fact that this is a copy of a large scale fresco, formerly in the Nigaristan Palace in Teheran, the coarseness of execution is remarkable. This is indeed painting by the yard. The clothing of virtually every courtier – women are conspicuously absent – exhibits the same folds in the same place. Happily this monotonous symmetry stops short of identical beards and costume. Yet this painting was certainly intended – as were several other enthronement scenes noted by 19th century travellers – as a serious and comprehensive statement of royal splendour.

In conception and execution alike the painting has much in common with modern primitives. It has the same apparently naive delight in strong clashing colours and the same almost complete disregard for the third dimension. In no sense can this array of marionettes be termed a portrait gallery of the Qajar court.

In this, almost the last manifestation of court art in Iran, the tradition has returned to its Sasanian sources and refurbished them with splendid pomp and circumstance. It is therefore fitting that the Court should be represented in

strength – 118 people in all, disposed in the same tiered arrangement as the Sasanians had used – and that the royal trappings of war and feasting should be ceremonially displayed. Even foreign ambassadors are present. The group to the left has been identified with the British trio of Ouseley, Jones and Malcolm, all of them notable Persian scholars. At the centre of all, surrounded by twelve of his many sons, sits Fath 'Ali Shah himself, on the dais-like throne that so often appears on official portraits.

90
An archer on horseback
Miniature painting
Isfahan, c. 1685; collected in Persia between 1684 and 1688 by Englebert Kaempfer
London, British Museum, no. 1928 3-23 02; transferred from Department of Manuscripts (Sloane Collection no. 5292.247)
Dimensions: 214 x 134 mm
Previously exhibited: London 1949, 1959
Published: Titley, *Catalogue*, no. 404 (128)

For general information about this and similar drawings see **91**. The theme here, as in the case of the dancer with castanets, is ancient. The piebald horse provides the ideal outlet for the painter's expressionist tendencies. It seems quite likely that such paintings were produced to order, in quantity – in fact that they are quintessential bazaar work.

91
A woman dancing
Miniature painting
Isfahan, c. 1685; collected in Persia between 1684 and 1688 by Englebert Kaempfer
London, British Museum, no. 1928 3-23 01; transferred from Department of Manuscripts (Sloane Collection no. 5292.363)
Dimensions: 227 x 125 mm
Previously exhibited: London 1949, 1959
Published: Titley, *Catalogue*, no. 404 (127)

The cycle of royal life was of course depicted in many media besides book painting. The wall paintings which survive from Safavid Isfahan give a good idea of the range of these subjects: banquets, scenes of dalliance, picnics in gardens, embassies and battles. Many of these paintings have vanished, as was to be the fate of numerous similar scenes in the following two centuries. This drawing and its companion pieces in the British Museum (**90** and nos. 1928 3-23 05, 06, depicting – with rather less panache – a seated lady and a standing youth) have no pretensions to fine art, but they are valuable as contemporary records of vanished material. Perhaps in their bold, confident drawing and in the rather slapdash application of bright

paint they capture some of the characteristics of lost Safavid wall paintings (for an up-to-date account of the subject see E. J. Grube, "Wall paintings in the seventeenth century monuments of Isfahan", *Iranian Studies* VII (1974), 511-42).

92
A boy and two girls dancing
Miniature painting
Perhaps Tehran, early 19th century
London, British Museum, no. 1934 12-3 02; given by E. Croft-Murray, C.B.E. Formerly in the collection of Sir Henry Willock, Chargé d'Affaires at Tehran 1815-26; his collection is well represented in the British Museum.
Dimensions: 217 x 323 mm
Previously exhibited: London 1936, 1949, 1959

The langourous sleepy manner cultivated in oil paintings of the Qajar period was almost equally successful with more traditional pigments. Time-honoured canons of beauty only partially account for these figures – tradition has been revamped into a kind of visual hyperbole of wasp waists, sloe eyes and cupid's-bow mouths. Western influences are responsible for the modelling and the timid cast shadows, but the plain background and frozen movement show that these influences are only half-understood.

Such dancing displays were a prominent feature of Safavid court life, as the murals in the Chihil Sutun palace at Isfahan show, and the castanets, sashes and trailing ribbons are all accessories of the dance.

93
Seated musician
Miniature painting
Bukhara style, late 16th century
Artist, Sadiq-i Afshar
New York, Metropolitan Museum of Art. Gift of Mrs. John Campbell White, no. 59.45
Dimensions: 205 x 160 mm.

The musician depicted here has doffed his turban, with its spectacular aigrette, to reveal a skull completely shaven but for the fashionable lovelock (*zulf*) by his ear. Here the artist, true to the often realistic tendency of Bukhara painting, has deftly captured his absorbed expression. But the thick outlines shading off into indistinctness are an unhappy compromise between drawing and painting.

The musician plays the *rabab* or spike fiddle, a precursor of the European violin. Arched wooden bows of this kind with a resined horsehair string are still in use in some parts of the Islamic world. A remarkable variety of *rababs* can be share the small resonator and the long neck. Such instruments were used to accompany recitations of epic poetry. Nevertheless, in medieval Persian courts poets and musicians performed seen on Persian miniatures but they all distinct functions – the Sasanian tradition in which the poet was also a musician and singer seems to have lapsed. Moreover, perhaps as a result of religious prejudices against music, the professional musician had a comparatively low social status.

94
A court dwarf

Drawing; possibly Istanbul, later 16th century
The signature Vali Jan is probably a later attribution
Boston, Museum of Fine Arts, no. 14. 696 (formerly in Martin and Goloubew collections)
Dimensions: 123 x 70 mm.
Previously exhibited: Venice 1963
Published: Martin, *PM*, 65-6 and pl. 120; Coomaraswamy, *Goloubew*, 67, no. 107 and pl. LIII; Schroeder, *Fogg*, 102; Grube, *MMP*, no. 80; I. Stchoukine, *La Peinture turque d'apres les manuscrits illustres* I (Paris, 1966), 34-5

Dwarfs were an institution at the Ottoman court. Like their colleagues in contemporary Europe, they enjoyed a privileged position as intimates of the ruler, and could on occasions play a political role. They received both kicks and ha'pence from the Sultan. Contemporary accounts place them with the numerous mutes with whom the monarch communicated in sign language.

This dwarf may be compared with one depicted in a drawing in the Fogg Art Museum. As with the Fogg drawing, provenance and authorship are alike uncertain; an attribution to Qazvin could well be defended. The figure is almost certainly a court dwarf, for the popular dwarfs depicted in the Turkish shadow plays (*Karagoz*) do not wear turbans but jesters' caps loosely based on European models. Again like his European counterpart, he carries the attribute of his trade, the long staff which ultimately derives from the wooden sword used by comic actors in antiquity. The drawing is distinguished by an enviable economy: a few sure and graceful lines cruelly expose, indeed accentuate, his gross obesity, while the more thoroughly worked features express a sharp intelligence and perhaps pathos. The Shi'ite turban that he wears is, as Schroeder notes, a jibe at the state religion of the Safavids, the arch-enemies of the Ottoman sultans in the Islamic world.

95
Palace scene

Miniature painting; parent manuscript has 440 ff. and 38 miniatures
Anthology; this leaf is taken from the *Khamsa* of Nizami (*Makhzan al-Asrar*)
Probably Shiraz, 813/1410-11
Copyists, Mahamud b. Murtaza b. Ahmad al-Hafiz al-Husaini and Hasan al-Hafiz
Dedicated to Iskandar Sultan

Lisbon, Calouste Gulbenkian Foundation Museum no. L.A. 161, f. 12

The text in the body of the page is the *Khamsa* of Nizami; that in the margins is the *Mantiq al-Tair* of 'Attar. This disposition of the script has allowed the artist to extend his picture at an angle to the left, thereby creating an illusion of impressive depth and height. This tall, extremely narrow format is a curiousity. Every detail in the architecture and in the placing of figures conspires to make it seem higher still. The lovingly detailed interior, with each type of decoration carefully distinguished from the next, makes an admirable background for this format. Such work recurs on a much larger scale in a whole series of manuscripts dated between 1396 and 1427, usually with the accent on height rather than breadth. Full use is made of the high horizon in that two servants occupy the foreground, while the lady gazing at the scene from an upper floor serves further to accentuate the loftiness of the building. These details of the design also recur in numerous early Timurid manuscripts. In short, the picture represents an ingenious response to an unorthodox picture space. The triangular panels of ornament at the outer corners should be seen simply as elegant end-pieces which serve to round off the calligraphy (cf. **194**). They are not thumbpieces as are the triangular ornamented panels found in other anthologies of the period.

96
Banquet scene

Miniature painting
Probably Firdausi, *Shahnama*, frontispiece
Shiraz, c. 1444

Cleveland, The Cleveland Museum of Art, nos. 56.10 and 45.169; part of the frontispiece was formerly in Schulz and Goloubew collections

Dimensions:
(a) 56.10: leaf 327 x 217 mm.; painting 263 x 207 mm.
(b) 45.169: leaf 322 x 220 mm.; painting 261 x 206 mm.

Previously exhibited: Munich 1910, Detroit 1935, San Francisco 1937, New York 1940, Rome 1956, Paris 1961, Venice 1962

Published: for an excellent bibliography, see Grube, *MMP*, no. 34; cf. also Blochet, *Peintures*, 166 and B. W. Robinson in *OA* IV/3 (1958), 114

Schulz identified the subject as the marriage between the physically unprepossessing Ghazan Khan (who ruled 1295-1304) and Kiramun Khatun. He gave no grounds for this identification, but it would help to explain the curiously resolute manner in which the prince woos his lady. This central tableau does suggest that the subject is more than a banquet scene. It seems generally agreed that these sundered leaves, which belong together as a double-page frontispiece, are from a manuscript of the *Shahnama* – dated 848/1444 and copied by Muhammad al-Sultani – in the Bibliothèque Nationale, Paris (suppl. persan 494). But it seems impossible to reconcile this theory with the subject matter proposed by Schulz.

Few Persian miniatures have caught the spirit of royal merry-making as faithfully as these. Here is the quintessence of court life. As usual, nature participates in the festivities: trees and flowers alike are in blossom. Chinese clouds sail serenely across a gold sky. The expulsion of bystanders by an officious chamberlain, a standard feature of such scenes, stresses the exclusiveness of royal pleasures. Conspicuous consumption is the keynote. It explains the presence of numerous spectators, and of the court officials carrying the emblems of their rank. Hence, too, the references to courtly pastimes: musicians, falconer and the groom with a cheetah. Costly ceramics and carpets are prominently displayed. Even the court ladies, their heads drooping on swan necks, function principally as exquisite objects.

These miniatures are also of central importance in that they represent the final maturity of the Timurid style of Shiraz. The earlier characteristics of the style are now refined. Figures are still large, but no longer lumbering; they are placed close together but the groups are varied in size and arrangement, with ample space around them. As is common with such frontispieces, the artist has spread himself over two pages rather than depicting two separate scenes. Their unity is emphasised by the way that almost every glance is focussed on the royal pair to the far right.

97
Shah Bahram enthroned
Miniature painting
Firdausi, *Shahnama*
Shiraz school, c. 1440-45

Private collection
Dimensions: page 221 x 289 mm; decorated area 159 x 204 mm

The painting is remarkable for its detailed architectural setting. In many ways this echoes contemporary decoration: high dadoes of hexagonal tiles, spiral columns and campaniform plinths are regular features of Timurid architecture, while lightly painted floral and other designs on a white ground were found in palaces and religious buildings alike (cf. *54*). Only the profile of the arch is anachronistic, for it has the *dur-i 'ajamana* (a depressed four-centred arch) form of Saljuq buildings.

Behind the Shah stand his sword-bearer and quiver-bearer, whose functions continued into the Qajar period (cf. *89*). They wear the tall conical hats which are so frequently found in Shiraz painting between c. 1425 and c. 1450. Some of the courtiers clamp their arms firmly to their chests, perhaps as a sign of respect. The differences in scale between them emphasise that the major scene takes place inside.

98
A princely couple with attendants under a flowering tree
Miniature painting on silk
Probably Herat, c. 1450

Boston, Museum of Fine Arts, no. 14.545; formerly in Goloubew collection
Dimensions: 314 x 232 mm.
Exhibited: Munich 1910, Paris 1912, New York, 1968
Published: the bibliography up to 1928 is given in Coomaraswamy, *Goloubew*, 37-40 (with pls. XXX-XXXI); among later discussions, see Kühnel in *SPA*, 1854; Robinson, *PD* 132 and pl. 21 (in colour); Grube, *KdO* V (1967), 4-5 and Abb. 1; Grube, *Classical Style*, 25-6, 186 and pl. 15

It would be difficult to evoke the Persian courtly ideal more succinctly than this artist has done. Paradoxically, however, the painting is unusually Chinese in spirit. Indeed, it is the end product of 150 years of intermittent chinoiserie. The artist has responded to the economy of Chinese painting by reducing detail to a minimum. He places the few objects he needs with an exact sense of interval. These objects, like the people themselves, have a primarily symbolic value: they are fixtures of the court. It seems likely, in view of the disproportion in scale between the upper and lower sections, that in its original form this painting on silk copied an imported Chinese work and comprised only the bird and the branch. Perhaps a later artist added the courtly scene. Other theories hold that the entire painting is by a single hand. It is in any event noteworthy that this juxtaposition of an archetypal Chinese theme with an essentially Islamic one can be achieved with so little sense of incongruity. Chinese influence was a cyclical phenomenon in Persian painting, especially in the Mongol and Timurid periods, and it was a potent factor in the formation of the mature Timurid style. Thus it would be mistaken to think only in terms of a massive influx of Chinese techniques and motifs in the early 14th century which weakened with time and was absorbed into the native tradition. Embassies were exchanged and there was a constant flow of artifacts from east to west. In this case the use of silk as a medium must have accentuated that natural affinity for Chinese painting which many Timurid artists displayed. The court scene does not trespass into the upper part of the picture, nor does it make the design crowded. Rather does it complement the Chinese theme in its choice of the same muted colours.

The girl musician plays the *rabab* or spike fiddle, an instrument which has changed little over the centuries. It appears frequently in scenes of music-making at court and in court poetry; compare the 11th century poet Manuchihri: *Ma mard-i sharabim va kababim va rababim* – "We're men of drinking and feasting and music-making".

99
Courtiers by a stream

Miniature painting
Firdausi, *Shahnama*
London, British Museum, no. 1948
12-11 04; formerly in Anet and Eckstein collections
Dimensions: leaf 268 x 198 mm.; painting 108 x 000 mm.
Previously exhibited: Paris 1912, London 1931, New York 1940, London 1949, 1959, 1963, 1967
Published: C. Anet in *BM* XXII (1912;, 9-17 and pl. IIIH; Marteau and Vever, *MP* I, pl. VI (colour;; Kxhnel, *MIO*, 55 and pl. 38; Ro`binson, *PMP*, no. 107 (with bibliography of other dispersed leaves from this manuscript;; Titley, *Catalogue*, no. 146
Varied dates and provenances have been suggested for this mutilated miniature. A mid-15th century date now seems generally accepted, while recent attributions favour a Western Indian provenance. Not enough information is yet available to settle the question. In fact the leaf has points of contact with several schools. The hills of this remarkably high horizon are mantled in red, recalling work

commonly associated with Herat, while the tight massing of near-identical, broad-faced figures echoes the Timurid style of Shiraz. Chinese influence makes itself felt in unusual ways, notably in the escutcheons of the pages' clothing and the prominent blossoming tree. This tree serves to close off the far side of the picture and also to emphasise the direction in which the company gazes. The companion leaf (Museum of Fine Arts, Boston, no. 14.544) depicts a king enthroned. Some ceremony, perhaps of initiation or promotion, is being enacted, for a courtier presents to the ruler a page whose turban sets him apart from his fellows. Indeed, dress is deliberately used to point distinctions of rank.

100
Khusrau before his father Hurmuzd

Manuscript: 356 ff. and 19 miniatures. According to Schulz there were formerly 35
Nizami, *Khamsa* (*Khusrau u Shirin*)
Perhaps Isfahan; 868/1463-4 (?)
Copyist: Darvish 'Abdallah al-Isfahani (?)
Dublin, Chester Beatty Library and Gallery of Oriental Art: Pers.
Ms. 137, f. 31; formerly in Sambon, Schulz and Goloubew collections
Dimensions: page 324 x 217 mm
Previously exhibited: London 1931
Schulz, *PM* I, 87-8 and II, pls. 38-40, 42-6; Blochet, *Peintures*, 165-7; Kuhnel, *MIO*, 26, 56 and pl. 45; Sakisian, *LMP*, 36; *London 1931*, no. 540C; *BWG*, 78, no 59 and pl. LX, A, B; Kühnel in *SPA*, 1856; Robinson, *AO* I (1954), 105; Stchoukine, *MT*, 60, 62, 101, 109 and 119; Robinson, *Bodleian*, 30, 70 and 80; CB *Catalogue* I, 67-9; Robinson, *PD*, 139 and pl. 79; B. W. Robinson, in *Pope Memorial Volume* (forthcoming)

The Sasanian King Hurmuzd proclaimed that anyone who harmed his neighbour would suffer the rigours of the law. He was therefore incensed when his son Khusrau transgressed the edict. He ordered that the prince should have his horse, his slave and even his clothes taken away from him. A naked torso in Persian painting is a common symbol for a slave, and the feeling of disgrace is made keener still by the prince surrendering his sword.

Despite their outstanding quality, the miniatures of this manuscript are

101

very hard to localise. Their finesse and grasp of detail is worthy of Herati work, but the figure types differ from that school, as do the cool colours. The design consistently extends into the margin, another detail not easily paralleled as a regular feature of a manuscript. Schulz, the former owner of the manuscript, gave the date and the name of the copyist but the colophon which contained this information is now lost. It may have belonged to the *Khamsa* of Amir Khusrau which was formerly bound together with this work. Much detailed research is still needed on Persian painting of the middle years of the 15th century; recent work has already established hitherto unknown schools at Samarqand and Yazd which were active in this period.

The king is a strikingly youthful figure, but his imposing presence easily dominates the scene. Khusrau cuts a puny figure beside him. Such dispropositions of scale are of course deliberate. Standing watch at the door and holding his mace of office is the chamberlain, already a crucial figure at the Sasanian court.

101
The King of the East with two ladies
Miniature painting
Maulana Muhammad b. Husam al-Din,
  Khavar Nama, f. 183
Perhaps Shiraz, 881/1477
Signed "the least of the slaves, Farhad.
  881"/1477

Dublin, Chester Beatty Library, and
  Galley of Oriental Art Pers.
  Ms. 293, no. 4
  Dimensions: 400 x 280 mm.
Published: for the parent manuscript
  and its dispersed leaves, see **16**.
  For this leaf, see CB *Catalogue* III, 61

This sumptuous interior illustrates the enviable range of Farhad. The main interest of the scene lies in the detailed information which it gives about the decoration and furnishings of contemporary palaces. No examples have survived of the dais or the four-light windows with stucco infill, though the latter seem to have been a popular feature of Timurid buildings (cf. **28**;. The Chinese motifs on some of the robes and the dais drapery accord well with the fashion for chinoiserie that marked much of the 15th century in Persia. Equally typical of the period are the geometric designs of the woodwork and the floral patterns stencilled on the walls.

102
Garden scene
Miniature painting
Herat school, c. 1485
Cleveland, the Cleveland Museum of
  Art, no. 44.490; formerly in
  Ricketts and Hofer collections
Dimensions: leaf 263 x 160 mm.;
  painting 233 x 142 mm.
Previously exhibited: London 1931,
  New York 1933, New York 1955,
  Rome 1956, Paris 1961, Venice 1962,

New York 1968
Published: Martin, *MP II*, pl. 68;
London **1931**, no. 482; *BWG*, **97-8**,
no. 82 and pl. LXXIZ; Diamond,
Guide, 31 and fig. 19; A. Sakisian, in
Syria XII (1931;, 169 and pl.
XXXVI; Kxhnel, *SPA*, 1863 and
pl 889 (in colour;; H. C. Hollis in
Bulletin of the Cleveland Museum of Art
XXXII (1945;, 35-9; *Mostra d' Arte
Iranica*, no. 510; *Cleveland Handbook,
Handbook*, no. 723; *Sept mille and
d'art en Iran* (P ris, 1961;, no. 1080;
Grube, *MMP*, no. 53; Grube,
Classical Style, 191 and pl. 37

Although both subject and treament are fairly conventional, certain details are worth noting. The open-air grille over which a spitted bird is being roasted has certain affinities with Timurid cauldrons, but objects of this precise kind seem not to have survived.

Bihzad's habit of including a Negro in his paintings for reasons of colour contrast may find an echo here. Persian notions of vertical perspective are typified by the superposed figures to the left. Reading from the top downwards, the musicians are playing the lute, harp, long lute, and end-blown flute respectively. But it is the unfinished state of the picture which yields the most valuable information. It shows that very careful and detailed drawing underlies the painting proper and that figures were left to the last. Perhaps they were for the master to complete, while junior members of the atelier might execute the tapestried garden setting. The relationship between this unfinished painting and a virtually identical finished painting often attributed to Bihzad, in the Gulistan Palace Library, Teheran, was discussed by Binyon, Wilkinson and Gray (*BWG*,

no. 81 and pl. LXVII, in colour). They conclude tentatively that this is a copy of the finished work, which formed the left hand part of a double-page frontispiece showing Sultan Husain Baiqara and ladies in a garden.

103
Prince and attendants in a garden pavilion

Tinted drawing
Qazvin style, c. 1590
London, by permission of the Director of India Office Library and Records, no. J. 28-11
Dimensions: page 365 x 235 mm.; painting 200 x 130 mm.
Previously exhibited: London 1951, 1967
Published: Robinson, *VAM* 1951, no. 102; Robinson, *VAM* 1952, pl. 23; Robinson, *PM*, pl. XVIII; Robinson *PMP*, no. 180; Robinson, *IOL*, no. 210

Picnics are still an everyday feature of Persian life, and they have been a stock convention of Persian literature from early medieval times. Similarly, the poetic cliché which compares the beloved to a cypress may well have induced the artist to echo the curved, tapering sweep of the tree in the silhouettes of the courtiers. The iconography is equally time-honoured. In this harmonious regrouping of familiar elements the only unfinished feature is the corner panels left blank for a text. The reeling courtier in loud yellow leggings may strike a discordant note amidst this elegance but he serves as a reminder that this is a drinking party.

The awning or baldachin under which the prince sits may seem no more than a delightful caprice of the artist, and certainly no surviving structure of this type is known. Artistic licence alone keeps it upright, but the accounts of European travellers to the Safavid court show that temporary edifices for garden festivities and entertainments were put up in large quantities. The translation of such flimsy structures into more durable form is illustrated by the palaces and garden pavilions in Isfahan and – significantly enough for this drawing – in Qazvin.

104
Preparation for a royal meal: figure of a youth

Manuscript; ooff., 5 miniatures and 1 drawing
Hatifi, *Shirin u Khusrau*
Khurasan, c. 1575
London, Royal Asiatic Society of Great Britain and Ireland
Codrington 244
Dimensions: 260 x 163 mm.
Previously exhibited: London 1951, 1967
Published: Morley, *Catalogue*, 244; Robinson, *VAM* 1951, no. 82; Robinson, *PMP*, no. 172

(a) *The painting*) In this unusually relaxed scene, genre elements for once

prevail over royal ones. The artist has no pretentions to very refined detail, and his colours are cheerful rather than subtle. His forte is clean, confident drawing and a sure sense of composition. Thus each figure has a different pose and has ample room to move. Such work is a simplified version of the contemporary style of Qazvin and its very simplicity points to Khurasan rather than to Shiraz.

(b) *The drawing*) The presence of a tinted drawing rather than a painting opposite the royal couple enthroned may simply mean that the patron could not afford a frontispiece of the usual kind (e.g. **177**). The youth depicted here displays the same confident but somewhat wooden drawing style that marks the painting opposite. In the margins of both pages are rather coarse floral sprays in gold.

105
A page in European dress holding a flask and glass

Miniature painting, partly drawn in ink

Isfahan style, about 1590
By Mir Yusuf, according to the inscription in the lower left corner
London, British Museum no. 1948 12-11 015; formerly in Anet and Eckstein collections. In the lower right corner is the obliterated seal of a previous owner
Dimensions: leaf 312 x 177 mm.; painting 162 x 102 mm.
Previously exhibited: London 1949, 1959
Published: Martin, *MP*, pl. 156; Gray, *BMQ* XVII (1952;, 18; Titley, *Catalogue*, no. 404 (209;

This young exquisite with his kohl-rimmed eyes, his earring and trailing locks personifies the Safavid ideal of male beauty. Blatant disproportions were an essential part of that ideal; hence the contrast between massive thighs and etiolated hands and feet. He holds a ceramic ewer with a portrait of a lady, a type of pottery common in later Safavid times. Though clearly Persian, the page is clad in European dress, following in this a vogue at the

Safavid court. Europeans reciprocated:
the portraits of Tavernier and Sir
Robert Sherley in Persian dress are
justly celebrated. But the details here
are not entirely correct. The chic
feathered hat and the cloak are
unexceptionable, but the breeches,
with black blossoms and white Chinese
tai forms against the gold, have nothing
European in their patterning.

The beardless cupbearer depicted
here is probably one of the corps of
slaves (*ghilman*) – young eunuchs and
pages – who served in the private
household of the Shah.

106
Recumbent semi-nude
Miniature painting from the album of
the Amir of Bukhara (21 ff.)
Bukhara, c. 1550
New York, Pierpont Morgan Library,
Ms. 386-5 (18 miniatures in all)
Dimensions: leaf 241 x 378 mm.;
painting including borders 135 x
228 mm.; painting excluding
borders 67 x 152 mm.
Previously exhibited: San Francisco
1937, Venice 1962, New York 1968
Published: Martin, *MP*, 54 and
pl. 120; San Francisco, *Cat.*, 32 and
pl. 65; Grube, *MMP*, no. 72; Grube,
Classical Style, 32, 193 and pl. 50

Although the female nude appears
sporadically in earlier Persian art it is
not until the 16th century that this
theme is treated in isolation, for its
own sake. Even then it is typical that
this figure, which is as realistic as the
artistic canons of the time permitted,
should be embowered within floral
ornament of a highly fanciful character.
The calligraphy is a reminder that this
leaf was prized for more than its figure
drawing and its floral scrolls. In
traditional style, the lady is
ostentatiously unfettered by the frame.
A typically Persian gift for abstraction

has inspired the treatment of the whole
figure. The complexities of anatomy are
here reduced to a few splendidly
assured curves. Technically, the link
with later Safarid painting is thus
manifest; but odalisques of this kind
were to become a favourite theme of
Ottoman art.

107
Distribution of New Year presents
by Shah Sultan Husain
Miniature painting
Artist: Muhammad 'Ali, son of
Muhammad Zaman
Dated 1133/1721-22
London, British Museum, no. 1920
9-17 0299 (transferred from
Department of Oriental Printed
Books and Manuscripts, album Or.
1372, f. 47)
Dimensions: leaf 277 x 419 mm.;
painting 245 x 350 mm.
Previously exhibited: London 1939,
1949, 1959, 1967, 1971
Published: Robinson, *PMP*, no. 88;
Royal Persia, no. 243 and illustration
on endpapers

Scenes such as this became popular in
late Safavid times – Shah Sultan
Husain ruled from 1694 to the fall of
the dynasty in 1722. Surprisingly
enough, they owe more in their layout
and intent to pre-Islamic traditions
than to more recent work. The central
figure of the ruler flanked on each side
by three tiers of courtiers is a familiar
stereotype of Sasanian rock reliefs.
But this image was unaccountably
submerged in post-Sasanian
iconography, which preferred more
informal renderings of the monarch.
The return to these Sasanian images
continued for the next century and a
half and even led to the carving of
"pseudo"-Sasanian rock reliefs in the
Qajar period, the first examples of this
art form in Islamic Persia. This

conscious revival of past imperial
glories coincided with Iran's political
decline.

Nau Ruz, the Iranian New Year, is
celebrated at the beginning of spring
and like Christmas in the west is an
occasion for the exchange of gifts. The
Persepolis reliefs of the 6th century
B.C. depict the subject peoples of the
Persian empire bringing their New
Year gifts to the ruler. The Sasanian
monarchs received and distributed
gifts at this time and the custom
continued into Islamic times. To this
day the Shah gives presents to high-
ranking officials in a special Nau Ruz
ceremony. The symbolic distribution
of largesse is of course a function of the
monarchy in many cultures.

Shah Sultan Husain is sufficiently
identified by his robe and turban
but the painting is almost surely
intended as an actual portrait.
The placing of the courtiers may
reflect distinctions of rank, though
their uniformly glazed expressions
make it hard to identify them more
closely. The ceremony takes place in a
talar, the portico in front of a house or
palace.

European techniques of painting
had been popularised in Persia by the
father of this artist. Their effect on the
carefully contrived conventions of
Persian painting can be gauged here. A
livid light plays over the scene. This
rippling light, rather like shot silk in its
effect is a signature of Muhammad
Zaman and his son. The uneasy
mixture of linear outline and internal
modelling indicates that the artist, like
many of his contemporaries, had
learned a trick rather than absorbed a
new way of seeing. Highlights are
treated as an element of surface
pattern, another speciality of father and
son, while the colours have lost their
strength through over-blending.

The Ruler and his Duties

بدین کشت روشن بیاساما

سیاوش بیامد بہ میدان شبنگ

بفا کنم شاد مشک کدبان

ودرانیدک هشتم انیرگاه

خروشی برآمد ز نزدیک شهر

همی خواست کو را بنای برد

سیاوش بیان که آمد آبش

اگر آب بودی و مک نرسد

جواز کو و آمش بها مون

یکی شاد دما زیندا مذجهان

جهانیان خروشان واشونا

یکی خود ز دین بناه بش

پهاد شفانش اب وه نغاذ

جهان آفرین یم بیارد گاه

فم آمد جهان او اذ کام

عمی نوبه جوشان بیا نرد کرد

نوکفتی که با آبش اشت

ز نری و جوجه نی نوشل

دوذ و

خرو شیدن آمنه شهر

سین کهان و میان جهان

مراشر جمه وبش کیان شنده

یکی بارک بر نشسته سیاه

دخ شاه کو س بره ودنه

بندن وی به اندان مکی مش

سیاوش سید ربا نده تاتت

زنر سو رباز می جوشنده

یکی پش با دینکان پرخ

جهان آمذا سیانای سولد

سواران لشکر برا گحید

عمی زاده مزه یکی باد کن

بوی پره ز نعفنه ردلی بیاینده

محی کره نغش با مذهما

پهم کسنتش انیس نزم ون

کزین کوه آمش بیایم سکی مش

بشک سگ دل شاه سا ننذ

کسی ایشه وقا سیا شنذ

کناا کی آینه نازشن و

توکشی هنز داشت انند

عدوشت پیش عم رنغت

که خشوء برا کنده دا ذ کن

هشیوا راجا جای پسنده

بلک کند کا نو بد موش

سیاوش مرا و آمش ننذا

سری ورزشم نهانی کناا

جواز دشت سوه اید ودا

جهانی نغاه به کاره سه م

جوفنا یش بك رنده آنند

بلی پدنفنذ دلی ایشد

جان جزمزو رسم وساکلن

کزین جهان بود کره شرنت

اکزین کام رعایی مرا

برا مندا مؤان واش ذا

نمای براذ آش کنت ودملینش

که آمذز آش برد ن شمانو

دم آمش باه یکان بده

The Ruler and his Duties

The duties of the medieval Iranian ruler were manifold. It was impossible for him to plead ignorance as to their nature, for an entire literary genre was devoted to listing them. These manuals of statecraft – the "Mirrors for Princes" – perpetuated a Sasanian tradition. They laid down the proper balance between business and pleasure and treated the king's choice of boon companions with the same seriousness as matters of high state policy. The moral was often pointed by some edifying tale of transparent allegory. An example of the first category is the story of the old woman who upbraided Sultan Sanjar for exercising so little control over his men that they could rob poor people such as herself with impunity (195a). How then could he call himself a just ruler? The story of Bahram and the shepherd has a similar burden (114), while the tale of Nushirvan and the birds conveys the same message by more roundabout means (125).

The king was the ultimate repository of justice in the land and it was his duty to make himself available to any of his subjects who had a just complaint. In practice it was commoner for the king to set aside certain hours when he would hear such complaints. A chain was hung across the threshold of his palace and those seeking redress would grasp it. Executions would often be carried out in his presence (cf. 127 and numerous scenes in 139): the fatal leather mat would be spread before his throne and sand would be sprinkled to absorb the blood. Numerous forms of execution are depicted in Persian painting. The victims were shot with arrows, burned over a slow fire, decapitated; limbs were amputated (129) and throats cut.

Another major function of the ruler was to build widely for the public good. His viziers and certain wealthy nobles shared this task with him and such building activities became a traditional focus of rivalry between the highest officials of the land (e.g. the viziers of Malikshah and of Öljeitü). Caravansarais, hostels and theological colleges are the categories of such buildings most frequently encountered. Many rulers – such as Mas'ud of Ghazna and Ghazan Khan – participated in the buildings they themselves financed by drawing the plans and supervising certain sections of the work. Others, like Shah 'Abbas and especially Timur, took a close and at times Draconian interest in building operations, meting out severe punishment if the work was not completed according to schedule (119). Often the palaces shown in Persian painting display the titles of the ruler over the doors. Works of civil engineering such as bridges and fortifications (121) also fell to the ruler's lot and he may be seen directing the workmen on such tasks.

Poets and literary men in general were dependent on royal or official patronage for their living (116, 117).

Sometimes, as in the celebrated case of Firdausi and Mahmud of Ghazna, the patron was less than generous – although it is recorded that he gave the poet a house decorated with paintings of *Shahnama* scenes. But Mahmud unwisely stinted his presents of money and convertible assets and the poet vented his spleen by writing a bitter denunciatory preface to the epic; he also scrawled a caustic epigram on the wall of the great mosque at Ghazna.

Nizami was more fortunate, for he was sent 5000 dinars in red gold, and a camel laden with precious stuffs, by the prince to whom he dedicated the first book of his *Khamsa*, while Hafiz was sent a thousand dinars for one of his poems from an Indian prince even though he himself never travelled to that country. No doubt the prospect of such rewards inspired the fulsome eulogies of their patron with which medieval poets larded their work.

108
The greedy dervish
Miniature painting; the present manuscript has 56 ff. and 8 miniatures
Sa'di, *Gulistan* (text, tr. Gladwin, 22-4)
Herat, 830/1426-7
Copyist, Ja'far al-Baisunghuri
Patron: probably Baisunghur b. Shah Rukh; the manuscript has the seal of the library of Sultan Baisunghur Bahadur Khan

Dublin, Chester Beatty Library and Gallery of Oriental Art MS Persian 119, f. 9
Dimensions: 203 x 138 mm.
Previously exhibited: London 1931, Cairo 1935 and London 1967
Published: for a bibliography up to 1967, see Robinson, *PMP,* no 17; see also Kirketerp-Møller, *Bogmaleri,* 116-7

A king who turned night into day in pursuit of pleasure and preened himself on his good fortune was rebuked for his thoughtlessness by a shivering dervish outside his palace. The contrite monarch gave him lavish alms but when the impudent dervish squandered all and quickly returned for more, he was sent packing. The artist evokes the early part of this cautionary tale by numerous subtle devices. Courtiers gaze curiously at the dervish but no-one lifts a finger to help him. They are all safely within or beside the palace; he alone is outside its orbit in symbolic isolation. The warm brickwork of the palace provides an appropriate foil for the chill tonality of the pale blue landscape in which the dervish shivers. Every detail of the palace is fastidiously choice – inscriptions, glazed tiles, ornamental brickwork and even the gold and indigo robe of the young coutier. This ostentatious wealth heightens the forlorn state of the hunched, half-naked dervish. Similar devices are used in the scene of the distressed poet from the same manuscript. In both leaves the delight in detail, finish and colour is subordinate to the desire to tell the story effectively.

109
King Jamshid teaching crafts
Miniature painting; the original manuscript has   ff. and three other miniatures
Tabari, *Annals,* in Persian translation
Turkoman Court style (?), Sha'ban 874/February 1470
Copyist, Badi' al Zaman

Dublin, Chester Beatty Library and Gallery of Oriental Art Pers. 144, f. 20a
Dimensions: 350 x 240 mm.
Previously exhibited: London 1931
Published: *London 1931,* no. 476 (a); *Souvenir,* 39; *BWG,* no. 71; Wiet, *Exposition,* 91; Kühnel in *SPA,* 1855 and pl. 880; Stchoukine, *MT,* no. LXIX; Kühnel, *PM,* 13 and pl. 24 CB *Catalogue* I, no. 144 Robinson, *PD* 132 and pl. 20 (in colour); B. W. Robinson in *Pope Memorial Volume* (forthcoming)

The text, like so many other Islamic chronicles, combines mythical and historical material. Jamshid, the legendary king whom Persian tradition still popularly identifies with Persepolis, was celebrated for teaching mankind useful crafts. The activities and tools illustrated here have remained virtually unchanged in Persia into modern times. For their 20th century equivalents see H. E. Wulff, *The Traditional Crafts of Persia* (Cambridge, Mass. 1966), 19 (bellows); 34, 51 (anvils); 56-7 (scissors); 58 (honing stone); 185-8 (spinning wheel) and 199, 214 (loom).

The painting marks the transition between the Juki *Shahnama* (28) and the fully fledged style of the Bihzad atelier. Hints of this later school include the burgeoning interest in facial types, the varied poses and the array of separately conceived self-contained vignettes. In its largely pastel tones, however, the painting differs from the intense contrasting colours favoured by the next generation of Herati painters. Its real place probably lies, as B. W. Robinson suggests, within a school termed "imperial Turkoman" or "Turkoman court" to distinguish it from the simpler and more clearly defined Turkoman school

110
Sultan Mahmud turns fisherman
Manuscript; 208 ff. and 9 miniatures
'Attar, *Mantiq al Tair* (text, tr. Nott, 47-8)
Probably Herat, c. 1490-1500
London, British Library, Add. 7735, f. 68a
Dimensions: page 248 x 346 mm.; painting 128 x 120 mm.
Previously exhibited: London 1967, 1971, 1973, 1976
Published: Rieu, *Catalogue* II, 577-8; Meredith-Owens, *PIM*, 20 and pl. XII; M. G. Lukens, *BMMA* 1967, 328 and fig. 9; Robinson, *PMP*, no. 31 and pl. 16; *Royal Persia*, no. 164; M. L. Swietochowski in *IAMMA*, 41, 47, 49, 50-1, 56, 63, 65-7, 71 and pls. 6, 11, 21, 35 and 37 (the latter is the opening depicted here); *Oriental Manuscripts*, no. 102 and pl. 9; Hayward Gallery Catalogue, no. 584
Titley, *Catalogue*, no. 91

In this allegorical poem the various stages of the mystic path are described. Its Sufi teaching is pointed by anecdotes. One of them concerns the effect of good luck. Sultan Mahmud of Ghazna, separated from his army by chance, came across a boy who was dejected because he had caught no fish. The Sultan offered to help and when he himself cast the net he brought in a hundred fish. Next day, when the boy came to visit him, Mahmud seated his visitor beside him on the throne. When an indignant courtier remonstrated the boy replied, "Joy has come, and sorrow is past, because I met with a fortunate monarch". Mahmud makes numerous appearances in the poem, for he was regarded as a model both as ruler and lover.

Even though this is one of the larger miniatures in the manuscript, setting and detail alike are simplified. Within the configurations of the rocks bordering the pool are concealed human and animal faces, a conceit much in vogue from the later 15th century onwards in both metropolitan and provincial work. Landscape and figure details identify this painting as dependent on the Bihzad atelier.

111
Sultan Mahmud and the woodcutter
Manuscript; 172 ff. and 7 miniatures
'Attar, *Mantiq al Tair* (text, tr. Nott, 48-9)
Probably Shiraz, 898/1492-3
Copyist, Na'im Din al Shirazi

Oxford Curators of the Bodleian Library, MS. Elliott 246, f. 63a
Dimensions: book 265 x 160 mm.; painting 115 x 78 mm.
Exhibited: London 1951, 1967; Oxford 1972
Published: Sachau and Ethé, *Catalogue*, no. 628; Robinson *VAM* 1951, no. 18; Robinson, *Bodleian*, 47-8 and pl. VI; Robinson, *PD*, 139 and pl. 81 (in colour); Robinson, *PMP*, no. 132; Robinson and Gray, *PAB*, 13; M. L. Swietochowski, *IAMMA*, 41, 47, 49-50, 53, 59-60, 63, 66-7, 69-71 and illustrations of all 7 miniatures in figs. 5, 10, 16, 25 (the opening exhibited here), 30, 31 and 40

For general remarks on this poem, see **110**. In this scene, as in **110**, the theme is the monarch as the "bringer of good luck". Sultan Mahmud, seeing an old man whose donkey had stumbled and thrown its load of thorns, strapped the burden onto its back and sent them on their way. Later, when the old man met him again and recognised him as the Sultan, he demanded a purse of gold for his thorns for "when a lucky man like the Sultan puts his hands to my bundle of thorns they become bunches of roses".

Few Turkoman paintings use colour in such seductive combinations as the illustrations in this manuscript. Here deep blue, green and gold create a satisfying harmony further enriched by paler shades such as the mousey robe of the old man. This richly embroidered robe is, like the coat of the boy in **110**, oddly at variance with his expressed poverty. In both cases the urge to decorate overrides any stirrings of naturalism. Similarly, it is the rich colour of the foliage that counts rather than the summary vertical lines that define it.

112
King Dara and the herdsman
Manuscript; 62 ff. and 3 miniatures
Probably Tabriz, c. 1520
Sa'di, *Bustan* (text, tr. Clarke, 57-9)

Oxford Curators of the Bodleian Library, MS. Marsh 517
Dimensions: book 245 x 170 mm.; painting 152 x 98 mm.
Previously exhibited: London 1951, 1967; Oxford 1972
Published: Sachau and Ethé, *Catalogue*, no. 1983; Robinson, *VAM* 1951, no. 34; Robinson, *Bodleian*, 82-3 and pl. X; Stchoukine, *MS*, no. 163; Robinson, *PMP*, no. 32; Robinson and Gray, *PAB*, 16-7

King Dara (Darius III) once came unawares upon the herdsman tending the royal horses and, taking him to be an enemy, prepared to shoot him. The

herdsman rebuked the King for not recognising his servants and for his indifference to their welfare.

Published opinions differ as to whether the paintings in this manuscript can be attributed to Bihzad. The fact that two of them copy earlier works of the master is itself no indication of his authorship; it was standard practice for figures, landscape details and entire compositions to be freely re-used not only by their creator but also by others. Both earlier (1488/9) and later (1535) versions of this particular scene are known. Only in comparison with the rich circumstantial detail of the 1488/9 *Bustan* in Cairo (Mustafa, *PM*, pl. 3) does this painting seem impoverished. Moreover, it displays subtleties of design and observation quite different from those of the Cairo manuscript. Thus the curving silhouettes of the horses ease the transition between the upper and lower sections, as does the flowing loop of the stream. The splayed forelegs of the mare giving suck have a lively naturalism while the vegetation bordering the brook is rendered with microscopic definition. In its gold ground and blue sky the painting reverses accepted colour schemes, an arresting detail; indeed, from first to last the painting owes its impact to its brilliant blaze of colour.

113
King Dara and the herdsman
Miniature painting
Sa'di, *Bustan* (text, tr. Clarke, 57-9)
Bukhara style, c. 1540

Cambridge, Fitzwilliam Museum, P.D. 202-1948
Dimensions: leaf 406 x 279 mm.; painting 162 x 100 mm.
Previously exhibited: London 1951, 1967
Published: Robinson, *VAM* 1951, no. 71; Robinson, *PMP*, no. 161

For the subject, see **112**. The painting exhibits the brilliant colours which had become traditional for this scene. Dark shades predominate but the many flowers, the rocks and the striped blue breeches of the herdsman provide lighter accents. The basis of the design, a horizontal division into tiers, lacks the subtlety of earlier versions of this theme, though the use of the stream to separate ruler from shepherd is unexpected. The artist has also departed from his model in the mannered convention he adopts for the horses, with their elongated backs and small heads. A touch of humour, welcome in so sentential a subject, is provided by the emaciated horse which turns its head to gaze at the bird perched on its rump.

The miniature is typical of the Bukhara style in its continuation of Herati modes, especially in its colours, figure types and use of detail. A comparison with **112**, produced perhaps a generation earlier, is

tent underline this courtly atmosphere. At the same time, realistic observation controls the choice of subject. Everyone pursues their daily round, oblivious of the noble horseman above – for the conventional high horizon is actually used here to suggest that the shepherd and Bahram Gur are on higher ground than the women, not just further away. The work is typical of its time in the prominence given to genre scenes. Equally typical is the corollary – that the ostensible subject of the drawing is tucked away in an area of secondary importance.

115

The sages of China bringing books on history to Ghazan Khan

Miniature painting
Hafiz-i Abru, *Majma' al-Tawarikh*
Probably Herat, c. 1425

London, British Museum, no. 1966
10-10 and 013
Dimensions: leaf 427 x 332 mm.;
painting 242 x 227 mm.
Published: *Sotheby*, 11.7.1966, lot 26;
Titley, *Catalogue*, no. 341; for a
general discussion of the parent
manuscript and its dispersed
miniatures see Ettinghausen, *KdO* 11
(1955), 30-44 and the bibliography
given in **67**

Reminiscences of the Ilkhanid style of the Rashid al-Din manuscripts include the varied headgear, the plain robe with parallel folds of drapery, and the gnarled tree with its linear shading and a jagged secondary silhouette at the base. But the model is transformed by the emphasis on colour, applied in large blocks and scarcely affected by modelling (though the sky is an astonishing ultramarine streaked with red). Natural features are repeatedly co-opted as compositional devices.

Ghazan, who ruled Iran from 1295 to 1304, was noted for his patronage of scholars, for whom he endowed numerous buildings in his capital, Tabriz. He commissioned his vizier Rashid al-Din to write the so-called "World Chronicle" (*Jami' al-Tawarikh*) and himself provided for it much of the information on Mongol history. The seat of the senior Mongol ruler, the Great Khan, was at Peking and for generations his authority was acknowledged by the Mongol empire to the west. Ghazan broke with this tradition, as his coins show, and the Great Khan's representative left Tabriz. But there is no reason to doubt that cultural contacts with China continued, as this miniature suggests.

116

A poet presents his work to the king

Miniature painting
Maulana Muhammad b. Husam
al-Din, *Khavar Nama*, f. 139
Probably Shiraz, c. 881/1477

Cambridge, Mass., Fogg Museum of
Art, no. 1956. 23
Dimensions: page 395 x 286 mm.

instructive – already the echoes of Herat are weaker. This leaf was formerly f. 18 of Fitzwilliam MS. 262-1949; it is now mounted on light brown paper speckled with gold.

114

Bahram Gur and the Shepherd

Drawing
Nizami, *Khamsa* (*Haft Paikar*; text, tr. Wilson, 257-60, 274)
Qazvin style, c. 1550
Signed "Work of Mir . . ." or, according to Stchoukine, "work of Ustad . . ."

Boston, Museum of Fine Arts,
no. 14. 589; formerly in Goloubew
collection
Dimensions: 450 x 295 mm.
Previously exhibited
Published: Coomaraswamy, *Goloubew*,
42 and pl. XXXIV; Stchoukine,
MS. no. 35; R. Ettinghausen,

Drawings in the Islamic World in I. Moskowitz, *Great Drawings of All Time* IV (New York, 1962), no 869; Robinson *PD*, 135 and pl. 39; Robinson, *PMP*, 56

Bahram Gur, thirsty while out hunting, stopped at a shepherd's tent for some refreshment. Noticing the shepherd's dog suspended from a tree he was told that the animal had betrayed his trust by allowing a wolf to steal the sheep. Bahram took the hint and returning home arraigned his vizier and rewarded the shepherd. Such cautionary tales were a time-honoured oriental device for imparting home truths to the ruler (cf. **125**).

This evocation of a rustic encampment is something of a conceit, as the immaculate appearance of the women shows. The squalor and hardship of daily life is transfigured into romance. Even the dragons embroidered on the

Published: for a bibliography of the manuscript in general, see **16**

Certain details of execution are curiously maladroit, notably some of the junctions between text and painting, the angle of the inscribed doorway and the profile of the extreme right-hand arch. Moreover, the entire left margin seems to have been left unfinished. Otherwise the painting has the sumptuously detailed setting found in other interior scenes in this manuscript. The same flamboyant colours. The intrusive rock formation is an unexpected feature presumably introduced as a contrasting texture. A particular hallmark of this artist is his predilection for hair-thin lines in drawing faces. Indeed, the fineness of line in these paintings is remarkable in view of their large size. This combination of features seems to be rather unusual in the Turkoman style (the outstanding exception is the "Sleeping Rustam" of c. 1505 in the British Museum).

For other leaves from this manuscript, see **16, 101, 181, 187** and **198**.

117
The King Qizil Arslan embraces the poet Nizami

Manuscript; 250 ff. and 18 miniatures
Nizami, *Khusrau u Shirin*
Isfahan style, Jumada I 1091/June 1680 (an error for 1041/1631)
Copyist, 'Abd al-Jabbar
Signed by Riza-yi 'Abbasi, one miniature dated 6 Safar 1042/23 Aug 1632

London, Victoria and Albert Museum, no. A.M. 364-1885, f. 246a
Dimensions: page 243 x 137 mm
Previously exhibited: London 1951, 1967
Published: Sir T. W. Arnold, *BM* XXXVIII (1921), 59-67 and two plates; Arnold and Grohmann, *IB*, pls. 71-4; Gray, *PP* 1930, pl. 15; Robinson, *VAM 1951*, no. 119; Robinson, *VAM 1965*, 17 and pls. 33-4; Stchoukine, *SA*, 132; Robinson, *PMP*, no. 71; Welch, *Isfahan*, no. 51

Rulers often rewarded poets richly for their work, but the King here pays Nizami a signal honour – he descends from his throne to embrace the poet. As so often in this manuscript (cf. ff. 34a, 99a and 123a, for example), the scene is witnessed by a courtier on each side, their bodies inclining slightly forward in a manner characteristic of these illustrations. Equally typical is the use of paired text panels of uneven size at the top and bottom of the painting. These serve to break up the picture space and perhaps to mitigate the rather formal layout. In common with most of the paintings in the book, the design is marked by a notable economy. Riza achieves this principally by limiting himself to a few large figures, their bodies described by sweeping curves. Half a dozen colours, again used *en bloc*, suffice, but most of the robes are lightly dusted with gold for added richness. Landscape is also simplified and even facial expressions tend to be uniform. It is perhaps justifiable to infer from these standardised features that book painting did not capture Riza's imagination.

118
Portrait of Riza–i 'Abbasi

Miniature painting
Probably Isfahan; completed 14 Ramadan 1084/24 December 1673
Signed Mu'in Musavvir

Princeton, University Library, no. 96G (formerly Quaritch collection)
Dimensions: page 301 x 213 mm.; painting 187 x 103 mm.
Previously exhibited: Venice 1962, New York 1973, Cambridge, Mass., 1974
Published: Martin, *MP* I, 72 and fig. 32 Schulz, *PMI* 186-7; T. W. Arnold, *The Journal of Indian Art and Industry* XVII (1916), 69-70 and pl. Ib (in colour); Sakisian, *LMP*, 136, 142-3 and pl. C; Arnold and Grohmann, *IB*, pl. 75; *BWG*, 178; Kühnel in *SPA*, 1892-3; Moghadam and Armajani, *Catalogue*, 88, no. 200; E. Kühnel in *Pantheon* 29 (1942), 108, fig. 2; Grube, *MMP*, no. 118; Stchoukine, *SA*, 67, 88-9, 225; Welch, *Isfahan*, no. 76

This drawing and its twin, which is dated 5 Safar 1087/19 April 1676, are interesting on several counts. They may perhaps claim to be the only authentic likeness preserved of a Persian painter. It is thus all the more fortunate that the painter in question should be the supreme Persian artist of the 17th century. The old maestro is shown peering through his pince-nez as he works on one of the single leaves which were the staple of his art in his later years. Since he did not have a regular stipend as a permanent member of the royal scriptorium, he was constrained

to sell individual leaves to make a living. Indian merchants were eager patrons of such work. Riza appears to use no model for his painting; such subjects came into the category of things known rather than things seen. He is caught in a typical attitude, unassuming and therefore convincing; he is too absorbed to be self-conscious. Perhaps other Persian paintings were executed in an equally unpromising posture. Certainly this slumped pose is still typical of modern exponents of the art. Before Riza lie brushes, sketches, pencase and saucers of paint, while in his sash is the knife used for trimming paper. In the affectionate homage which the pupil Mu'in here offers to the memory of his master one may sense that intimate relationship between *ustad* and *shagird*, master and apprentice, which was traditional in painting as in other Persian crafts. Riza died in the year that this portrait was sketched and a valedictory mood seems to permeate the painting. It is remarkable that Mu'in should have returned to this subject some 38 years later (the inscription states that he did so "in accordance with the wish of my son") and still fostered the illusion that this was an informal, so to speak contemporary, portrait.

Technically, too, the painting is of interest. Side by side with a rather crass linear emphasis (e.g. in the foot) one may note the subtle, restrained modelling of jowl, neck and brow. Indeed, the painting is far less linear than the Boston drawing (**167**) or even his manuscript illustrations (**79**). The execution is uneven, ranging from the awkward junction of left arm and shoulder or the hurried daub on which Riza works to the practised ease of line and broad expanses of colour in the lower half of his body.

119
Construction of Khawarnaq
Manuscript; 203 ff.; one double-page
　and 20 single miniatures
Nizami, *Khamsa*
Herat, 900/1494-5
Attributions to Bihzad, Mirak, Qasim
　'Ali and 'Abd al-Razzaq
Patron, Amir 'Ali Farsi Barlas
London, British Library, Or. 6810,
　f. 154b
Dimensions: open book 250 x 350 mm;
　painting 175 x 115 mm
Previously exhibited: London 1967,
　1973, 1976, 1977
Published: for the extensive literature
　up to 1967, see Robinson, *PMP*,
　no. 29; later publications include
　M. G. Lukens in *BMMA* (May 1967),
　passim; Grube, *WI*, p. 59;
　Kirketerp-Møller, *Bogmaleir*, 122-3,
　125-6; Rice, *IP*, 130 and pl. 57;
　M. L. Swietochowski in *IAMMA*,
　57; Hayward Gallery Catalogue,
　no. 582

This is among the finest of all 15th century manuscripts. It is a typical work of the Bihzad atelier, but no two

scholars have agreed on how to apportion the paintings between the master, his colleagues and his pupils. Certainly Bihzad's skill in drawing bearded faces, of which the Mughal emperor Babur speaks, is well exemplified here. So too is his capacity for devising new and seductive combinations of colour. Equally typical is the fertile invention which creates a seemingly endless variety of natural poses for these labourers.

The palace of Khawarnaq symbolised, like the arch of Ctesiphon, the magnificence of pre-Islamic civilisation and became a *topos* of Islamic literature. Presumably Khawarnaq is depicted here because Bahram Gur, the hero of the *Haft Paikar,* spent his youth with the Yemenite Arab ruler Nu'man, who lived in it. The model for this scene (which was later to be copied with painful fidelity in India) may well have been a painting also frequently attributed to Bihzad – the "Building of the Bibi Khanum Mosque" in the Baltimore *Zafar Nama*. Both paintings illustrate building practices which have changed little over the centuries. Examples include the adzes used to cut bricks, the wooden scaffolding and the lack of centring for the arch. Only in one respect is it exceptional. The entire building, like a teeming anthill, swarms with workmen. The parallel with Samarqand a century earlier is irresistible – for it is recorded of Timur that he once threatened to execute the entire work force if a certain building was not completed, from scratch, within ten days.

120
**Iskandar (Alexander) with
　representatives of Gog and
　Magog**
Miniature painting; parent manuscript
　has 000 ff. and 000 miniatures
Anthology, including the *Khamsa* of
　Nizami
Probably Isfahan, 838-40/1435-6
Copyists, 'Ali Pagir al-Ashtarjani and
　Zain al-Isfahani
Dublin, Chester Beatty Library and
　Gallery of Oriental Art Pers. Ms.
　124, II, f. 168
Dimensions: 270 x 170 mm
Previously exhibited: London 1931;
　Cairo 1935; London 1967
Published: see **38**

In Islamic tradition Iskandar was not regarded simply as a conqueror but as a searcher after wisdom, a prophet and a traveller whose insatiable curiosity took him to the ends of the earth. He was also a conscientious ruler; thus he built a wall to protect his people from the savage tribes of Gog and Magog. These northern peoples, who have been equated with the Tartars and the Huns, play a prominent role in Muslim eschatology and folklore. They were a byword for filthiness. In this scene, Iskandar observes their table manners, but the outlandish appearance with

which Islamic tradition credits them is not reflected here. Indeed, the artist has taken a rather reprehensible short cut by reproducing the layout of a standard courtly enthronement scene. Every inch of space is decorated, while the colours have the same washed quality as **38**. Window grilles of the type (though not the colour) depicted were a standard feature of Timurid mosques.

121
**Iskandar building the wall against
　Gog and Magog**
Manuscript; 569 ff. and 56 miniatures
Firdausi, *Shahnama* (text, tr. Warner,
　VI, 163-5)
Shiraz style, c. 1590
London: By permission of the Director
　of India Office Library and Records,
　Ethé 2992, f. 390a
Dimensions: leaf 460 x 295 mm;
　painting 305 x 230 mm
Previously exhibited: London 1931,
　1951, 1967
Published: *BWG*, no. 264; Robinson,
　VAM 1951, no. 55; Robinson,
　VAM 1952, pl. 26; Stchoukine,
　MS, no. 147, pls. LXXXII-
　LXXXIII; Robinson, *PD*, 140 and
　pl. 93; Robinson, *IOL*, 124-36, and
　no. 418

In Persia – as elsewhere in the Islamic world – it was an accepted principle, emphasised in numerous manuals of statecraft, that the ruler should build widely for the public good. Literally hundreds of inscriptions which survive on medieval Iranian buildings testify that many rulers discharged this duty. The national epic has no difficulty fitting Alexander the Great into this traditional pattern. The inhabitants of a city appealed to him for help against the monsters who each spring rampaged through their land. These monsters, the race of Yajuj and Majuj (Gog and Magog), lost their ferocity in winter time and became pale and thin – hence their puny appearance here. Iskandar caused walls to be built so that the pass through which they came was blocked.

The technique of building depicted here has changed little over the centuries. Masons still squat on walls as they build them and apprentices, men and boys, throw the bricks up to them in time to a rhythmical chant. Even the long-handled spade (*bil*) is still in use. The contrast between the simple dress and bare feet of the workmen and the richly costumed courtiers is well exploited. With unobtrusive skill the artist has accommodated well over a score of figures in the picture, but the king's dark chestnut mount and the knot of courtiers below him ensure that he stands out. The syncopated rhythms of the colour scheme are a particular strength of this manuscript. Formerly owned by Warren Hastings, it is typical of the large-scale illustrated copies of the *Shahnama* produced in Shiraz during the later sixteenth century.

power to its limited range of strong colours, a forte of earlier Shiraz painting. It is a daring stroke to clothe Siyavush in orange (not white as the text demands) as he rides through fire. The disregard for detail manifest in the repeated careless overpainting, and the generally coarse execution, underline the remoteness of this particular Shiraz school from the contemporary Jala'irid court style practised at Baghdad and elsewhere. But its preference for large figures and its sense of dramatic colour was to reappear in the paintings executed for Ibrahim Sultan (e.g. the Bodleian *Shahnama* of c. 1433-4, Ouseley Add. 176) and other Shiraz work of that time (e.g. **69, 141** and **194d**).

124
The fire ordeal of Siyavush
Manuscript; 229 ff. and 5 miniatures
Firdausi, *Shahnama* (text, tr. Warner, II, 219-21)
Probably Shiraz, 800/1397-8
Copyist, Muhammad b. Sa'id al-Qari
Dublin, Chester Beatty Library and Gallery of Oriental Art, Persian Ms. 114, f. 14b.
Dimensions: 250 x 160 mm
Previously exhibited: London 1931; New York 1933; London 1967
Published: See **159**

For the story illustrated here, see **123**.

The date and the name of the copyist are given in the collection of epics in the British Library (**159**); both books were originally part of the same larger work. They are crucial documents in the formation of the Timurid style, especially that version of the style associated with Shiraz. In place of the minute detail of the Khwaju Kirmani manuscript in the British Library (dated 798/1396) is a new sense of scale. The landscape, though not rendered in great detail, imposes itself by its large masses of colour. This particular combination of gold sky and mauve ground recurs in ff. 38 and 151. Even more effective is the silhouette of the coal-black horse against the scarlet-tipped tongues of flame.

Earlier versions of the Siyavush story favoured a horizontal format; here, the artist has recast the traditional iconography to emphasise verticality. This idea was copied almost within the decade by the artist who painted the same scene in the *Anthology* made for Iskandar Sultan (British Library, Add. 27261, f. 295 b). In the Dublin manuscript the men prostrate before Siyavush are an unusual feature of the scene though they are fully in the spirit of the text. This is the most tightly organised painting in the book; text and composition are more carefully dovetailed than in the other pictures. The narrow rectangular format recurs repeatedly in early Timurid painting, and echoes the newly fashionable shape of the books themselves. It is often associated – as here – with a high building to one side. Here the palace

122
The fire ordeal of Siyavush
Miniature painting
Firdausi, *Shahnama* (text, tr. Warner, II, 219)
Shiraz, 741/1340-1
Patron, the Wazir al-Hasan Qiwam al-Daula wa'l-Din
Montreal, M'Gill University, M'Gill Persian 33a
Dimensions: leaf 288 x 243 mm; painting 105 x 000
This particular leaf is unpublished. For a full discussion and bibliography of the parent manuscript, which is the key document for an understanding of the Inju style, see Grube, *MMP*, 31-2

For this subject, see **123**.

It shows that the custom of undergoing an ordeal as a proof of innocence was not confined to medieval Europe. Siyavush is clad in white, as the text demands; this detail is frequently ignored. The dominant red and yellowish tones which are a hallmark of Shiraz work in the 14th century are a very apt choice for this painting. The arches of the palace have a segmental, re-entrant profile typical of Ilkhanid architecture in Iran.

123
The fire ordeal of Siyavush
Miniature painting
Firdausi, *Shahnama* (text, tr. Warner II, 219-21)
Probably Shiraz, late 14th century
London, British Museum, no. 1923 1-15 01
Dimensions: 87 x 247 mm
Previously exhibited: London, B.M. 1931 and 1959
Published: Titley, *Catalogue*, no. 135

Sudaba, the wife of King Kai Kaus, fell in love with Siyavush, the king's son by another princess. When he rejected her overtures she told the king that Siyavush had tried to rape her; she then attempted to implicate him in another plot. Eventually Kai Kaus decreed that Siyavush should prove his innocence by riding between two great fires. He duly emerged unharmed.

The restrictive horizontal format is a survival of Tabriz practice earlier in the century, while the large figures echo earlier Shiraz work (cf. too Ipsiroglu, *PCM*, figs. 6-7). These features determine the diagrammatic treatment of the scene. Figures crowd into the frontal plane and display a rather forced symmetry. The picture owes its extends to the full height of the picture, and seems higher still because the text panel has been shortened to accommodate it. The contrast between finely worked architectural detail and open landscape was to be a hallmark of the Baisunghur school (**194**).

125
Nushirvan at the ruined village
Manuscript: 306 ff. and 23 miniatures
Nizami, *Khamsa* (*Makhzan al-Asrar*; text, tr. Darab, 157-9)
Baghdad, 788/1386-7 and 790/1388
Copyist, Mahmud b. Muhammad
Patron: possibly Sultan Ahmad Jala'ir

London, British Library, Or. 13297, f. 14a
Dimensions: open book 242 x 335; painting 105 x 130 mm
Exhibited: London 1971, 1973
Published: N. M. Titley in *BMQ* XXXVI (1971-2), 8-11; E. G. Sims in *aarp* 6 (1974), 57, 63-4; E. G. Sims in *Sanat Tarih Yilligi* VI (1976), 394, 396; Titley, *Catalogue*, no. 324A

The miniature illustrates a cautionary tale typical of the "Mirror for Princes"

genre. Nushirvan the Just chanced upon a ruined village while hunting with his vizier and was curious to know what the two birds among the ruins were saying to each other. The minister replied that they were haggling over a marriage contract. One was demanding some ruined villages as the dowry and the other was promising that if the king's tyranny continued he would soon be able to give away a hundred thousand such villages. Nushirvan, grief-stricken, made speedy reparation.

In this, apparently the earliest illustrated Nizami manuscript known, the scenes favoured in later iconography are already established – notably Sultan Sanjar and the old woman (**195a**) "practice makes perfect" (**34, 35**) and Khusrau espying Shirin (**23**). But the innovatory nature of the manuscript is revealed by the presence of several scenes which later dropped out of the accepted canon of illustrations. Stylistically it also illustrates a period of transition. Pointers to the developed Timurid style include the marshy tufts of the landscape, the facial types and the high horizon. The artist prefers cool,

sober colours, well exemplified by the bleak grey-green landscape and the slate-blue sky. This landscape is not encountered elsewhere in the manuscript. In most of the other miniatures the sky is gold; here gold is reserved for the accoutrements of the king. This picture may therefore be the work of a different artist. His draughtsmanship is careful rather than fine, as in the painstaking rendering of the bricks or the way that the horses are distinguished from each other.

126
The lady and the banker
Miniature painting; the original manuscript has ooff. and 12 other miniatures
Amir Khusrau, *Khamsa* (scene from *Hasht Bihisht*)
Probably Herat, 1 Rajab 890/14 July 1485
Copyist, Muhammad b. Azhar
Attributed to Bihzad
Dublin, Chester Beatty Library and Gallery of Oriental Art formerly in Martin collection
Dimensions: leaf 250 x 160 mm
Previously exhibited: London 1931, Cairo 1935, London 1967
Published: Martin, *MP*, 44-5 and pl. 75; Martin, *MB*, 5th unnumbered page and pl. 21; *London 1931* 478 (m); *BWG*, no. 78 (m); Wiet, *Exposition*, 93 and pl. 65; Stchoukine, *MT*, no. LXXI; CB *Catalogue* I, no. 163; Robinson, *VAM 1965*, 13 and pl. 19; Robinson, *PD*, 133 and pl. 24 (in colour); Robinson, *PMP*, no. 28

A courtesan brought a suit against a banker who, having enjoyed her favours only in a dream, was naturally reluctant to pay her. The king, taking the form of a parrot, symbol of wisdom, handed down a Solomonic decision: that the lady should taste the same evanescent pleasure as the youth by watching in a mirror as he counted out her fee.

Echoes of Chinese influence include the flowering trees and perhaps the border design on the carpet, but otherwise the sumptuous setting is wholly Islamic. The languid silhouettes of the three ladies form a loosely linked group which in turn quietly complements the trio of men. Bihzad, as is well known, enjoyed playing with such compositional problems and indeed some have attributed this miniature to him. The panels of calligraphy lack margins, but are not therefore unfinished. Since each contains only a single hemistich written diagonally, the text stands out with rare éclat.

127
Badr and Mushtari about to be executed
Miniature painting
'Assar, *Mihr u Mushtari*
Shiraz, c. 1540
Private collection
Dimensions: leaf 300 x 250 mm; painting 175 x 145 mm

Previously exhibited: London 1967
Published: Robinson, *PMP*, no. 142
and pl. 48

This romatic poem recounts the
adventures of the sons of Shapur and
his vizier, named Mihr ("Sun") and
Mushtari ("Jupiter") respectively.
Their pure and selfless devotion to each
other became a legend. Shapur, however, was led to believe that this love
was unnatural and ordered their separa-
tion. Mushtari then began a secret
correspondence with Mihr, which was
discovered. The king thereupon
commanded the executioner to behead
Mushtari and his go-between Badr,
and only the intercession of his
nephew Bihzad saved them, as it later
saved the life of Mihr himself.

In medieval times a leather mat was
spread in front of the monarch before
an execution and the victims were
forced to kneel on it. This detail is
missing here. Both colour and
compositional devices are deployed to
focus attention on the principal scene.
It is sandwiched between panels of text
and compressed even further by the
blue and white wall behind. The outer
wall of the palace and the courtyard
with trees beyond it close it off
vertically. This ability to compose a
picture in large blocks, only later to be
filled in with detail, is characteristic of
Shiraz work in the Safavid period.

128
The rival poets

Manuscript; 106 ff. and 8 miniatures
Asadi: *Garshaspnama*
Qazvin, 981 1573-4
Copyist: 'Imad al-Husaini
Paintings signed by Muzaffar 'Ali
(f. 5a); Sadiqi Beg (f. 45b); and Zain
al 'Abidin (f. 90b). The remaining
paintings are unsigned but are
probably the work of one or other of
these artists

London, British Library, Or. 12985,
f. 5a
Dimensions: page 350 x 470 mm.;
painting 220 x 180 mm. plus
marginal extension
Previously exhibited: London 1967,
1976
Published: N.M. Titley, *BMQ* XXI 1-2
(1967), 27-32; Robinson, *PMP*, no.
48; Robinson in *BM* CX (1968), 77;
Meredith-Owens, *Handlist*, 76;
Hayward Gallery Catalogue, no. 613;
Welch, *Artists*, 57, 75-7, 162, 197
and 20; Titley, *Catalogue*, no. 86

Sultan Mahmud of Ghazna (994-1030),
who wanted a verse history of pre-
Islamic Persia, invited the major poets
of the time to compose specimen
sections. The laureate 'Unsuri won
and with three fellow poets he repaired
to a garden to celebrate his triumph.
Chance dictated that Firdausi, newly
arrived at Ghazna, should also arrive
there. In order to test Firdausi's claim
that he too was a poet a competition
was proposed in which each in turn
should extemporise a line ending in the

same rhyme. To render the newcomer's
discomfiture certain, 'Unsuri chose a
rhyme shared by only three words in
the language; his friends duly used up
the remaining two. Unabashed,
Firdausi drew on his store of legend to
find a proper name that would fit, and
quickly capped the last line. He never
looked back.

For once poets are depicted
informally, far from the inhibiting
presence of their patron. In typically
Persian fashion they take their ease in a
garden, itself the favoured setting for
so much Persian lyric poetry. Such
poetic gatherings have not entirely
died in Persian society.

The venerable Muzaffar 'Ali, whose
signature the painting bears, was a
nephew and pupil of Bihzad and the
deep saturated colours owe more to
Herat than to Tabriz or Qazvin.

129
The execution of al-Hallaj

Manuscript; 179 ff. and 25 miniatures
al-Biruni, *Kitab al-athar al-baqiya 'an
al-qurun al-khaliya* ("The book of the
vestiges which survive of past
times"; text, tr. Sachau, 194-5)
Possibly Tabriz, 707/1307-8
Copyist, Ibn al-Qutbi

Edinburgh University Library Or. Ms.
161, f. 94a
Dimensions: leaf 320 x 200 mm
Previously exhibited: London 1931,
1951, 1967 and 1976 (Science
Museum)
Published: a full bibliography up to
1967 is given in Robinson, *PMP*,
no. 3. Cf. also D. T. Rice in *Scottish
Arts Review* VII/I (1959), 4-7; Rice, *IP*,
82-3, 85-7, fig. 32 and colour plate II.
Since then a full-length study of the
miniatures has appeared: P. P.
Soucek, in "*The Scholar and the Saint,*
Studies in Commemoration of
Abu'l-Rayhan al-Birnuni and Jalal
al-Din al-Rumi" (*sic*), ed. P. J.
Chelkowski (New York, 1975),

103-68, with further bibliographical
references in notes 2 and 3

Al-Hallaj (c. 858-922) was one of the
most controversial figures in the
history of Islamic mysticism. Indeed,
he is classed in this text as one of the
"pseudo-prophets". He lived at a time
of intense theological debate and his
highly-charged statements about his
mystical experiences, in which he
believed his own identity to have been
submerged in that of God, goaded the
authorities into arresting him. On the
orders of the Caliph al-Muqtadir
bi'llah he had his arms and legs cut off
and was crucified. He endured these
and other tortures without flinching
and even forgave those who had
accused him. The painter has movingly
captured this passive fortitude.

This miniature illustrates the
fundamental role of the Baghdad
school in the formation of Persian
painting. The painter delights in
tortuous drapery folds delineated in a
Byzantine manner by white
highlights and modelled colours. He
crams his figures side by side into the
frontal plane and several of them fill the
entire height of the panel. This leaves
little room for background detail,
which is confined to a single cloud, of
ultimately Chinese type, with the
trailing pointed wisp that is a signature
of this artist. Every figure, with the
significant exception of al-Hallaj, has a
halo. Normally in Baghdad painting
this feature is used indiscriminately,
often simply to make the head stand
out. In this case, however, the painter
may have wished to avert the slightest
suspicion that al-Hallaj was in any
sense holy. A later reader of the
manuscript seems to have disagreed,
for the faces of the executioners have
been rubbed out.

When Arabs are depicted in Persian
miniatures their turbans are usually
looped under the chin; this painting
is no exception.

The battle scenes of medieval Persian book painting veer from depictions of the up-to-date military methods used by the Mongols (143) to pictures of the heroic single combats described in the *Shahnama* (135, 136, 138). Firdausi's text recounts the sonorous challenges and counter-challenges which so unfailingly evoke the atmosphere of a medieval tourney. A millennium earlier the Sasanian kings had perfected an even more powerful formula for single combats. In bas-reliefs on the cliffs near Persepolis gigantic figures clash with shattering impact, and popular legend has transposed these rock-hewn heroes to the world of myth where they properly belong. It is entirely apt that the local name for this picture gallery of epic deeds should be Naqsh-i Rustam – "picture of Rustam". The "small" *Shahnamas* perpetuate this tradition in a different medium and on a tiny scale. But while such combats are the very stuff of epic poetry, they have little to do with a real battle. When Ilkhanid painters tackled a battle scene they betrayed the traumatic impact which the Mongol invasions had had on the Iranian psyche. The Muslims had been quite unprepared for the novel methods

of siege warfare which the Mongols, fresh from Chinese tutelage, had employed. Battering rams, catapults, fire floats, smoking out, the destruction of irrigation systems, and, perhaps worst of all, the sight of their own compatriots being herded into the front line by the Mongols – all contributed to the speedy fall of one Iranian city after another. The Rashid al-Din codices (especially 131) illustrate many of these instruments of war. This technical expertise was backed up by a fearsome discipline which may be reflected in some of the massed cavalry charges depicted in 14th century painting. The Mongol army was arranged on the decimal system and the chain of command was crystal clear. Cowardice was punished by death.

Not surprisingly, memories of the reign of terror which the Mongol military machine had inflicted on Persia grew less keen as the 14th century

advanced. A strong sense of discipline pervades many battle scenes of Shiraz and Herat painting from the 1420's onwards (140), but these pictures have lost the immediacy of the early 14th century Tabriz school. By the Safavid period it was common to depict a battle as a mêlée (148).

Major changes can also be detected in types of costume and armour in this period of some two hundred years. In early 14th century manuscripts the Mongol cavalry are shown wearing leather armour in overlapping folds; their horses were similarly accoutred. This same armour then appears on soldiers in battles which took place before the Mongol invasion (e.g. 131; this miniature, however, shows a war elephant, which was a standard feature of the Ghaznavid armies but was never used by the Mongols). Shiraz warriors of the 1420's onwards use greaves, armpieces and helmets of distinctive form. In Safavid battle scenes the figures unaccountably wear much less armour and despite the gory action a certain blitheness, perhaps the result of the tiny gesticulating figures and bright colours, pervades the field of war.

130

The followers of a false prophet are besieged

Manuscript; 179 ff. and 25 miniatures al-Biruni, *Kitab al-athar al-baqiya 'an al-qurun al-khaliya* ("The book of the vestiges which survive of past times"; text, tr. Sachau, 194)
Possibly Tabriz, 707/1307-8
Copyist, Ibn al-Qutbi
Edinburgh University Library, Or. Ms. 161, f. 93b
Dimensions: leaf 320 x 200 mm.
Previously exhibited: London 1931, 1951, 1967 and 1976 (Science Museum)
Published: see previous entry

Among many millennial sects which flourished in Persia during the early centuries of Islam was a group which worshipped a self-styled prophet known as al-Muqanna', "the veiled one". He was finally besieged and killed in 169/786 by the troops of the caliph al-Mahdi.

The combination of calligraphy and painting on this page is startlingly effective. Huge black letters stand out like banner headlines against the white ground. The same concern for immediate impact governs the design of the painting. Castle, besiegers and besieged are reduced to schemata, but so arranged as to tell the story with the utmost clarity. As in 129, borrowings from Baghdad painting are legion. They include the facial type used for the bearded man, the highly stylised plants and the vibrant colours. The architecture of the castle, on the other hand, reflects Persian practice, especially in the ornamental joints between the bricks. The horses closely

resemble the Mongol ponies depicted in the Rashid al-Din manuscript dated to the previous year (131).

131

Fighting between the sons of Sebuktigin

Manuscript; 277 ff. and 70 miniatures Rashid al-Din, *Jami' al-Tawarikh* ("Compendium of Histories")
Tabriz, 706/1306-7
Edinburgh, University Library, Or. Ms. 20, f. 119a
Dimensions: page 460 x 340 mm
Previously exhibited: London 1931, 1951, 1954
Published: the most significant publications up to 1967 are given in Robinson, *PMP*, no. 1. To these may now be added D. T. Rice in *Scottish Arts Review* VII/I (1959), 4-7; G. Inal in *AO* V (1963), 163-75; Ipsiroglu, *PCM*, 48, 51; D. T. Rice in *Central Asiatic Journal* XIV (1970), 181-5; Rice, *IP*, 88-94, figs. 33-6; B. W. Robinson in J. Sourdel-Thomine and B. Spuler, *Die Kunst des Islam* (Berlin, 1973), no. 273; R. Hillenbrand in *University of Edinburgh Journal* XXVI/4 (1974), 330-33; Kirketerp-Møller, *Bogmaleri*, 87-9, 91, 98-100; G. Inal in *KdO* X/1-2 (1976), 000-00; D. T. Rice, *The illustrations to the 'World History' of Rashid al-Din*, ed. B. Gray (Edinburgh, 1976); J. Trilling, *The Times Literary Supplement*, 15.4.1977, 465-6

This volume and its companion in the collection of the Royal Asiatic Society (170) together comprise the major surviving monument of early Persian painting. Both are incomplete

portions of the *Jami' al-Tawarikh* ("Compendium of Chronicles" or, more loosely, "World History") written by the Mongol vizier Rashid al-Din. The world-wide scope of the text is symptomatic of the Mongol outlook. Both codices were illustrated in Tabriz, which in the early decades of the 14th century was one of the great metropoles of Asia. Here thronged Chinese scholars and Italian merchants, Byzantines and Arabs, Uighurs and Indians. The Christian presence, represented by Armenians and Nestorians, was strong. This cosmopolitan setting helps to explain the Byzantine, Far Eastern and other foreign elements in these paintings. Their dramatic and virtually unprecedented style, with its emphasis on drawing rather than colour, and their very large, usually oblong format, had little posterity. Later painters, with their much less varied subject matter, developed rather different conventions of iconography and style.

The painting depicts the succession struggle between Mahmud and Isma'il, the sons of the Turkish general Sebüktigin who founded the Ghaznavid dynasty in the late 10th century. The use of Mongol armour, pennants, accoutements, ponies and ethnic types is something of an anachronism in a battle which occurred c. 997. But the artist does show an accurate historical sense in depicting elephants, for while the Mongols do not seem to have used elephants, the Ghaznavids maintained in the Helmand basin one of the rare elephant parks in Central and Western Asia. Mahmud must have learned much of the military uses of elephants in his seventeen campaigns in India. It seems likely, however, that the artist had no first-hand knowledge of that animal, as its reduced size, hirsute hide, corrugated trunk and blunted paws reveal. Even worse travesties of the elephant are known in Islamic art (e.g. the St. Josse silk).

Serpentine dust clouds swirl around this terrifyingly alien beast and are a clear signal of Chinese influence. So too is the convention whereby the opposing cavalry squads are cut off by the margin, a technique which presumably derives from a manuscript in roll form. The device lends a fierce immediacy to the action. Sharp opposing diagonals of lances and banners conjure up the cut and thrust of battle. The main tonality is brown, enlivened by bright patches of red for the horsehair banners and the tassel swinging from the elephant's rump – a feature with Sasanian antecedents. Drapery folds exhibit a fine shading which tones down the hard outlines, and for which a Chinese source is indicated.

132
Shah Shapur besieges Ta'ir the Arab
Firdausi, *Shahnama* (text, tr. Warner, VI, 330-35)
Probably Tabriz, early 14th century

Geneva, collection of Prince Sadruddin Aga Khan, no. Ir. M. 1/A
Dimensions: leaf 159 x 127 mm.
Bibliography: Welch, *Collection* I, 40-44 and pl. on 49

The scene depicts the Ghassanid prince Ta'ir being besieged in his Yemenite fortress by Shapur. Beside him at the window is his daughter Malika. This is a reference to the next stage of the story, for she becomes enamoured of Shapur and betrays the castle into his hands. This pre-Islamic setting is of course transposed into contemporary terms. A Mongol cavalcade streams past the fortress; no Iranian of the time would have needed reminding that the Mongols, profiting by their experiences in China, were masters of siege warfare. These horsemen form an action-packed predella to the scene. The upper tiers of the picture space are smoothly synchronised with the panels of text. Especially effective is the isolation of the doomed Ta'ir in the centre of the picture, appraisingly regarded by the treacherous Malika beside him. The painting well illustrates the delicate judgement whereby the artists of these small *Shahnamas* adjusted their compositions to exploit the available space.

133
Isfandiyar unhorsing Gurgsar
Miniature painting
Firdausi, *Shahnama* (text: Warner V, 111-12)
Probably Tabriz, first half of 14th century
London, British Museum, no. 1948

12-11 022; formerly in Eckstein collection
Dimensions: leaf 298 x 199 mm; painting 42 x 81 mm
Previously exhibited: London 1949, 1955, 1959, 1963, 1967
Published: B. W. Robinson in *Apollo* 5, 16 (1949), 89, fig. 1; Barrett, *PP*, 7; Robinson, *PMP*, no. 6; Titley, *Catalogue*, no. 150 and pl.

Paintings such as this have close stylistic links with Saljuq painted pottery and thus shed valuable light on Saljuq painting, which has mostly vanished. At the same time in the cavalry galloping headlong out of the frame, the quick glances backwards, the Mongol horses and the streaming pennants the link with the Rashid al-Din codices is patent. But major changes have occurred. The artist's field of endeavour is now much reduced, both in the page size and in the role of the picture on the page. Bright jewelled colours catch the eye. Lastly, the quality of personal emotion that invests so many of the battle scenes in the Rashid al-Din pages has gone.

The painting furnishes valuable details of customs in the Mongol army, notably the knotted tails of the horses (a practice followed by the Sasanians and the Umayyads) and the standards. One of them, depicting three fluttering bands, remotely echoes the banner of Chingiz Khan himself, with its nine yaks' tails.

134
Rustam flees from Isfandiyar
Miniature painting
Firdausi, *Shahnama* (text, tr. Warner, V, 229-31)
Shiraz school, c. 1335
Cincinnati Art Museum, no. 1947.498
Dimensions: leaf 260 x 184 mm; painting 86 x 133 mm
Published: Grube, *MMP*, 21-3

Apart from the otiose warrior in white the artist follows the text closely. The wounded Rustam, intent on flight, pays no heed to the taunts of Isfandiyar while his horse Rakhsh gallops off. Although Rustam is depicted in his traditional tiger – or leopard-skin garb as early as 1306 (**131**, f. 6b), he is given no distinguishing attribute here. Delicate trees with stellar blossoms and

a grossly inflated plant (a borrowing from the Mesopotamian school) eke out the composition. As in other miniatures from this manuscript, the artist overcomes the inherent disadvantages of the small format by using strong contrasting colours.

In the context of a lengthy volume which is punctuated only by small illustrations, variations in their shape and size come as a welcome relief. The irregular format of this panel provides a clue as to how scribe and painter cooperated in preparing an illustrated manuscript. Numerous panels left blank for painting in unfinished post-14th century books show that the scribe finished his task first. Presumably the same practice was followed in the 14th century. This leaf shows that, even at the planning stage, the artist must have had a fairly clear idea of the ultimate layout of his pictures. Here, as in other versions of the theme, Rustam's escape into the hills is expressed by a stepped format.

135
Piran slain by Gudarz
Miniature painting
Firdausi, *Shahnama* (text: Warner IV, 106-9) Probably Tabriz, early 14th century
London, British Museum
Dimensions: leaf 298 x 199 mm. painting 42 x 81 mm
Previously exhibited: London 1949, 1955, 1959, 1963
Published: Titley, *Catalogue,* no. 149

Despite the small size of the picture, the artist has managed to render the setting in four receding planes and has found room for mountains, plants and clouds. His real forte, however, is equipment. The tooled leather of the horse trappings, flowered undercoats, Pickelhauber helmets and overlapping scale armour all evince a remarkable eye for detail. The subject is the last of some 11 single combats between Iranian and Turanian heroes. Finally the two aged generals themselves take the field. The defeat of the Turanian Piran is expressed in purely symbolic language. No blood or sign of a struggle can be seen, but the vanquished *rukh* and his horse fall headlong. Both are muffled almost to immobility in their armour.

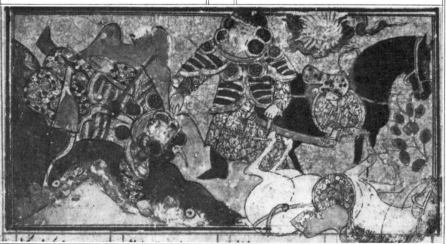

Bulky and threatening as samurai, these ungainly figures nevertheless accord with contemporary Christian accounts of Mongol military equipment.

136
Combat between Piran and Gudarz

Miniature painting

Firdausi, *Shahnama* (text, tr. Warner, IV, 106-9) Shiraz 741/1340-1

Patron: Wazir al-Hasan Qiwam al-Daula wa'l-Din

Cleveland Museum of Art, no. 44.479; formerly in Nazare Aga collection

Dimensions: leaf 367 x 300 mm.; painting 290 x 245 mm

Previously exhibited: London 1931, Vienna 1935, Ann Arbor 1959

Published: *London 1931*, no. 533A; *BWG*, no. 24(b); Kühnel, in *SPA*, 1834 and pl. 834A; Ann Arbor, *Catalogue*, 42

For the subject, see **135**.

As early as the period of the Sasanian rock reliefs, Persian artists favoured the theme of single combat. This acquired an especially epic quality when each champion battled on behalf of an entire army. Such combats are a staple of the *Shahnama*. The iconography used here was also used for other single combats, such as the duel between Rustam and Isfandiyar (**134**).

Overlapping triangles represent the hilly country. This feature is ultimately of Chinese origin but the symbols for grass and trees derive from the Baghdad school of the 13th century. The garish colours are a hallmark of the Shiraz style in this period.

137
Fariburz leads the Iranians against the Turanians

Miniature painting

Firdausi, *Shahnama*

Shiraz, 741/1340-1

Patron the Wazir al-Hasan Qiwam al-Daula wa'l-Din

Montreal, Museum of Fine Arts, no. 954. Ea.1

Dimensions: page 346 x 454 mm

In its loud colours and childlike symbols for landscape the Inju style might be likened to folk art; but as with most 14th century battle scenes the clangour of war is vividly evoked. The origin of such pictures might well be sought in wall painting. Other small *Shahnamas* of more sophisticated type (e.g. Istanbul, Topkapu Saray Museum, Hazine 1479) still retain the convention of showing mountains as a series of brightly-coloured diminishing triangles.

138
Afrasiyab fighting Naudar

Miniature painting

Firdausi, *Shahnama* (text: tr. Warner I, 350-55)

Shiraz, 741/1340-1

Patron: the Wazir al-Hasan Qiwam al-Daula wa'l-Din

Baltimore, Walters Art Gallery, no. W. 677d.

Dimensions: leaf 285 x 240 mm

The painting owes a heavy debt to the battle scenes of the Rashid al-Din codices (**131**, **170**), notably in the bold frontal rendering of one horse with its flailing hoofs (cf. Talbot Rice, *World History*, pl. 49). Awkward though it is, the twisted pose captures the violent action of the battlefield. The opposing side are not distinguished by details of armour and equipment and these details do not necessarily conform to contemporary practice. Indeed the, horse of the warrior with a shield is equipped in a style which recalls Sasanian practice.

139
A multiple slaughter

Manuscript; 335 ff. and 39 miniatures

Sadaqa b. Abu'l-Qasim Shirazi: *Kitab-i Samak ʿAyyar* ("The book of the ruffian Samak")

Inju style of Shiraz, c. 1330–40

Oxford, Curators of the Bodleian Library, MS. Ouseley 381, f. 283 b

Dimensions: page 300 x 194 mm; painting 127 x 148 mm

Previously exhibited: London 1931, 1951, 1967; Oxford 1972

Published: Sachau and Ethé, *Catalogue*, no. 442; *London 1931*, no. 531A, B; *BWG*, no. 17 and pls. XII–XIII; Stchoukine, *PI*, no. XX; Robinson, *VAM 1951*, no. 6; Barrett, *PP*, 5, 12, cover and pl. 5; Robinson, *Bodleian*, 2–7 and pls. II–III; Robinson, *PMP*, no. 103; Robinson and Gray, *PAB*, nos. 4–6

This scene is taken from a rare early Persian novel, a very lengthy tale full of blood and thunder and marvellous happenings (for a sample, see R. Levy, *The Three Dervishes and Other Tales* [Oxford, 1923], 175-210;).

It shows how a certain Taj-Dukht kills four men and takes away a fifth. The severed heads of the victims stacked one upon the next make a grisly sight – scenes of carnage and torture are a particular feature of this manuscript. But the centrepiece of the picture is the superb tent. Its splendidly vigorous Kufic inscription leaps to the eye. Such coarse but bold decoration is far more likely to have been in common use than the delicately embroidered arabesques and calligraphy of the tents shown in later miniatures (cf. **96**). The huge stencilled patterns of the tent and its bulging irregular outline also carry conviction as a realistic rendering of contemporary tents. Discordant colours echo the violent action of these miniatures. In this scene mauves and reds predominate – elsewhere in the manuscript yellow plays a major role. Such is the gusto of the artist that he does not attempt fine detail, accurate drawing or subtle colour harmonies. But his sense of composition is strong – note for example, how the trees are not simply stock notations for a landscape but entwine to form an arbour over the tent, thus making it even more the focus of attention. It is a pity that this Inju style, for which origins in wall painting have been suggested, disappeared so quickly. No doubt it was too raw for the refined susceptibilities of later patrons.

140
The defeat of Pir Padishah and Sultan ʿAli by the army of Shah Rukh in 1405

Miniature painting

Hafiz-i Abru, *Majmaʿ al-Tawarikh*

Probably Herat, c. 1430

London, Victoria and Albert Museum, E.5499-1958; formerly in Robinson collection

Dimensions: 244 x 161 mm

Previously exhibited: London 1951, Zürich and the Hague 1962, London 1967

Published: Robinson, *VAM* 1951, no. 11; Robinson, *Connoisseur*, December 1951, 177, fig. III; Stchoukine, *MT*, no. XXI, pl. XXXII; *Kunstschätze aus Iran*, no. 991; Robinson, *VAM* 1965, 9 and pl. I; Robinson, *PMP*, no. 16

The painting is unusual in its limited range of drab colours – dun, beige and grey. The brassy sheen of armour and the gold sky itself make little headway against this prevailing tonality. Robinson argues for an attribution to Herat rather than Shiraz because the author worked for the ruler of Herat and because the crowded battle scene is more typical of Herat than of Shiraz. Faces are flat and expressionless and the action is equally stylised, symbolised as it is by regimented lines of horsemen, weapons and trumpets. The battle rages above a grisly predella of maimed bodies and severed limbs. Shields of the type used here were still used by Turkish troops in the late 17th century and have survived as part of the booty taken then.

An exceptional feature of the painting, noted by Robinson, is that it represents an actual historical event fairly soon after it occurred.

141
Timur fords Ra's al-'Ain

Miniature painting

Sharaf al-Din 'Ali Yazdi, *Zafar Nama* ("Book of Victory")

Shiraz, 839/1435-6

Copyist, Ya'qub b. Hasan called Siraj al-Husaini al-Sultani

Montreal, Museum of Fine Arts F. Cleveland Morgan Collection, 962.Ea 38

Dimensions: page 257 x 178 mm

Published: for the manuscript in general, see **69**. For this leaf, see *London 1931*, no. 464; *BWG*, no. 41; *Islamic Art. Selected Examples from the Loan Exhibition of Islamic Art at the Cleveland Museum of Art* (Cleveland, 1944), pl. 13; B. Gray in *East and West* 14 (1963), fig. 3

The text is a biography of Timur in which great stress is naturally laid on his campaigns. Ra's al-'Ain ('Ain Warda) is a town in northern 'Iraq which Timur sacked at the end of the 14th century. As its name indicates, the site is well watered; in fact the many springs there form the principal source of the River Khabur.

In his technique for representing water – an imbricated pattern interspersed with rosettes – the artist has hit on a pleasing novelty. Equally striking is the figure of Timur's horse lunging forward into the torrent. The narrow torso of the conqueror and the tall hats are typical features of the Shiraz school associated with Ibrahim Sultan.

142
The siege of Alamut

Manuscript: 188 ff. and 6 paintings; other leaves are dispersed in European and American collections

'Ata Malik Juvaini *Tarikh-i Jahan Gusha* ("History of the World Conqueror")

Copyist, Abu Ishaq b. Ahmad al-Sufi al-Samarqandi

Probably Shiraz; completed 16 Shawwal 841/12 April 1438

Paris, Bibliothèque Nationale, Supp. pers. 206, f. 149a

Dimensions: page 270 x 170 mm.

Previously exhibited: Paris 1938

Published: for references to the manuscript in general and to the other dispersed leaves, see **70**. For this particular miniature, see Blochet, *Inventaire*, 38; Blochet, *Enluminures*, 89, pl. XLI; Blochet, *MP*, pl. XCIV; Blochet, *Catalogue*, no. 444

Alamut, the "Eagle's Nest", was the principal fortress of the Isma'ilis, the Order of the Assassins. They represented the last vestige of Muslim opposition to the second wave of Mongol conquests from 1255 onwards. Hülegü, the first Mongol Ilkhan (1256-65), spent three years reducing their mountain fortresses in the Alburz range encircling the Caspain Sea. The Isma'ili chief Rukn al-Din Khurshah, who had earlier capitulated to Hülegü finally persuaded the defenders of Alamut to surrender.

Alamut is celebrated to this day for its inaccessibility, and Juvaini describes its setting in the text accompanying this miniature (J. A. Boyle, *The History of the World Conqueror* (Manchester, 1958), 719). Yet the artist ignores both oral and written sources in order to follow the established iconographical tradition for representing sieges. He even improves on his model. The castle, far from being perched on an impregnable peak, actually has a moat complete with drawbridge. Moreover, the vertical format is well exploited, as the lofty ramparts, high horizon and superposed tiers of bodies show. When he had to depict a similar scene in a square picture space (**143**) he used quite different means.

Despite its formal quality, the picture vividly captures the panoply of war. But the decorative embellishment of the castle, including the corbelled towers, is pure fantasy. In earlier paintings, memories of the Mongols were still vivid enough to make the artist observe distinctions of dress – here, besiegers and besieged are dressed alike.

143
Siege of a fortress

Miniature painting

Juvaini, *Tarikh-i Jahan Gusha* ("History of the World Conqueror"). The body of the manuscript, with 6 miniatures, is in the Bibliothèque Nationale, Paris, Sup. Pers. 206 (**142**); other detached leaves are in the

British Museum and various public and private collections in Europe and the U.S.A.
Copyist, Abu Ishaq b. Ahmad al-Sufi al-Samarqandi
Probably Shiraz; completed to Shawwal 841/12 April 1438
London, British Museum, no. 1948 12-1106; formerly in Anet and Eckstein collections
Dimensions: leaf 265 x 176 mm.; painting 154 x 163 mm
Previously exhibited: London 1931, 1949, 1959
Published: for a general bibliography, see 70. For this leaf in particular, see BWG, no. 55a; Titley, Catalogue, no. 225

Unlike its companion piece in the British Museum (70), this miniature is unfinished. It thus sheds some light on how a manuscript was illustrated, for the evidence clearly indicates that in this case, at least, the text was completed first. Even the margins of the text panels are ruled in their final form, while parts of the painting are still quite blank.

An origin in Shiraz is suggested by the faces – long, rectangular and with tightly fitting pointed helmets – and by the trick of massing rows of identical faces, in this case peering timidly over the walls. This device is psychologically effective here in that it suggests the trapped feeling of the besieged penned within their walls. The Mongol attackers shelter behind wooden constructions which are probably a legacy of Chinese siegecraft.

Persian artists were rarely concerned to produce replicas of actual building types. They preferred to embellish them with fastidious ornament of their own devision. This painter was no exception. His polygonal fortress, built of brick with a base of greenish stone and geometric decoration in glazed brick, reproduces a familiar type of Mongol mausoleum in north-west Iran.

144
The combat between Gudarz and Piran

Miniature painting
Firdausi, Shahnama (text, tr. Warner, IV, 106-9)
Possibly Western Indian Art, second quarter of 15th century
Cambridge, Fogg Museum, Harvard University, Cambridge, Mass., Wetzel Bequest. no. 1919.137; formerly Wetzel collection. Twelve paintings from the same ms. are in the Metropolitan Museum of Art, New York and others in the Vever collection, Paris
Dimensions: 178 x 183 mm
Previously exhibited: New York, 1940; Rome, 1956
Published: Ackerman, Guide, 249; Schroeder, Fogg, no. X Mostra d'Arte Iranica, no. 502; I. Fraad and R. Ettinghausen, in Chhavi: The Golden Jubilee Volume of the Bharat

Kala Bhavan (Banaras, 1972), 48-66 and pls. 133-61, place this and related works in the orbit of the western Indian Sultanates

For the subject, see 135. The artist has used the large space granted him to expand the traditional iconography. He sets this last of the setpiece duels between champions of Iran and Turan in its full dramatic context. A sloping horizon of undulating rocks bisects the picture. Below sits the Iranian cavalry, stock-still in suspense. Most of them have their eye fixed on the central horseman who watches the progress of the fight. Above, Gudarz taunts the fleeing Piran, whose broken hand hangs slackly as he scrabbles frantically up the mountainside. Schroeder believes that Piran is already dead, but his eyes suggest the opposite and no trace of the javelin thrown by Gudarz can be seen. Moreover, this section of the picture is much closer to the traditional iconography of the episode, which shows pursuer and pursued (cf. 136), than to the moment of the kill (cf. 135). At all events, powerful gestures and flying feet make this scene the antithesis of the frozen tableau beneath.

As with much other work recently attributed to western India, several Shirazi elements can be noted. Here the sense of space, as well as the convention for figure and vegetation, accord well with that school.

145
Bizhan forces Farud to retire

Miniature painting
Firdausi, Shahnama (text, tr. Warner, III, 63-4)
Possibly Western Indian, c. 1450
New York, Metropolitan Museum of Art Bequest of William Milne Grinnel, 1920. no. 20. 120. 247
Dimensions: 198 x 180 mm
Published: Robinson, PD, 138 and pl. 76 (colour plate of this leaf); for this manuscript as a whole and related works see the article by Fraad and Ettinghausen cited in 144

In one of the many incidents of the ancestral war between Iran and Turan, Farud, the son of Siyavush (cf. 123) wreaked havoc among the Iranian champions until the hero Bizhan worsted him and forced him to seek shelter behind his castle walls.

The artist has kept closely to the text, even including the detail of Farud's wounded horse. Clear story-telling demands that the Iranian hero should dominate the design and should tower half as high as the castle walls. The defenders clustered on the battlements perpetuate an old iconographical tradition (cf. 130). Perhaps the most novel feature is the single tree whose sinuous branches neatly contrive to occupy the only major empty area in the picture. This painter shows commendable ingenuity in devising fancifully shaped trees as space fillers – cf. the two further examples in the companion miniature of Rustam

catching Rakhsh, no. 20. 120. 240. In this detail, as in the facial types or the plain green ground, the picture seems somewhat alien to other Timurid provincial work and its current attribution to western India (cf. 2, 41, 99 and 144) seems tenable. The nearest parallel for such painting within Iran itself seems to be the school of Shiraz; the distinctive trees already mentioned seem prefigured in the previous generation of Shiraz work (e.g., 194, f. 12). For other miniatures from this manuscript, see 99 and 144.

146
Bizhan rides to aid Gustaham

Miniature painting
Firdausi, Shahnama (text, tr. Warner, IV, 120)
Gilani school 899/1493-4
Copyist, Salik b. Sa'id Patron, Sultan 'Ali Mirza of Gilan

Geneva, collection of Prince Sadruddin Aga Khan, no. Ir.M.17/B
Dimensions: leaf 242 x 235 mm
Bibliography: Welch, Collection I, 127-8, 133 and colour plate on 135; for related works, see the bibliography cited in 71

Every so often a vigorous element of caricature intrudes into the exquisitely refined courtly atmosphere of Persian painting. The work of the so-called "Siyah Qalam" affords an outstanding example of this. Such paintings are so remote in spirit from the preoccupations of court painting that it is easy to believe that they were produced in the borders of the Islamic world. The leaf shown here is typical of the so-called "big-head" Turkman style which flourished in Gilan, again near the borders of Islamic territory, with the Christian lands of the Caucasus to the north. Other leaves from this manuscript are found in the Keir collection (Robinson, Keir, 159-62, pl. 36 and colour plates 15-17). The vigour and simplicity of the style, its penchant for bright contrasting colours and for large, rather wooden figures, and finally its static quality, all point to a link with early Ottoman painting, which so often draws on the Turkoman style. Drapery folds are rendered by pale, even white, strokes placed parallel to each other in a way that recalls late Byzantine painting at Mistra and elsewhere. This device is at all events foreign to the painter's style, for the other parts of the picture are innocent of modelling. Indeed, there is something primitive in the repetitive handling of men and animals alike. The latter resemble rocking horses to a degree unusual even in Persian painting and this lifeless quality is made even more pronounced by the almost identical treatment of pose, expression and accoutrement. The riders, too, are dummies, their coarse ruddy faces identically bearded and their teeth bared in ferocious grimaces. This treatment directly contradicts the text, for it suggests that one paladin has roused the other's wrath – graphically caught in his startling eyes – by grasping the bridle of his horse, presumably restraining it. But the laboured style weakens the sense of vigorous action. The artist has sacrificed finesse for immediate impact – the painting is as direct as a poster – but his technique seems inadequate to express his imagination to the full.

147
Battle scene

Manuscript; 184 ff. and 13 miniatures
Qasimi, *Shahnama-yi Isma'il* (a poetical history of Shah Isma'il)
Tabriz style, 948/1541-2
Copyist, Ibrahim al-Munshi

London, British Library, Add. 7784, f. 107b
Dimensions: open book 260 x 335 mm.; painting 152 x 107 mm. with continuations in the margins
Published: Rich, *Catalogue* II, 660-1; Meredith-Owens, *PIM,* 22-3 and pl. XVII; Titley, *Catalogue,* no. 231

The subject matter of the miniatures in this manuscript is limited to scenes of war, the chase and the court. Here the artist has caught the excitement of war above all in the frenzied charging horses and he has used them boldly to

open up a hitherto hackneyed theme. Similar horses in headlong career recur on f. 46b, while the splendidly vigorous drummer and trumpeter are repeated on f. 169b. Banners are a feature of five other miniatures in the manuscript. This painter was therefore economical of invention, however effective the results were. The picture goes far to corroborate the statement of contemporary sources that hand-guns as well as artillery were being used in the reign of Shah Isma'il. Musketeers feature in the battle scenes of ff. 117b, 160a and 169b, but it seems highly unlikely that they were a major fighting force in the Safavid army at this time. In all the miniatures of this manuscript more traditional methods of carnage dominate. A leitmotif of the text is the military prowess of Shah Isma'il and to this day his tomb at Ardabil is crowned by a finial of the same general type as those shown on the banners here.

Some memories of the Turkoman style linger in the coloured stones bordering the stream and in the greenery of that area. Despite his penchant for violent action, the artist arranges even minor details with careful casualness. Thus the tarnished silver stream retains its unbroken line only because the flowers on its near side all grow upside down. Elsewhere,

helmets roll aside unregarded but their plumes artfully trail into the margins.

148
Battle between Bahram Chubina and Khusrau Parviz

Miniature painting
Nizami, *Khamsa (Khusrau u Shirin)*; it has been suggested that this leaf was intended for the royal Nizami in the British Museum (**23**)
Tabriz, c. 1540

Edinburgh, Royal Scottish Museum, no. 1896-70
Dimensions: 395 x 295 mm
Previously exhibited: London 1931, 1951; Rome 1956; London 1967
Published: *London 1931,* no. 511; *BWG,* no. 166, pl. XCIVA; Kühnel, in *SPA,* 1876; *V AM 1951,* no. 39; Stchoukine *MS,* no. 15; Gray, *PP 1961,* 134 (colour plate) and 141; Robinson, *PMP,* no. 40; Rice, *IP,* 146 and pl. 66

Persian painters were rarely preoccupied with historical accuracy. Thus the turbans and other details of costume and military gear in this depiction of a pre-Islamic battle are those of the early Safavid period. So too is the flag with its Arabic legend "Help is from God and victory is near" (Qur'an LI, v. 13), a text found on banners in other 16th century manuscripts (**147**, f. 26a) and also on surviving Turkish banners of the 17th century. Beside the elephant, a venerable old man raises aloft an astrolabe, a precision instrument used in astrology as well as astronomy. Perhaps he is the chief astrologer of the court, a post which was of some importance. Presumably his calculations have proved that this is an auspicious moment to fight.

This frantic mêlée is typical of Safavid battle scenes, and differs substantially from most Timurid practice. No open space remains, and in place of the clash of tightly massed cavalry the battle resolves itself into a series of individual combats. The effect is designedly chaotic. Much the same can be said of the riotous profusion of colour. In comparable Timurid work (e.g. the Juki *Shahnama*) a greater degree of symmetry in action and colour is apparent.

149
Soldiers Sack a Town

Manuscript; 87 ff., one double page and 7 single miniatures
Timur Nama by Hatifi ("Book of Timur")
Bukhara school c. 1560

London, British Library, Add. 22703, f 2b
Dimensions: open book 288 x 370 mm.; painting 195 x 127 mm
Previously exhibited: London 1967
Published: Rieu, *Cat.* II 654; Titley *Catalogue,* no. 183; Robinson, *PMP,* no. 164

Although battle scenes are a staple of

147

appears to be a shrine while a soldier grasps him by the belt and brandishes a sword. If the building is indeed a shrine the youth is no doubt trying to claim sanctuary (*bast*) within it. This is a time-honoured right in Persian society and one which has been frequently exercised even in modern times.

150
Duels between Fariburz and Kulbad (above and Giv and Gurvi (below)
Manuscript; 285 ff. and 88 miniatures
Firdausi, *Shahnama* (text, tr. Warner, IV, 99-100)
Probably Qazvin, c. 1585

By gracious permission of Her Majesty Queen Elizabeth II, MS. A/5, f. 120a
Dimensions: written surface of page 240 x 170 mm
Previously exhibited: London 1951, 1967
Published: Holmes, *Specimens*, no. 150; Robinson, *VAM 1951*, no. 84; B.W. Robinson, *The Connoisseur* CXXVIII (1951), 179-80 and pls. VII-VIII; Stchoukine, *SA* 136 and pl. VII; Robinson, *PMP*, no. 57; Robinson, *BMCX* (1968), 73-8 and figs. 12-39

The painting shows two of the 11 (or 12) duels fought between Iranian and Turanian champions to avoid mass bloodshed. For further details see (**136**).

This manuscript was acquired in India by Warren Hastings, who presented it to his sovereign, and it shared the fate of many Persian manuscripts in that country. Many of its pictures were overpainted, while its leaves were remarginated and shoddily rebound in total disorder. It was probably executed for a royal patron, perhaps at a time when the palace atelier was being reorganised, for Robinson has demonstrated the coexistence of the Qazvin and Shiraz styles in the paintings.

This leaf, attributed to a Shirazi artist, is typical of the numerous experimental page layouts of the manuscript. The interrelationship between text and painting varies from one folio to the next. Here the text is used simply enough to divide the two combats. But the text panels do not bisect the page completely, so that on the left an uninterrupted vertical shaft, extended by the banner which breaks through the upper margin, establishes the picture space. Thus the viewer can discount the text panels visually and complete the picture in his mind's eye. This device ensures that the two scenes are not unduly cramped. Given this subtle spatial organisation it is strange that the artist has used so little of the page.

151
Rustam attacks the palace of Afrasiyab by night
Miniature painting

Persian paintings, it is much rarer for artists to depict the aftermath of war. This originality is a feature of illustrations in *Timur Nama* manuscripts, where the predominantly military career of the conqueror forced artists to devise numerous variations on a rather limited theme. Moreover, the text did not have centuries of iconographic tradition behind it, and this too encouraged innovation. Here the horrors of war are evoked in a series of independent cameos. In these vivid snapshots there is no hint of the impersonal pageantry of battle; instead, the accent is on the human drama of each situation. By exploiting the convention of the high horizon the artist is able to present each episode in terse, almost diagrammatic, form without danger of overlap into the adjoining scene. The same device allows him to construct a remarkably varied setting for the action—a palace, a garden, a shrine and a tent combine to suggest a city in microcosm.

Within this formal ordered setting soldiers run amok. Some slaughter prisoners; it was a feature of the Mongol and Timurid invasions that each soldier would be detailed to kill a set number of captives. Others seize women, or lurch off under a load of booty. Some citizens, their torsos stripped to denote that they are now slaves, are clustered pathetically together. Elsewhere, two women try to drag a youth into a building which

Firdausi, *Shahnama* (text tr. Warner, III, 347-8)
Qazvin style, c. 1590
London, British Museum, no. 1948 12-11 07; formerly in Eckstein collection
Dimensions: leaf 419 x 282mm; painting 229 x 155mm
Previously exhibited: London 1949, 1959, 1967
Published: Robinson, *PMP,* no. 58; Titley, *Catalogue,* no. 147

Afrasiyab, king of Turan, had mal-treated his son-in-law Bizhan and Rustam, accompanied by seven Iranian cavaliers, raided his palace in revenge. Rustam wields a mace although the hyperbole of the text demands that he shatter the gate with his bare hands. The warring figures are carefully disposed to avoid overlapping and to give each vignette its full weight. The artist has filled the empty spaces with a novel leitmotif – the unwound turbans of the dead. Below this gory scene bystanders converse casually, a contrast typical of Safavid painting.

152
Captive on a camel
Manuscript; ff. and 10 miniatures
Mirkhwand, *Raudat al-safa* ("Garden of Purity") IV
Shiraz style, c. 1580
London, Royal Asiatic Society of Great Britain & Ireland
P. Codrington 38
Dimensions: 316 x 209 mm
Published: Robinson, *VAM 1965,* 15-16 and pl. 26

The aftermath of battle is rarely de-picted in Persian miniatures. Here a jubilant cavalcade canters across the picture, framed by rejoicing mucisians and soldiers below and by caricatured onlookers above. Many of the specta-tors bite their index fingers in a time-honoured gesture of astonishment. All focus on the dejected figure, bound and barefoot, who slumps on a shambling camel. Only the prisoner rides a camel, perhaps as a mark of his shame. Apart from the furled standard the most interesting detail of military equipment is the wide variety of shields depicted here.

The manuscript is part of an encyclopaedic history stretching from the Creation to the death of Sultan Husain Baiqara in 1505.

153
A prisoner
Miniature painting from the album of the Amir of Bukhara (21 ff.)
Bukhara, c. 1550
New York, Pierpont Morgan Library, MS. 386-2 (18 miniatures in all)
Dimensions: leaf 378 x 241mm; painting including borders: 261 x 133mm; painting excluding borders, 171 x 114mm
Previously exhibited: New York 1933, Venice 1962, New York 1968
Published: Dimand, *Guide,* 41 and pl. 32; Grube, *MMP,* no. 71; Grube,

Classical Style, 32, 194 and pl. 52; M. S. Young, "A Medieval Garland", *Apollo* Feb. 1969, 182, fig. 3

The theme of the seated prisoner enjoyed a great vogue in the 16th century, especially in the school of Bukhara. The reasons for this have yet to be explained satisfactorily. He is usually shown, as here, armed to the teeth and fettered by a yoked device which may derive from Far Eastern models. The lobed arch which frames him is elaborated beyond any require-ment of architecture, while grotesque human and animal heads proliferate in its floral borders. These heads may be related to the paintings of creatures composed of animals and men (**204**), a fashion which is well represented in the Bukhara school.

154
Two youths duelling
Miniature painting
Qazvin style, late 16th century
Indian Office Library, no. J. 56-13
Dimensions: leaf 245 x 165 mm; painting 90 x 115 mm
Previously exhibited: London 1931, 1951
Published: *London 1931,* no. 621B; *BWG,* no. 193 and pl. CVIIA; Robinson, *VAM 1951,* no. 99; Robinson, *IOL,* no. 207 (illustrated)

For the latter half of the sixteenth century the Safavid capital was at Qazvin, and here a fashion for single-leaf paintings or – more often – tinted drawings, blossomed. This fashion extended in the same period to the Shaibanid court at Bukhara, with the difference that the Bukharan painters developed colour at the expense of line (e.g. **10**).

This drawing illustrates both the strength and the weakness of such work. Its forte is sureness of line and elimination of extraneous detail. A plain background distances the action; but its bareness is mitigated at key points by irregularly lobed pyramidal cartouches filled with scrollwork. This very bareness, however, makes it hard for the artist to achieve some rational rapport between the figures, especially as their glances do not meet. The fluid line cannot disguise their stiff poses. The inherent weakness of the style is apparent not only in the graceful but facile convention used for the feet (note the disregarded pentimenti) but also in the alarmingly deformed set of the shoulders in the right-hand figure. Drapery folds occur almost exclusively at the joints, as if indeed the rest of the garment were entirely smooth.

The youths are probably engaged in a training bout, of the kind that was a common feature of princely education (compare the description of Bahram Gur's education in the *Shahnama,* tr. Warner, VI, 379). One figure wears a kind of tracksuit, ideal for such a work-out, while the other has improvised a shield by bundling some clothes round his hand.

155
Rustam lassoes Kamus
Miniature painting
Firdausi, *Shahnama* (text, tr. Warner, III, 188-90)
Probably Qazvin, c. 1576
Signed by Siyavush (cf. **46**)
Private collection; formerly in Paul R. Loewi collection
Dimensions: 440 x 310 mm
Previously exhibited: Paris 1912 (the parent manuscript); this leaf: London 1951; Zürich and the Hague, 1962; London 1967
Published: the parent manuscript was broken up some time after 1912 and its miniatures dispersed. The most complete bibliography available of these separate leaves is contained in B.W. Robinson, *Iran* XIV (1976), 1-8, in which an attempt is made to reconstruct the original order of the miniatures. For this particular leaf see Robinson, *VAM 1951,* no. 62; B.W. Robinson, "Persian Painting", in *The Concise Encyclopaedia of Antiques* V, ed. L. G. G. Ramsay (London 1961), 77 and pl. 55D; B.W. Robinson, in *The Complete Encyclopaedia of Antiques,* ed. L. G. G. Ramsay (London, 1962), 817 and pl. 296C; *Kunstschütze aus Iran,* no. 1004; Robinson *VAM 1965,* 16 and pl. 28; Robinson, *PD,* 135 and pl. 43 (in colour); Robinson, *PMP,* no. 56 (c); Robinson, *Iran* XIV (1976), no. 36; Welch, *Artists,* 22, 25 and fig. 1
Robinson *VAM 1965,* 16 and pl. 28; Robinson, *PD,* 135 and pl. 43 (in colour); Robinson, *PMP,* no. 56 (c); Robinson, *Iran* XIV (1976), no. 36; Welch, *Artists,* 22, 25 and fig. 1

In one of the many rounds of single combat described in the *Shahnama,* Rustam lassoed the boastful Kamus of Kushan, pulled him from the saddle and carried him back to camp under his arm. There he was hacked to pieces in his bonds by the Iranians. Once again the artist has taken numerous liberties with the text, notably in giving Kamus a black steed instead of a dun one and in failing to show the body armour of Rustam's horse. But the atmosphere of the medieval tourney with which the story is charged is imaginatively exploited. Banners wave, trumpets blare and the horsemen gallop in opposite directions. Figures are dis-posed symmetrically, even to details of colour, so that the opposing sides are clear for all to see.

In colour and design the painting is traditional enough, as the repeated breaking of the margin indicates. But the suppression of detail, the sense of space and the relatively large size of the figures all announce a change of direction. This transitional painting foreshadows the mature Isfahan style. The career of Siyavush the Georgian has recently been described at length by Anthony Welch (*Artists, passim* but especially 15-28).

Genre

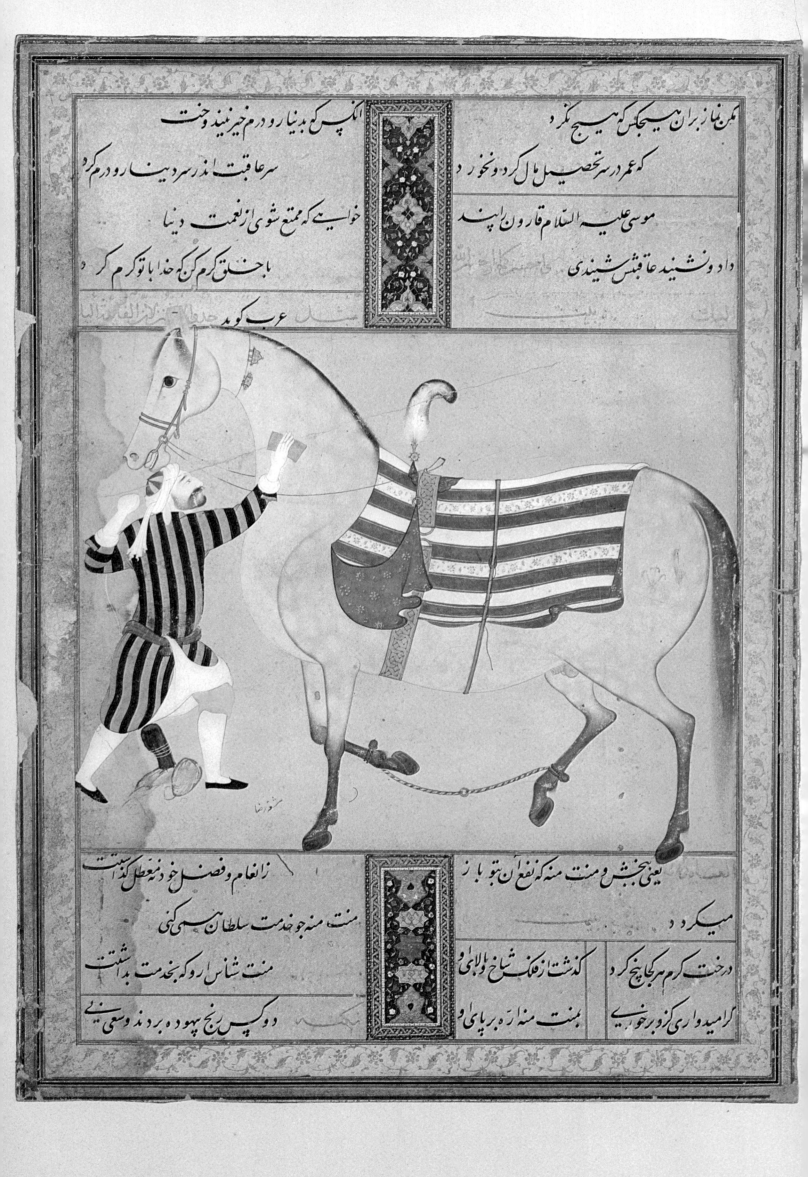

من باز بر آن هیچکس که هیچ نکرد و
که عمر در سه تحصیل مال کرد و نخورد

ازبس که بدنیار و درم خیر نمی‌بخت و خست
سرعاقبت اندر سر دینار و درم کرد

موسی علیه السلام قارون را پند
داد و نشنید عاقبتش شنیدی

خواهی که متمتع شوی از نعمت دنیا
با خلق کرم کن که خدا با تو کرم کرد

شد عرب کو مدصدای... ملاذ الغابة الیا

یعنی بخشش و منت منه که نفعان بتو باز
می‌کرد و

زا نعام و فضل خود منعطل کند ست

منت منه جو خدمت سلطان همی کنی
منت شناس او را که بخدمت بداشت

کدست از فلک شیخ والایی و
بخت منارة بر پایی او

درخت کرم هر کجا پیچ کرد
کرامیدواری کزو برخوری

دو کس رنج بیهوده برد و سعی بینی

This section embraces much more diverse material than the other parts of the catalogue and even the title of "Genre" is not wholly appropriate for it. Most of the paintings do, however, show that the ruler participated in the daily life of his subjects to a marked degree. The section entitled "religion" provides further evidence on this score.

Despite the prohibition of drinking alcohol which has operated throughout Islam from the time of Muhammad, it was far from rare for princes and commoners alike to ignore this tenet. Spirits as well as wine were drunk. Several of the Ilkhanid and Timurid princes were addicted to drink and the Mongol Khan Arghun seems even to have suffered from delirium tremens. The illustrious career of Baisunghur as perhaps the greatest patron of 15th century painting was abruptly terminated by his death from drink. But Sultan Husain Baiqara, for example, got drunk once a week only. In Islamic mysticism wine is a symbol of religious ecstacy, but it is a moot point whether the drinking poems of Hafiz and so many other Persian poets should be interpreted in this esoteric way. Dervishes are frequently shown rather the worse for wear as a result of drink. Even under the rule of a bigot as stern as Tahmasp the authorities still had to post public notices (even on the dynas-

tic shrine of Ardabil) forbidding the consumption of wine and threatening offenders with heavy penalties.

Both the Mongols and Timurids were originally nomads and even when they had settled they maintained some of their ancestral traditions. Thus Timur often held court at Samarquand in a tented palace rather than in the permanent structures that he had ordered to be built in the same city. The Mongol rulers erected entire tent cities which could hold populations estimated at 50,000. For these princes the term "tent" did not imply something simple and makeshift. One of the royal tents used by Ghazan took two years to make and a month to erect, while another Mongol prince had an audience tent which could hold two thousand people. No satisfactory modern parallels exist for such structures. The more ambitious examples had architectural features such as doors, windows and porches, and even their ornament copied contemporary architecture in its use of inscriptions and foliage or geometric borders (**139**). Their materials were costly: satin with gold and

silver embroidery and a sprinkling of precious stones. Carpets would bedeck the interior. Such tents were favourite gifts to and from royalty and they form a curious contrast to the scenes of everyday life enacted around them (**114**). But these scenes are keenly observed and they show, not surprisingly, that the essence of nomadic life has changed very little over the centuries. This is true, for example, of the methods used in preparing dairy products, grinding corn or making bread (**161**). A tribe of nomads on the move loads its baggage in much the same way today as in 1397 (**159**). In rendering such scenes Persian artists often display a marked naturalism which may even verge on caricature. This latter trait recurs frequently in the work of Riza-yi 'Abbasi, who was noted for his treatment of low life (**169**). But in the broad context of Persian painting this approach was exceptional; it was much commoner for genre scenes to act as a kind of sub-plot in depictions of courtly activities and pastimes (**56**). In numerous miniatures, however, the opportunity for lively detail of genre type is not taken (**58**); in this respect Persian painting offers no ready parallel for the panoramic depiction of daily life in certain 13th century manuscripts of al-Hariri's *Maqamat* produced by painters of the Baghdad school.

156
A drinking party in the mountains
Tinted drawing
Qazvin, c. 1575
Probably by Muhammadi;
Boston, Museum of Fine Arts, no. 14.649 (formerly in Goloubew collection)
Dimensions: 210 x 134 mm.
Previously exhibited: New York, 1973; Cambridge, Mass., 1974
Published: Coomaraswamy, *Goloubew*, 35, no. 48 and pl. XXVI; Gray, *PP 1961*, 159 and colour plate on 157; Welch, *Isfahan*, no. 4

Muhammadi is particularly noted for his pastoral scenes and the drawing here belongs *grosso modo* to that category. The casual overlapping of figures, every one in a different attitude, creates an animated scene. The pale washes of colour are nicely attuned to this peaceful meditative scene. It is hard to equate the artist who handles subdued colours in this discreet way with the master of the technicolour hawking scene (**51**). Yet if Muhammadi did indeed produce both works, that would not make him a freak, for several major Persian artists seem to have assumed remarkably distinct styles for drawing and painting. Certain oddities can be detected in this drawing. Two modest groups of buildings nestle in the folds of the hills in a fashion that argues quite unexpected classical influence – in Byzantine art, such conventions for architecture and townscapes were

widespread. In the rugged, contorted outline of the tree, which is the major colour accent of the picture, the artist explores and glories in those irregularities of nature which seem banished from the consistently smooth outlines of his figures. Such a contrast is rather too marked to carry conviction. Yet despite the suave unruffled line which defines these figures, close observation verging on caricature has produced some arresting portraits, such as the bald man washing his hands and the two men in blue. This element of caricature applies particularly to those who have partaken not wisely but too well. Such details, and the flavour of everyday life which clings to the drawing, suggest that this is a gently satirical rendering of a meeting of some dervish confraternity.

The bowls for drinking and washing accurately reflect the shapes and designs of contemporary Safavid ware.

157
A Drinking Party
Tinted drawing in ink
Probably Isfahan, c. 1630
London, British Museum, no. 1948 10-9 060
Dimensions: leaf 200 x 148 mm; drawing 142 x 90 mm
Previously exhibited: London 1949, 1959
Published: Titley, *Catalogue*, no. 404 (195)

This satirical drawing shows the range

of the mature Safavid style. Its curving, lurching lines suggest not grace but abandon and debauch. These are not the gilded youths of the court, sipping wine with friend or beloved. They are middle-aged, if not old, they have run to fat, and the wine-cups into which they gaze disconsolately are empty. One of them wears the high cap of the dervish. This may provide the clue to the drawing, for in some dervish dances the participants donned goat-skins, complete with heads (cf. B. Gray, *BMQ* IX (1935), 89. The goat in the background may be intended as an ironic comment on such practices. Its wispy hair, bulging cranium and vacant expression parodies the men themselves.

158
A Picnic at night
Tinted drawing in ink
Isfahan, 17th century
London, British Museum, no. 1920 9-17 0275; transferred from Department of Oriental Printed Books and Manuscripts (album Or. 1372, f.23)
Dimensions: leaf 418 x 266 mm.; painting 251 x 173 mm
Previously exhibited: London BM
Published: Titley, *Catalogue*, no. 404 (94) 1931, 1949

It was never the ambition of the Persian artist to paint night scenes realistically. Every detail of the scene had to be clear, and this overriding aim allowed

113, 145 and pls. XIII–XV; Robinson, *PM*, pl. II and text opposite; Kuhnel, *PM*, 11, 58 and pl. 14; Gray *PP 1961*, 67–8 and pl. on 66; Meredith-Owens, *PIM*, 14 and pl. II (colour plate of the opening exhibited here); Robinson, *PD*, 131 and pl. 8; Robinson *PMP*, nos. 9–10; Rice, *IP*, 112 and pl. *Royal Persia*, no. 169; Kirketerp-Møller, *Bogmaleri*, 106–8; E.G. Sims in *aarp* 6 (1974), 56–57; Titley, *Catalogue*, no. 99

The theme is an episode from Mongol history dating from the period before their career of world conquest had started. They are shown riding through a mountain pass behind their chieftain Börtechinua. Even after they had become rulers of Persia, the Mongols maintained a quasi-nomadic way of life for generations, travelling to summer and winter pastures and erecting entire cities of tents there.

Unlike many later depictions of camp life, this is treated simply as a genre scene. The atmosphere authentically captures the bustle of moving camp. Details are equally accurate – the humble tent, the striped rope and the sprigged cloth wrapped round bundles are all articles in common use to this day in Iran. Fantasy takes over in the treatment of the rocks, but the sense of activity is accentuated by their rippling masses. The four seperately coloured coulisses which they form are an integral part of the action, for they conjure up the twisting defile through which the Mongols move. But the artist is also swayed by the colour and texture of these coulisses and in this he foreshadows much 15th century work (c.f. **210**, or numerous miniatures from **28**). His trick of showing figures only in part was enthusiastically copied in Shiraz work of the next generation.

160
An encampment

Manuscript: 77 ff. and 8 miniatures, of which 6 are on three double page openings

Jami, *Baharistan* ("Spring-land")

Bukhara, completed 954/1547–8; the miniatures themselves can be dated c. 1525–30

Dedicated to 'Abd al-'Aziz Bahadur, governor of Bukhara 1540–49; the dedication to Sultan Husain Baiqara and the date of 1498 are both spurious

Lisbon, Calouste Gulbenkian Foundation Museum, no. L.A. 169, f.45

Dimensions: leaf 310 x 200 mm

Previously exhibited: Lisbon 1963

Published: for the manuscript in general, see **20**

While **184** and **185** reflect the legacy of Bihzad as a figure painter and as a master of detail, this painting shows that later artists imitated his genre scenes with equal readiness. Subjects

---

for no complex experiments in chiaroscuro; hence the bright daylight and pale blue sky. Only the candlesticks and braziers reveal that it is night-time.

Bold, obtrusive colours destroy the illusion of an unfinished quality which marked earlier tinted drawings. Moreover, the various details of the composition are too rehearsed, notably the rock-bordered brook and the drapery folds of turbans, sashes and wrists. The weak pointilliste background in the lower half of the picture, the unsubtle rendering of successive planes by lines of rocks and the way that the leaves are treated all betray a mechanical and tired approach.

The British Museum card catalogue entry on this painting attributes it to Muhammed Qasim and dates it c.1675, but the seal on the painting (between the tree and the horizon) apparently gives the date 1035/1624. It might therefore be best to leave the question of date open for the time being, especially as the drapery convention used here has certain parallels in work

executed between 1625 and 1650 (e.g. the seated youth in the Fitzwilliam Museum; Robinson, *PMP*, no. 74 and pl. 33).

159
Nomadic Mongols on the move

Manuscript; 243 ff. and 11 miniatures

Collection of epics: *Garshaspnama, Shahanshahnama, Bahmannama* and *Kushnama*. The book is open at the *Shahanshahnama* of Ahmad of Tabriz

Shiraz style, 800/1397–8

Copyist: Muhammad b. Sa'id b. Sa'd al-Hafiz al-Qari

London, British Library, Or. 2780, f.44b

Dimensions: leaf 255 x 260 mm.; painting 210 x 122 mm

Previously exhibited: London 1967, 1971, 1973

Published: Rieu, *Supplement*, 133; Gray, *PP* **1930**, 48–50 and pl. 4; *BWG*, 62–3; Kühnel, *SPA*, 1845 and pls. 857, 941B; B.W. Robinson, in *Journal of the Iran Society* I (1951), 82; Barrett, *PP*, 22, 24 and pl. 10; Stchoukine, *MT*, no. XIII, like nomadic encampments were perhaps judged unsuitable for the microscopically detailed treatment given to more solemn scenes. Against a single-colour sky and background the colours of the tents and especially of the animals stand out in unblemished purity. Within a generation painters had lost the art of using colours with this degree of intensity.

Echoes of the much-vaunted realism of Bihzad, notably in the handling of the animals, can also be detected. Despite the detailed nature of these studies, the animals are essentially isolated against a neutral ground, so that their very realism acquires a frozen, unnatural quality. They are conceived, in fact, as separate vignettes, and given only a minimal context.

Few paintings illustrate so graphically the use of the high horizon as a perspective device. The zig-zagging silhouette of the tents in particular creates an elegant and satisfying pattern.

This painting, like **20**, has suffered considerably over the years.

161
An encampment
Manuscript; 178 ff., one double page and 12 single miniatures
Jami, *Yusufu Zulaikha* (text, tr. Griffith, 158–60)
Shiraz, c. 1575
Copyist, Shah Mahmud al-katib

London, British Library, Or. 4122, f. 87b
Dimensions: open book 408 x 560mm; painting 324 x 198mm
Previously exhibited: London 1967, 1976
Published: Rieu, *Supplement*, 189; Stchoukine, *MS*, no. 125, pp. 145, 156, 164, 183, 195 and pls. XLIX–LI; Robinson, *PMP*, no. 153; Hayward Gallery Catalogue, no. 614; Titley, *Catalogue*, no. 214

The text corresponding to this miniature describes how Zulaikha

eagerly satisfies Yusuf's wish to become a shepherd. But there is no sign of the "careful guardians" she sent to watch him; instead, the artist has freely embroidered the story and made it a busy genre scene.

The sheer size of the picture enables the artist to exploit with a rare thoroughness the device of the high horizon as a symbol for recession. At least seven planes, one piled upon the next, can be distinguished. The artist patiently chronicles the multifarious activities of daily life, but his grasp of detail is uneven (e.g. the yellow blobs that do duty for flowers) and too many colours compete for attention. It is only possible to identify Joseph in this farrago because of his flame halo. The people themselves are no longer the diminutive figures of late Timurid and early Safavid painting but have become larger. This trend was to continue until in the 17th century the figures often seem inappropriately large for book illustration.

162
Adultery unmasked
Miniature painting
From a *Kalila wa Dimna* (text: V. Kubičkova, *Persian Fables*, tr. G. Theiner [London, 1960], 92, 94)
Shiraz school, 1440–50

London, British Museum, no. 1955 7–9 02
Dimensions: leaf 231 x 145 mm; lower painting only, 102 x 89 mm.
Previously exhibited: London 1959
Published: Titley, *Catalogue*, no. 16

In the Sanskrit *Fables of Bidpai* (known in the Islamic world as the *Book of Kalila and Dimna*) animals are used, as in Aeşop, 'to point a moral and adorn a tale'. Occasionally, however, no such disguise is required. In this story a husband allowed his unfaithful wife to believe that she had blinded him. By this stratagem he caught the lovers together, thrashed the man and drove his wife out of the house, first cutting off her nose. Islamic law in fact punishes adulterous women by a severe beating or, in certain cases, death by stoning.

Small and markedly narrow in format, but packed with detail, the picture typifies the changes undergone by the later Timurid style in Shiraz. Figures lose their heroic quality, yet contrive to be graceful despite inherently clumsy attitudes, as the spreadeagled lover shows. Architecture is rendered in obsessive detail and with a fantasy which owes very little to actual buildings or their decoration. Subsequent damage may account for the dullness of some of the colours here, and perhaps for the rather coarse facial features. Bolsters and coverlets of the type depicted – though not with such Chinese decoration – are still used in Iran, but carpets of the type shown here are known only from miniatures.

تاجراتقضۀ شه عزام خوان تجر آن ری کی خان
بود ۀ کلی بیانه صد خریدار پشت پستا
تا جراز جمله پای پش نها
سع او در مژاه افتاده

کرو بر جه که سر کفت مراد
فرس خلالار لی لی ای تبدلا
وندران سروش ژو دوسکی
لیکه سید از رو بود مراد

Possibly Bukhara, later 16th century

London, Royal Asiatic Society of
  Great Britain & Ireland,
  Codrington 303a

Dimensions: 230 x 125 mm

For the earlier sections of this story
see **3** and **127**. Mushtari, banished by
his king, had the bad luck to fall in with
his calumniator Bahram. This villain
ill-treated Mushtari and his two
friends and finally put them on board
a ship about to embark on the Caspian
Sea. The three friends are here shown
suffering shipwreck.

The painting seems to be loosely
modelled on one of the numerous
scenes of Iskandar shooting waterfowl
(e.g. **56**). As a result, the six passengers
who converse casually form a bizarre
and disturbing contrast to the three
friends struggling for dear life in the
water. Otherwise the details of the ship
and its management are well observed.
Perhaps the most original stroke of the
artist is to show the sail projecting far
beyond the thick 9-line margin within
separate picture space of its own, itself
defined by a second though modest
and incomplete margin. The turban of
the lookout projects even beyond this,
a typically witty conceit. Persian
artists never tired of exploring the
various permutations of the links
between text and pictures.

Originally the contrast between
white sail, black boat and silver sea
must have been most effective. But
time has tarnished the sea black and
lent it a viscous consistency in which
fish and men seem immired.

165
Prince watching bathers in a pool
Miniature painting
Shiraz style, c. 1575

India Office Library, no. J.8.1

Dimensions: page 385 x 235;
  painting 130 x 75 mm

Previously exhibited: London 1951

Published: Robinson, *VAM* 1951,
  no. 61; Robinson, *IOL*, no. 532

This scene, which occurs in several
other manuscripts of the poet Saʿdi's
works (e.g. one in the India Office
Library datable perhaps c. 1575, Ethé
no. 1123) depicts the tomb of the poet
which, in medieval as in modern
times, was a popular resort of the
people of Shiraz. Saʿdi himself had
stipulated lavish appointments for his
place of burial, including marble
troughs for washing. The presence of
the prince, with his entourage of
musicians and half-naked women, and
above all the throngs of spectators,
suggests that some special and
essentially public spectacle or
ceremony is being enacted. A pool near
the tomb was popularly supposed to
possess healing virtues and the
inhabitants of Shiraz regularly bathed
in it on the Wednesday before the New
Year (Meredith-Owens, *PIM*, 26 and
pl. XXI). This is probably the scene
depicted here.

163
A Merchant Buys a Slave Girl
Miniature painting
Jami, *Haft Aurang* ("Seven Thrones")
Provincial school, mid 16th century

Private collection

Dimensions: painting, excluding
  margins, 163 x 106 mm.

Published: Maggs Bros Ltd.,
  Oriental Miniatures & Illumination,
  Bulletin No. 1 (December 1961),
  no. 1 (illustrated on cover and on
  first page, wrongly captioned "A
  Marriage Ceremony")

The story concerns a merchant who
bought a ravishingly beautiful woman
at an auction against heavy competition
and who, having bought her, gave
himself up to the good life. The
auctioneer is shown leading the girl to
the merchant while the unsuccessful
bidders – one of them quite woebegone
– condole with each other in a doorway.

The conceptual strain which this
painter affects is more pronounced in
this miniature than in its two
companion paintings (**29** and **192**).
Although the architectural setting
indicates that this is an interior
scene, no corroborative detail is
given. This bareness, like the large
expanses of unbroken colour, points to
Khurasan rather than to any of the
other provincial schools of the time.
The figure types, on the other hand,
are quite distinct from normal
Khurasani work of the time. It may
therefore be best to leave the question
of provenance open for the time being.

Slavery was an accepted feature of
medieval Persian life. Rulers derived
much revenue from the slave traffic
and slaves were a common gift to and
from royalty.

164
Mushtari shipwrecked
Manuscript; ff. and 2 miniatures
ʿAssar, *Mihr u Mushtari*

The miniature itself is scarcely worthy of its resplendent illuminated setting, whose intense dark blue and blazing gold tones physically engulf it. Illumination on this scale was customarily lavished on the frontispiece or the last double page opening of a manuscript. This was the right hand half of such a double page, though it is not certain whether it was at the front or the back of the book. In the *Kulliyat* of Sa'di mentioned above the corresponding scene occurs on the last folio of the book.

166
The caliph and the barber
Manuscript; 786 pages and 30 miniatures
Nizami, *Khamsa* (*Makhzan al-Asrar*; text, tr. Darab, 243–4)
Shiraz style; Safar 947/June 1540
Cambridge, St. John's College Library
Dimensions: page 320 x 200 mm
Published: E. G. Browne, *A supple-*

mentary handlist of the Muhammadan manuscripts . . . in the libraries of Cambridge . . . (Cambridge, 1922), 318, No. 1434; Robinson, *Bodleian*, 121

It was common for Muslims to shave their heads so that they could wear turbans in greater comfort. The operation was performed by the barber, who was also skilled in applying massages, emunctories, depilatories and the like. Hence, perhaps, his rather humble social status, which may account for his darker hue in the picture. The Caliph was therefore mortified when his barber repeatedly demanded his daughter in marriage. His wise Persian vizier explained this extraordinary conduct: the barber must be standing on a spot where treasure was buried, and this gave him, all unawares, delusions of grandeur. Next day the caliph ordered him to stand elsewhere, whereupon he at once showed due submissiveness. The

treasure was found as the vizier had predicted. The text tells this story of Harun al-Rashid but some versions, such as this one, substitute al-Ma'mun.

Baths throughout the Muslim world often had figural and even erotic paintings, but here modest stencilled abstract designs suffice. Details like the octagonal pool, the shapeless skirts of the bathers and the buckets of water with which they douse themselves are still common features of Islamic hammams. Total nudity was and is taboo.

The mechanical, over-precise geometric forms make this a curiously lifeless picture; it is in fact a simplified and rather weak copy (especially in its watery colours) of Bihzad's classic interpretation of this scene. Almost identical versions of this scene occur in roughly contemporary Nizami manuscripts in the Chester Beatty Library (CB *Catalogue II*, pl. 26) and in the Freer Gallery of Art (Guest, *Shiraz Painting*, pl. 3).

167
Young man killed by a lion
Tinted drawing
Isfahan, 3 February 1672
3 Shawwal 1082
Signed Mu'in Musavvir
Boston, Museum of Fine Arts, no. 14.620; formerly in Goloubev collection
Dimensions: page 199 x 313 mm; drawing 104 x 175 mm.
Previously exhibited: Venice 1962, New York 1973, Cambridge, Mass 1974
Published: Martin, *MP* II, pl. 158; Schulz, *PM* II, pl. 163; Coomaraswamy, *Goloubew*, 54–5 and pl. XLVII; 114; Schroeder, *Fogg*, 149; Grube, *MMP*, no. 117; Welch, *Isfahan*, no. 75; O. Grabar in *Iranian Studies* VII/1–2 (1974), 12–13 and fig. 1

It is virtually unprecedented in Persian art that a scene as specific as this should be recorded within a month or so of the event. Seen in the context of later Safavid art, however, it is rather less surprising. Other artists, notably Riza-i'Abbasi (cf. **169**) produced – side by side with highly stylised formal work for court consumption – studies of everyday scenes and people. It was not rare for inscriptions on such drawings to be longer and more informative than the terse signatures on "official" work. But this inscription is long even for Mu'in Musavvir. It gives the very day the drawing was done – though this inscription was added at least five days later – complains about the severe weather that winter, and mentions that ambassadors from Bukhara had come to Shah Sulaiman bringing gifts of wild animals. It finally explains the subject of the drawing – how one of the royal lions broke loose from the keepers, ran amok and savaged a youth who died on the

spot. All this authenticiates an extraordinary subject. Moreover, the inscription states that the artist produced the drawing to distract himself – not to please a patron. This is the work of a man who draws almost as naturally as he breathes. With the increased range of subject matter in the seventeenth century the artist can now record objectively the fatal irruption of the court on everyday life. At the same time, he is sufficiently within the bounds of convention to make the faces devoid of expression and to render the lion in such a Chinese spirit that it resembles a tiger.

168
Man grooming a horse
Miniature painting
Probably Qazvin, c. 1580-90
Painted by Rida/Riza (for discussion of the name, cf. Schroeder, *Fogg*, 116-34)
London, British Museum, no. 1948 12-11 014; formerly in Anet and Eckstein collections
Dimensions: leaf 335 x 239 mm.; painting 163 x 000 mm.
Previously exhibited: Paris 1912, London B.M. 1931, 1949, 1959, 1963
Published: For the most convenient bibliography see Stchoukine, *SA*, 130-1, to which may be added Schroeder, *Fogg*, 153; B. Gray in *BMQ* XVII (1952), 18; Titley, *Catalogue*, no. 398 (45)

The inscription identifying this as an early work of Aqa Riza/Riza-i 'Abbasi may well be genuine. It is perhaps a young man's picture in its deliberate assault on the eye. The leaf must be seen in its entirety, for its various parts complement each other. Densely massed illumination in the richest blue and gold is set off by paler colours. The calligraphy, in alternating black and gold, takes up about half the page. The vigorous activity of the groom and the sheer bulk of the horse cause them to break through the frame on all sides. The field itself is dominated by bold stripes. With these loud accents controlling the design the artist can well afford to leave the ground colour untouched and even to use a very similar colour for the delicately mottled coat of the horse. But none of the drama would succeed without the plain cinnamon ground to act as a foil.

That this is a royal horse is indicated by the splendour of its trappings, notably the huge feather at the pommel and the tooled girth, while the sign on his rump is perhaps the royal *tamgha* or brand.

169
Bagpipe player
Tinted drawing in an album containing 48 pages including endpapers
Isfahan, probably 1022/1613-14 (the date could also be read 1033/ 1623-4)
Signed Riza-i 'Abbasi

Cambridge, Fitzwilliam Museum, Marlay 40, f. 11 (formerly Marlay collection)
Dimensions: leaf 312 x 225 mm; painting 178 x 104 mm
Previously exhibited: London 1967
Published: Robinson, *PMP*, no. 90

Riza-i 'Abbasi was censured by the historian Iskandar Munshi because he foresook the cultured atmosphere of the court to associate with athletes and wrestlers. His drawings do indeed reflect an absorbed and satirical interest in low life. This bagpiper, for example, is clearly no embryonic court musician. His fur hat, baggy pantaloons and pointed yellow boots lay no claim to elegance. Moreover, he is not yet fully master of his instrument, to

judge by his face, suffused a deep red with the effort of blowing. Presumably the bagpipe did not have a sufficiently delicate timbre to accompany poetic recitations; at all events, it seems not to feature among the instruments played at court.

Since the genre element of the drawing is uppermost, background details are sketchy. Amidst the rocks on which the musician stands a face peers out, an echo of a long-outmoded fashion. These tumbled boulders are treated with the freedom of rocaille ornament and tinted blue and magenta. But the finest drawing is reserved for the figure itself; here the lines become thicker or thinner according to a beautifully controlled rhythm.

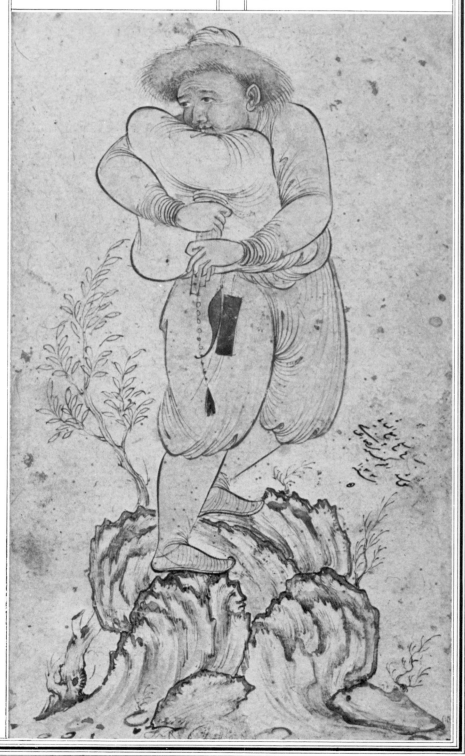

Religion

Religion

Paintings of religious subjects are quite common in the Persian tradition, although they are much more likely to be found in works of history than in more narrowly theological works like Qur'anic commentaries, collections of *hadiths* or of course the Qur'an. The *Shahnama* itself, though written almost four centuries after the Islamic conquest, has very little tincture of the Muslim faith.

The stories of the prophets made suitably edifying reading and were a popular theme for illustration. Sometimes they are given flame haloes (e.g. **174** and many of the depictions of Yusuf) but it was very common for the prophet not to be distinguished by any outward sign (**170** and **173**). In the course of the 16th century it became increasingly common to show Muhammad veiled. Even so, the painters carefully followed Islamic tradition in not exalting him above human status. Only in scenes of the *mi'raj* (**183** – Muhammad's miraculous night journey) is the supernatural aura that must envelop the Prophet fully exploited.

Religious observances and duties permeate the life of a Muslim and many of these practices are reflected in Persian painting. It is incumbent on the Muslim to wage holy war (*jihad*) against unbelievers (**187**) and this precept was even applied in wars between the various creeds. The career of the fanatical Isma'il I illustrates this (**79**). Many rulers made the pilgrimage to Mecca, and in Iran this was supplemented by pilgrimages to the great national Shi'ite shrines – Karbala, Najaf, Qum and Mashhad. Sometimes these pilgrimages were marked by a spectacular humility; it is recorded of Shah 'Abbas, for example, that he travelled on foot across the desert from Yazd to Mashhad. The Ka'ba is a favourite theme and the painters depict this, the central edifice of the Muslim world, with notable and consistent accuracy (**180**). Apart from pilgrimage, however, and scenes within mosques, the formal role of the monarch in cultic practices – e.g. leading divine worship or delivering the bidding prayer from the pulpit – is rarely depicted, perhaps because many rulers wished to minimise their own important role in public worship. The major religious festivals, too, are not often illustrated. It is conceivable that some inborn reluctance to explore overtly religious themes – with the important exceptions noted above – hindered the development of these subjects. Religious themes of a more private nature are frequently encountered. Thus the ruler is shown venerating a holy man (**186**) or conversing with a dervish. Scenes of dervish life, showing these Sufis dancing, meditating, begging, praying or drinking, became increasingly popular from the later 16th century onwards. But they do not always possess a distinctively religious quality; instead, they frequently incline towards genre. Even so, the wilder type of dervish, outlandishly dressed, with a tangled beard and a spectacularly emaciated appearance, is not a popular subject.

During the Mongol and Timurid periods orthodox Islam and even orthodox Shi'ism declined while Sufism and "folk Islam" flourished. These latter forms of religious life, despite an inclination towards such extreme practices as collective hypnosis, extensive fasting and even self-mutilation, nevertheless exerted a powerful appeal at a popular level. Through them unlettered Muslims could achieve a sense of personal communion with God which they might have felt was denied to them in orthodox Islam. The concern of the Sufis was to integrate into orthodox Islam some of the fundamental tenets of mysticism: the importance of the individual's relationship with God, the exercise of charity and the leading of a devotional life along ascetic lines. Individual mystics attracted followers and thus founded associations which were to become the dervish orders of medieval Islam. Safavid power originated in one such order and in the early years of the 16th century the Safavid monarchs showed sympathy for Sufi teachings. It was only later that the rulers came to realise that Sufism and official Shi'ism could not be reconciled. But the movement maintained much of its hold on the populace even when official support had been withdrawn.

170
Noah and the ark

Manuscript; 60 ff. and 36 miniatures
Rashid al-Din, *Jami' al-Tawarikh* ("Collection of Histories")
Tabriz, 714/1314–15

London, Royal Asiatic Society, no. A.27, f. 45a
Dimensions: page 425 x 300 mm.
Previously exhibited: London 1931, 1976
Published: the manuscript is usually discussed in conjunction with the Edinburgh version of the text. The basic bibliography given in Robinson, *PMP*, no. 2 should therefore be supplemented by the references cited in **131**. See also W. H. Morley, *A descriptive catalogue of the historical manuscripts in the Arabic and Persian languages preserved in the Library of the Royal Asiatic Society of Great Britain and Ireland* (London, 1854), 1–11; G. M. Meredith-Owens in *Journal of the Royal Asiatic Society* 1970/no. 2, 195–9 and pls. I–II; Hayward Gallery Catalogue, no. 530; B. Gray, *The World History of Rashid al-Din* (forthcoming)

The Qur'an refers repeatedly to Noah and Sura 71 bears his name. In Muslim tradition he is a prophet and numerous extra details, some taken from Jewish commentaries, later embellish the story. The text here mentions how Noah entered the Ark with his family at God's command, and also refers to the animals he took with him, but these are not shown.

For general comments on the historical and stylistic context of this manuscript, see **131**. No special attempt has been made to depict the 3-storey ark of Islamic legend with its body like a bird and its prow and stern in the shape of a cockerel. Instead the artist reproduces the medieval Persian stereotype of a boat. This does duty not only for the ark but also for a regular sea-going vessel (**73**, f. 50a) or even a pleasure craft (**56**). Indeed, Noah sprawls at his ease while a courtly atmosphere prevails: one son sits huddled beside him and two others wait on him deferentially. The undulating motion of the boat is well suggested by rhythmical scrolling waves rendered with superb panache. Similarly expressive conventions for waves are found elsewhere in 14th century painting – e.g. the scenes of Jonah and the whale in this manuscript (f. 59a) and in **172**, or a leaf in Istanbul showing Zal shooting a bird (Gray, *PP*, colour plate on 42). This work is closer to a tinted drawing than to a painting, but it gains unusual richness by the lavish use of silver.

171
Muhammad on a donkey accompanied by four men

Miniature painting
Unidentified historical text
Shiraz school, c. 1340

Princeton University Library, no. 92G
Dimensions: leaf 107 x 79 mm; painting 60 x 51 mm
Previously exhibited: New York 1940; Venice 1962
Published: Moghadam and Armajani, *Catalog*, no. 196; H. Buchthal, O. Kurz and R. Ettinghausen, *AI* VII (1940), 164, no. 16 of addenda; R. Ettinghausen, *AI* VII (1940), 111 and 121; Ackerman, *Guide*, 194; Grube, *MMP*, no. 27

The text illustrates a prophecy about Muhammad. Representations of the Prophet, still unveiled, occur frequently in manuscripts of the early 14th century. Quite often the context is a series of pictures of other prophets.

The bland, epicene facial types used here are familiar from Saljuq pottery while the bold, sketchy drawing and strong colour typify the Inju style. By a curious convention the hoofs of the donkey, which break out of the margin, are not coloured in. The figures themselves seem too large for the space they occupy and gross disproportions of scale are common – a characteristic example is Muhammad's elongated index finger. For another leaf from this manuscript, see **63**.

172
Jonah and the Whale
Miniature painting
Rashid al-Din, *Jami' al-Tawarikh*
Baghdad or Tabriz, c. 1390

New York, Metropolitan Museum of Art Purchase, Joseph Pullitzer Bequest, no. 33.113
Dimensions: 319 x 418 mm
Previously exhibited: New York, 1968
Published: *Art Treasures of the Metropolitan* (New York, 1952) pl. 206; Robinson, *MMA*, no. 3; Dimand, *PM*, 20 and pl. VI (in colour); Grube, *Classical Style*, 25, 186 and pl. 13; M. L. Swietochowski in *Iranian Studies* VII/1–2 (1974), 52 and fig. 1

Jonah is an important prophet in the Qur'an; Suralo is named after him. In some respects the iconography of this scene corresponds to earlier depictions in Christian art, notably in the gourd which God caused to grow over Jonah's head to protect him from the sun. In the Christian tradition his traumatic sojourn in the belly of the fish caused his hair to fall out and he is often shown bald. In this respect, as in the presence of an angel, this Islamic version departs from the Christian norm. Muslim and Christian artists alike gave their imaginations free rein in depicting the great fish. Sea-serpents, senmurvs and Chinese carps are merely some of the variants commonly encountered. Christian artists frequently telescoped the various elements of the Jonah cycle into a continuous narrative form – but in Islam this was apparently avoided. Painters preferred to concentrate on the single episode of Jonah and the whale. Notable versions of the theme, very different from this one, are found in the Rashid al-Din codices in Edinburgh and London. The large size of this painting, which illustrates the same text as these manuscripts, is a direct echo of them. Like them it combines Chinese elements – such as the knobbly tree trunk – with Mesopotamian ones, such as the fleshy plants. In this and other respects (notably Jonah's face) this is a curiously archaic painting, hard to equate with other Timurid work of c. 1400. This archaic quality perhaps suggests an origin in Baghdad rather than in Tabriz.

173
Moses about to kill 'Uj
Miniature painting
Hafiz-i Abru, *Majma' al-Tawarikh*
Herat school, c. 1425
Cincinnati Art Museum, no. 1947.501
(formerly in Tabbagh collection)

Dimensions: leaf 425 x 326 mm; painting 352 x 000 mm
Previously exhibited: Philadelphia 1926; London 1931; New York 1940; Venice 1962
Published: *London 1931*, no. 431d; *BWG*, no. 28(l); Kühnel, in *SPA*, 1840 and pl. 849 (in colour); Ackerman, *Guide*, 192 and illustration on 193; J. Pijoan, *Summa Artis; Historia general del Arte, XII; Arte Islamico* (Madrid, 1949), 343, pl. XVIII (colour); *Guide to the Collections of the Cincinnati Art Museum* (Cincinnati, 1956), 26; *Near Eastern Art. Ancient and Islamic* (Cincinnati, 1962), illustration no. 21; Grube, *MMP*, no. 40

'Uj is the Arabic name for Ogg, the giant King of Bashan. He is not mentioned in the Qur'an, but Muslim histories of the prophets amplify the Biblical account (Deuteronomy iii, 11 and Numbers XXI, 33–5). According to the Islamic sources, 'Uj wanted to win Pharaoh's daughter, so he took a huge rock to crush the Israelite camp. But God sent birds to bore a hole in it, so that the rock fell over his head like a collar. By making a great leap, Moses was able to kill him by a blow on the heel with his staff.

In choosing to portray the moment immediately before this, the artist exploits to the full the wonders related in his text. He contrives that even on this large page the frame cannot contain the giant. He restricts himself to the few colours and large expanses that the subject demands. But the grand scale exposes (as in the feet of 'Uj) the feeble draughtsmanship which mars other miniatures from this book. In an earlier painting illustrating this story (e.g. **131**, f. 9b – Talbot Rice, *World History*, pl. 13; cf. also Grube, *MI*, no. 65B) 'Uj is shown collapsing head over heels, his huge body

174

spreading over most of the limited picture space. One image evokes his dreadful power; the other symbolises his utter defeat.

174
King Namrud casts Abraham into the fire

Miniature painting; parent manuscript has 440 ff. and 38 miniatures
Anthology; this leaf is taken from Hamdallah Mustaufi al-Qazvini, *Tarikh-i Guzida*
Probably Shiraz, 813/1410–11
Copyists, Mahmud b. Murtaza b. Ahmad al-Hafiz al-Husaini and Hasan al-Hafiz
Dedicated to Iskandar Sultan

Lisbon, Calouste Gulbenkian Foundation Museum, ff. 326 b. and 327 a
Dimensions: 327a, 244 x 147 mm
Published; for a bibliography of this manuscript in general, see **45**.

These leaves have been published in Gray, *PP 1961*, 72 and colour plate of f. 327a on 79

King Namrud (Nimrod), disturbed by a prophecy that a child would be born that would oust him, reacted like Herod with the massacre of infants. Abraham escaped and in later life became a convinced monotheist and overturned the idols in Namrud's temple. A ballista designed by Iblis Satan) catapulted him into the flames at the royal command, but within the fire was an idyllic landscape of trees and streams. An angel (not shown here) came to comfort him and he emerged unharmed.

An earlier version of this scene in the Edinburgh *Jami' al-Tawarikh* (131, f. 3b; see Talbot Rice, *World History* pl. 7) condenses the action into a single oblong picture. In this expanded version, the artist has exploited the double-page opening with imagination: king and catapult occupy one page and Abraham the other. The gap between the two pages is thus turned to account; the format reinforces the sense of the subject matter. Although the picture can be appreciated on one level as a decorative set-piece of great dramatic power, it also has deeper resonances. The scene inevitably recalls the story of Shadrach, Meshach and Abednego saved in the fiery furnace. Traditionally they too have their hands raised in prayer. In their case, too, God intervened to save his chosen. The flames resemble some vast aureole within which Abraham sits embowered and in this context his flaming halo – an early occurrence of this feature in Islamic painting – is especially appropriate. Indeed the whole pyre is his crown. His pale face and hands are of the right intensity of colour to draw the eye and to act as the molten centre of the flames.

The quilted floral background to the prophet also refers to the miracle, for it bears no relationship to the landscape outside the flames. This drab landscape continues that of the picture opposite. But unlike the painting with King Namrud, the horizon is not shown in the scene depicting Abraham. By this means its background acquires a timeless quality, thereby emphasising the exemplary nature of the scene. Thus despite the immediate appeal to the senses which this picture exerts, its concentrated colours may well be intended to convey religious exaltation.

175
Yusuf and Zulaikha enter the pavilion of love

Manuscript; 76 ff. and 5 miniatures
Sa'di, *Bustan* (text, tr. Clarke, 393–4)
Tabriz school, c. 1540
Vienna, Nationalbibliothek, no. AF 103, f. 73a
Dimensions: page 251 x 168 mm
Previously exhibited: Vienna 1901, 1953
Published: Flügel, *Handschriften* I, 533, no. 537; *Katalog 1901*, no. 290; Holter, *Les principaux manuscrit*, 101–3, no. 8 and pl. XIXb; Holter, *PM*, 39 and pls. VI–VII; *BDM*, no. 103; Robinson, *Bodleian*, 85; Stchoukine, *MS*, no. 37 and p. 154

The attempted seduction of Yusuf (Joseph) by Zulaikha (Potiphar's wife) is given detailed treatment in Islamic sources. Zulaikha's nurse builds a pavilion in which walls, floor and ceiling are all covered with pictures of the pair as lovers. Zulaikha leads Yusuf there and he is on the point of yielding when he discovers that she keeps an idol in the room. This brings him to his senses and he flees from her. Zulaikha's love, sufferings and eventual happiness (for she marries Yusuf in due course) are, incidentally, not to be understood in a purely romantic sense for they are intended as an allegory of the soul's pilgrimage to God.

174

The conventions of perspective observed by the Persian artist obliged him to render architecture schematically. But it is easy to recognise this polygonal kiosk as a standard feature of Iranian palaces from medieval times if not earlier. These airy, open-plan structures had two or more storeys and were embellished with courtly or romantic wall paintings. Their interiors, as in this case, often contained poetic quotations in stylish *nasta'liq* script. Indeed, inscriptions are a leitmotif here. They range from simple repetitions of the name 'Ali to invocations like "O thou who art all-sufficient in matters of moment" and good wishes for the ruler, "may Allah Most High cause his sultanate to endure". The rendering of decoration posed fewer problems of representation for this painter than did architecture. Thus the Persian genius for surface ornament found ample scope in embellishing these card-house facades. As a result the techniques of tilework depicted here accurately reflect early Safavid architecture.

The painting is an excellent example of the court style of Safavid Tabriz.

176
Solomon and his court
Miniature painting
Unidentified text
Shiraz school, c. 1545
London, Victoria and Albert Museum, no. E. 2456–1929
Dimensions: 188 x 150 mm.

Previously exhibited: London 1951
Published: Robinson, *VAM 1951*, no. 58; Robinson, *VAM 1965*, 15 and pl. 24

Solomon was regarded as the epitome of the powerful king because he had dominion not only over all men but also over *jinns*, animals – whose speech he understood – and even the winds. By a natural transition "Solomon" became a generic term for "king" in poetry. He was also regarded as a prophet. In Iranian folk belief he was associated with numerous pre-Islamic monuments (cf. A.S. Melikian-Chirvani in *Le Monde Iranian et l'Islam* I(1971), 1–41); some were thought to have been built by *jinns* at his command. Solomon is often shown with the Queen of Sheba, Bilqis (e.g. the frontispiece of 212). Their meeting is recounted in Qu'ran xxvii. 22–45. She too became a byword: the great Timurid queen Gauhar Shad was dubbed the "Bilqis of the age".

In the more complex ensembles, as here, Solomon's status as a magician is explicit, for representatives of all creation surround him to do his bidding: birds real and fantastic, animals, reptiles and *jinn*, including demons. Tradition relates how at his command an *'ifrit* (demon) built a throne for Bilqis. In this miniature the parallel with an actual court is made explicit by the court dress of the attendants and by the presence of an old man, clearly intended as a vizier.

Even Solomon himself wears the characteristic Safavid turban. The lifelike imitation of gold tooling and other ornament on Solomon's throne (which tradition says was of solid gold) is the feature of the painting most typical of Shiraz. It contrasts strangely with the summary treatment accorded to the landscape or with the gauche frontality of one of the attendant *jinns*.

177
The court of Solomon
Manuscript; 243 ff. and 153 miniatures
Zakariya Qazvini, *al-Makjluqat wa Ghara'ib al-Maujudat' Aja'ib*
("The Wonders of Creation and the Prodigies of Everything in Existence")
Qazvin style; 16 Jumada II 974/29 December 1566
The Syndics of Cambridge, University Library, no. Nn. 3-74, frontispiece
Dimensions: 350 x 241 mm.
Previously exhibited: London 1931, 1951
Published: Browne, *Catalogue*, 208-10; *London 1931*, no. 720C; *BWG*, no. 204; Robinson, *VAM 1951*, no. 76; Robinson, *VAM 1952*, 7 and pl. 22; Stchoukine, *MS*, no. 67

Representations of Solomon are frequently found in double-page frontispiece, the place of honour in Persian manuscripts. Despite the change of subject the familiar iconography of the enthroned ruler is reproduced; the only change is that various types of *jinns* replace the courtiers. It is peculiarly fitting that

Solomon, with his unique power over nature (what other king commands the winds or speaks with the ant?) should introduce a book entitled "The Wonders of Creation".

The handling is broad rather than delicate, but the colours, reinforced by the illuminated border, are strong enough to justify this treatment. Throughout the manuscript the figures are few and large – clearly the artists preferred spacious uncluttered designs in which expanses of a single colour could dominate. These characteristics are also found in certain roughly contemporary work at Qazvin (e.g. 46 and 155).

For this subject in general, see 176.

178
Dancing dervishes
Manuscript: 445 ff. and 8 miniatures
Sa'di, *Kulliyat* ("Collected poems")
Shiraz style, Muharram 938/August 1531
The Provost and Fellows of Eton College Library, no. 16
Dimensions: page 244 x 150 mm
Previously exhibited: London 1951
Published: Robinson, *VAM 1951*, no. 44; Robinson, *Bodleian,* 120; cf. also Robinson, unpublished notes kept with the manuscript

Solemn dances were an established part of Sufi ritual and the *nai* or end-blown flute was, and still is, frequently used in such dances and in other dervish ceremonies. The formula of a few figures disposed with clarity against a

white background and a gold sky is followed in all the exterior scenes in this manuscript except one (f. 368 b, where the background is pink). This simplicity would accord well with the early phase of the Safavid style of Shiraz, when vestigial influences of the Turkoman style were still making themselves felt. Later Shiraz work is much more crowded and detailed than this, as are the more ambitious Shiraz paintings produced at this time (e.g. **195**).

179
The Armenian Clergy

Miniature painting
Hafiz-i Abru, *Majma' al-Tawarikh*
Herat, c. 1425

Kansas, William Rockhill Nelson Gallery of Art, no 46–40
Dimensions: page 328 x 231 mm; painting 269 x 224 mm
Previously exhibited: Syracuse 1967
Published: Arts Club of Chicago, "The Miniature in Persian Art", 9.4–9.5.1963, no. 42 (illustrated); *Handbook of the Collections in the William Rockhill Nelson Gallery of Art and Mary Atkins Museum of Fine Arts* (Kansas City, 1973), 161

The historian Hafiz-i Abru, writing in the 1420s, incorporated into his text the world chronicle written by Rashid al-Din a century before and this partly accounts for the emphasis on Mongol Ilkhanid history (1256–1336) in the text. It was precisely during the Ilkhanid period that the oriental Christian minorities enjoyed an Indian summer of power and prosperity, for several of the Mongol rulers had leanings towards Christianity. Moreover, the Armenians enjoyed special favour, not least because their contingents fought in the Mongol army. The Armenian King Hayton even acted as a Mongol ambassador to Europe.

The picture is placed immediately beneath the heading " "Chapter Two" which deals, according to the superscription, with the area within the borders of the province (*wilayat*) of the Armenians (presumably a diocese) between al-Mada'in and Diyagh.

Al-Mada'in, the ancient Ctesiphon a few miles south-east of Baghdad, was, with Baghdad, the major urban centre of the Christians in Mesopotamia.

In many respects the style of the painting echoes that of the great manuscripts of the *Jami' al-Tawarikh* of Rashid al-Din, just as the accompanying text subsumes the text of Rashid al-Din. The large size of the picture space, its stark simplicity and restraint – the painter sedulously avoids making the palm branches burst through the margins – and its lack of landscape detail all find analogies in the *Jami' al-Tawarikh* manuscripts of the early 14th century. But it is the figures themselves that display the most marked dependence on these prototypes. Slender, commandingly tall and facially of pronounced Mongol type, they have the same powerful presence as the figures in the Rashid al-Din manuscripts. Even such details as their boots and the recurrent vertical falls of drapery with the robe parted at the hem tally with the earlier work. The curious headgear and the voluminous sleeves (the latter recalling a Chinese fashion) are presumably intended to be characteristically Armenian. For a brief account of various texts of the manuscript itself see R. Ettinghausen in *KdO* II (1955), 30–44.

180
A dervish praying in the sanctuary at Mecca

Manuscript; 497 ff. and 17 miniatures
Sa'di, *Kulliyat* ("Collected works"; the manuscript is open at the *Gulistan*, "Rose Garden"; text, tr. Gladwin, 67–8)
Shiraz school, 964/556-7
Copyist, 'Inayatallah Shirazi

Edinburgh University Library, Or. MS 104, f. 145a
Dimensions: leaf 300 x 210 mm
Previously exhibited: London 1931, 1951
Published: M. Ashraf ul-Hukk, H. Ethé and E. Robertson, *A Descriptive Catalogue of Arabic and Persian Manuscripts in Edinburgh University Library* (Hertford, 1925), 81–9; *London 1931*, no 545C; *BWG*, no. 186; Robinson, *VAM 1951*, no. 48; Robinson, *Bodleian*, 122; Stchoukine, *MS*, no. 120

Chapter II of the *Gulistan* deals with the morals of dervishes and this miniature illustrates the second tale of that chapter. The text describes how a dervish "placed his forehead on the threshold of the Ka'ba" and abased himself before God, saying "Do unto me that which is worthy of thee, and treat me not according to my desert". The Ka'ba is the sacred enclosure at Mecca which all Muslims must visit at least once in their lives if they are able. The term is used especially of the oratory in the centre of the courtyard, towards which the prayers of all Muslims are directed. This structure

contains the Black Stone which, according to tradition, Gabriel brought from paradise to Abraham when he was building the Ka'ba. From medieval times onwards it became customary to drape the oratory in a black cloth – the *kiswa* – with embroidered inscriptions.

The work is typical of Shiraz in its plethora of figures and of colours. The scene is apparently not one of pilgrimage, for the men do not wear the seamless white robe (*ihram*) which is part of the rite. The large courtyard surrounding the Black Stone is well suggested, as are the corner minarets, the right hand one clearly of Ottoman type. An element of caricature can perhaps be detected in the youth depicted face on in the upper centre, and also in the figures wearing high black conical hats. These types are characteristic of this painter. The upper margins come to an uncertain end at the base of the minarets; other contemporary artists were more ready to exploit such projections from the picture space (cf. **35**).

For the depiction of the Ka'ba in Islamic art see R. Ettinghausen in ZDMG N.F. XII, 3/4 (1934) 111–37.

181
Battle watched by 'Ali

Miniature painting
Maulana Muhammad b. Husam al-Din, *Khavar Nama*, f. 265
Perhaps Shiraz, c. 1475–80

Dublin, Chester Beatty Library and Gallery of Oriental Art, Pers. Ms. 293, no. 8
Dimensions: page 400 x 280 mm
Published: For the parent manuscript and its dispersed leaves, see **16**. For this leaf, see CB *Catalogue* III, 61–2

In this obscure incident from the early Islamic wars Malik holds a yelping dog as he rides towards 'Ali, looking back at his pursuers. Elements of Far Eastern inspiration are prominent here: forms enclosing the auspicious *ju-i* motif of Chinese iconography, and the flaming aureole around the head of 'Ali (cf. J. Tavernor-Perry, BM XII (1907), 22). But they have been so thoroughly absorbed into the native tradition that they are little more than decorative details.

In this and the similar scenes of violent action which are his forte, the artist revives the heroic age of early Islam, when the few faithful were hemmed in by enemies. A strong centralised composition ensures that there is no loss of impetus by a dwelling on detail. The colours, too, are bold and direct rather than subtle. 'Ali, who holds his famed two-pointed sword Dhu'l-Faqar, is an especially striking figure on his pink dappled horse. The cavalry and onlookers are still firmly in the Shiraz tradition of two generations earlier, both in their tight masses and in the details of their armour. Among several audacious uses of the margin one might single out the horse which has turned tail and bolts incontinently

Isfahan style, c. 1600

The Provost and Fellows of Eton
  College Library, no. 767, f. 155a.
Dimensions: page 319 x 206 mm
Previously exhibited: London 1951
Published: Robinson, *VAM 1951*,
  no. 36; B. W. Robinson in *The
  Connoisseur* CXXVIII (1951), 178,
  no. VI; Robinson, *Bodleian*, cf. also
  Robinson, unpublished notes kept
  with the manuscript

A traditional feature of illustrated
copies of the *Khamsa* of Nizami is the
inclusion (unwarranted by the text) of
the celebrated *Mi'raj* (Night Journey)
of Muhammad. Its placing varies from
one manuscript to the next; it may be
put at the beginning or end of the *Laila
va Majnun*, or, as here, in the early part
of the *Haft Paikar*. The Qur'an says
that God "caused his servant to make a
journey by night from the sacred place
of worship". This text was understood
to refer to a journey which Muhammad
made in a single night between Mecca
and Jerusalem. Thence he ascended to
Heaven through the seven spheres of
the planets, mounted on his human-
headed horse Buraq and accompanied
by angels. This subject inspired some
of the most exalted of Islamic religious
paintings, and a few versions (e.g. that
in **23**) have such visionary intensity
that they may be intended to reflect a
mystical experience.

This miniature shows the scene as
Persian painters habitually visualised
it, though in somewhat reduced form.
Muhammad is accompanied by only
four angels and the fiery clouds which
usually surround him (and often in
medieval Christian art also serve as
references to paradise) play a very
minor role. But the extraordinarily
long wings of the angels, like tongues
of flame, compensate for this to some
extent. The background is a most
unusual pale blue. Muhammad is
shown veiled, a custom which had
become established in the course of the
16th century.

B. W. Robinson attributes this
painting to the better of the two artists
whose work he distinguishes in the
later miniatures, and notes that his
style is associated with that produced
by Aqa Riza/Riza-yi 'Abbasi in the last
decade of the 16th century. Like all of
the paintings in the manuscript, it has
been remounted, and like many others
it has suffered later damage.

184
Muhammad, his grandsons and
some of his Companions in a
mosque

Manuscript: 77 ff. and 8 miniatures of
  which 5 are on three double page
  openings; all of them are later
  insertions
Jami, *Baharistan* ("Spring-land")
Bukhara, completed 954:1547–8; the
  miniatures themselves can be dated
  c. 1525–30
Dedicated to 'Abd al-'Aziz Bahadur,
  governor of Bukhara 1540–49;

out of the frame, or the unusual multi-
coloured flag which breaks through the
text panel but is accommodated in the
empty column between the verses. Its
crowning device is the word *Allah* –
shown, perhaps as a deliberate oddity,
in reverse.

182
Victorious champion watched by
Muhammad

Miniature painting
Unidentified text
Tabriz style, c. 1550

Private collection
Dimensions: 200 x 125 mm
Previously exhibited: London 1951
Published: Robinson, *VAM 1951*,
  no. 40

The scene illustrates an unidentified
manuscript but the presence of
Muhammad suggests that the text was
of a historical nature. Although they
are divided by a coulisse, both armies
wear turbans and their standards are
not obviously differentiated (on this
subject in general, see V. A. Kratch-
kowskaya in *AI* iv (1937), 468–71. In

actual fact the Islamic armies at the time
of Muhammad used a standard bearing
the Roman eagle. In Islamic tradition
Muhammad, as the man who
approached God more closely than any
other, is customarily depicted with a
veiled face. His flame halo, on the
other hand, is common to other
prophets.

The starry sky was of course an
accepted symbol for night-time in
Persian painting but this feat of arms –
it is almost a joust – demands to be
seen, so perhaps the sky has a purely
decorative function here. The pinkish
mauve background is characteristic of
later 16th century manuscripts (cf.
152 and **155**).

183
The Night Journey of the Prophet

Manuscript; 322 ff. and 48 miniatures,
  of which two (ff. 14a and 272b) date
  from the early Safavid period, one
  (f. 75b) from the Qajar period and
  the remainder from the period
  around 1600
Nizami, *Khamsa* (the book is open at
  the *Haft Paikar*)

the dedication to Sultan Husain Baiqara and the date of 1498 are both spurious

Lisbon, Calouste Gulbenkian Foundation Museum, no. L.A. 169
Dimensions: leaf 310 x 200 mm
Previously exhibited: Lisbon 1963
Published: for a bibliography of this manuscript in general, see **20**; for this leaf, see Gray, *AOI*, no. 122 (illustrated)

The scene and its setting bears – as is to be expected in early Bukhara painting – a family resemblance to a Bihzadian composition. In fact the master used it several times (e.g. in a miniature dated 894/1489 in the Cairo *Bustan*; see Mustafa, *PM*, pl. 5). Nevertheless one detail suffices to fix its derivative character and later date – the columns of the mosque. Their wooden shafts, bell-shaped plinths and stalactite capitals have marked the Muslim architecture of Central Asia from the

10th century to modern times. On the other hand, they are extremely rare in the architecture of Iran proper and of Afghanistan, which was where Bihzad worked.

The Prophet Muhammad, some of his Companions, and his two grandsons Hasan and Husain are here shown communing in a mosque. The building is decorated in tile mosaic, the most lavish architectural ornament of the time in the Iranian world. Its three types of decoration – geometric, floral and epigraphic – are equally characteristic of contemporary work. Despite the Arabic text written above the *mihrab* in the centre ("and he prays standing in the *mihrab*") the Prophet is shown kneeling. But this was the usual iconography for depicting Muhammad with his grandsons.

In his subtle marshalling of the figures the artist has clearly profited from the spatial innovations of Bihzad. Each person is presented with clarity –

overlapping is kept to a minimum – and at the same time there is a sense of a relaxed relationship between the people depicted. It is a minor triumph of the artist to maintain this feeling of interchange while incorporating a large empty space between the groups.

185
A pious gathering

Manuscript; 77 ff. and three double-page plus two single miniatures; all the miniatures seem to predate the manuscript itself
Jami, *Baharistan* (Spring-land")
Bukhara, c. 1525–30
The manuscript is dedicated to 'Abd al-'Aziz Bahadur, governor of Bukhara 1540–49, and dated 954/1547. The dedication to Sultan Husain Baiqara and the date 1498 are both spurious

Lisbon, Calouste Gulbenkian Foundation Museum, no. L.A. 169 f. 30
Dimensions: page 310 x 200 mm
Exhibited: Lisbon 1963
Published: for a bibliography of this manuscript in general, see **20**.
For this leaf see Gray, *AOI*, no. 122 (illustrated)

Like the scene opposite depicting the Prophet in a mosque, this painting shows an almost total dependence on the manner of the Herat atelier of c. 1500. Bihzad had been pre-eminent in that school as an exponent of empty space and his methods are faithfully copied here. The placing of the figures is so assured that it seems inevitable, and each is individually characterised. Outside the enclosure, trees and flowers grow in colourful profusion. This section of the painting not only shows an entirely different facet of the artist's skill; it also serves to highlight by sheer contrast the orderly, disciplined activity of this circle of pious men.

The enclosure within which these scholars and divines sit is not a normal adjunct of a mosque (cf. Ettinghausen, *Berenson*, pl. VIII). It is probably a *hazira*, a typical feature of Timurid architecture in the eastern Iranian world. The *hazira* was an unroofed enclosure which contained the burial place of some holy man. Orthodox Islam prohibited the building of mausolea and indeed of any structure covering the grave because this was unnecessary ostentation. The *hazira* was an ideal compromise in that it marked the grave sufficiently but did not violate orthodoxy.

186
Prince and attendant visit holy man

Miniature painting
'Assar, *Mihr u Mushtari*
Shiraz or Isfahan, c. 1480
Private collection
Dimensions: leaf 200 x 120 mm; painting 130 x 70 mm.
Previously exhibited: Oxford 1966

The verses accompanying this miniature embody elaborate conceits to the

184

effect that one man kisses the saint's hand as does a sleeve, while another inclines towards him as does a skirt.

Orthodox Islamic theologians came to agree that a saint could act as a mediator between man and God. But popular belief was apt to invest the holy man with a quasi-divine aura. It was held that he could perform miracles and that through his agency prayers would be answered. Although the holy man was venerated in his life-time, he was credited with greatly increased powers after his death.

Persia has long been a major centre for the veneration of saints in the Islamic world, and numerous Persian paintings depict princes visiting holy men or hermits. Several details of this picture accord with the practices of the cult there. The saint is revered as he stands on the threshold of his hermit-age – "threshold" (*astana*) was pre-cisely the term used of a shrine. His foot is kissed – burial at the foot of a saint is often recorded, as in the case of several princes of the house of Timur. The holy man is poorly clad, with naked legs – this obvious poverty symbolised renunciation of the world. The build-

ing may well be a *khanqah* or a *zawiya*, a "convent" for Sufis. Sometimes these housed a single occupant. The enclosure is typical, as is the pool; often the water by a saint's dwelling was held to possess special virtue.

The melon dome depicted here was a typical and short-lived feature of 15th century architecture. Its combination of red and silver is a fancy of the painter. Stylistically the painting has affinities with some Shiraz painting of the later 15th century – the long waists indeed echo earlier work from that city. But neither the vegetation nor the figure types correspond to the ubiquitous Turkoman style of the period.

187
'Amr b. Umayya orders unbelievers to be drowned

Miniature painting; the original manuscript had over 600 ff. and 155 miniatures
Maulana Muhammad ibn Husam al-Din, *Khavar Nama*
Perhaps Shiraz, c. 1475–80
New York, Metropolitan Museum of Art Rogers Fund, 1955, no. 55.125.1

Dimensions: page 399 x 284; painting 168 x 275 mm
Previously exhibited: Venice 1962
Published: for the manuscript in general see **16**; for this leaf see Grube, *MMP*, no 47 (colour plate)

In the 15th century numerous Shi'ite principalities flourished in Iran, as if to set the stage for the adoption of Shi'ite Islam as the state religion by the Safavid Isma'il I in 1502. A typical manifestation of this Shi'ite fervour was the composition of the *Khavar Nama* by Ibn Husam al-Din in 1427. Modelled on the *Shahnama* itself, this epic poem glorifies the deeds of the early heroes of Islam, and of 'Ali in particular. An illustrated version of this rare text, dated 854/1450–1 accord-ing to a dubious colophon, is in the Museum of Decorative Arts in Teheran; some 100 of its miniatures, which originally numbered 155, remain. The rest are scattered among various collections in Europe and America. Several leaves dated 881/1476–7 are signed by a certain Farhad, a painter otherwise unknown, and the formula he employs suggests that the signature is authentic.

In these miniatures the Turkoman style achieves a rare stateliness and drama. The challenges of illustrating in such detail this comparatively recent text, for which virtually no icono-graphic models could have been available, produced an artist of rare originality. It is no wonder that a painter with such power of inventive-ness should work confidently on a large scale quite typical of Turkoman painting. Indeed, these miniatures mark the early apogee of that style alike in their strong colours and robust action. Certain later miniatures, it is true, excel them in finesse (14) but by that time the Turkoman style was already showing marked affinities with the court style of Safavid Tabriz.

This leaf illustrates an exploit of 'Amr b. Umayya, who enlists the help of a recent convert to Islam to cast overboard the infidels with whom he is sailing.

Brandishing a huge dagger, 'Amr personifies the duty of the pious Muslim to wage war on unbelievers. The artist clearly prefers to highlight the violent action of the scene rather than to linger over detail. Even so, the cloud nearly enclosing 'Amr's aigrette is a witty conceit, while the boat is seen primarily as a vehicle for ornament.

188
A Sufi

Tinted drawing
Probably Qazvin, late 16th century
Signed "Work of Mu'in al-Din"

Boston, Museum of Fine Arts, no. 14.616 (formerly Goloubew collection)
Dimensions: 155 x 90 mm
Previously exhibited: Venice 1962
Published: Martin, *MP*, 48 and pl.

88c; Schulz, *PIM*, 176, 200 and pl. 156; Coomaraswamy, *Goloubew*, 49, no. 76 and pl. XLIV; Grube, *MMP*, no. 98

Portraits of Sufis were a frequent theme of Safavid painting. The dynasty itself sprang from a Sufi order, and some of the Shahs themselves were members of such orders. In the early Safavid period especially, numerous Sufi organisations flourished and it was only later that the rulers came to regard the demands of Sufism and Shi'ism, the state religion, as incompatible. But even though the Sufi orders lost royal support, they remained a major expression of popular Islam.

The deliberate simplicity of the Sufi's garb focusses attention on his rather soulful face. A heavy beard and beetling brows lend it extra expressiveness. By contrast the rest of the work is stereotyped, and even – as in the treatment of the right arm – inaccurate.

189
Dervishes dancing in a glade

Qazvin, c. 1580

Geneva, collection of Prince Sadruddin Aga Khan, no. Ir. M. 70
Dimensions: leaf 195 x 125 mm
Bibliography: Welch, *Collection II*

This scene apparently depicts a group of "dervishes" – that is, members of some religious fraternity – performing their *dhikr* or religious ritual. Its immediate purpose was to bring on a state of religious exaltation or ecstasy in which the devotee could be made aware of the unseen world. Hence perhaps the raised faces of the dervishes in this picture. The ultimate aim of the dervish, as of the Sufi in general, was, however, to establish direct personal contact with God. Sufism stressed the worth of individual intuitive religious experience to a degree that orthodox Islam did not. Nevertheless, the Sufi creed enjoyed great popular support, not least in Iran, where dervishes were numerous and highly honoured. This picture, therefore, affords an insight into religious ceremonies which, though unorthodox, were extremely widespread in Iran until modern times.

The *dhikr* could take many forms; the most celebrated in the west is the whirling dance of the Mevlevi dervishes. Strictly speaking the *dhikr* was to be performed in the cloister or *khanqah* of the order, but here the ceremony is taking place in a forest glade. Some of the dervishes are attended by youths, perhaps by members of the order, who support them as they faint in ecstasy. One youth plays the tambourine. The slow dreamy movements of the raised sleeves of the dervishes, their undulating garments and their rapt expressions all vividly evoke an exalted mood. The skullcap of one dervish lies unregarded on the ground, a mute witness to, and comment on, the religious abandon depicted here. The lightly rendered landscape is a hallmark of Muhammadi

and his school and is peculiarly appropriate to the other-worldly associations of this scene. Two empty panels in the corners were no doubt intended to hold inscriptions; they show that in this case at least the role allotted to the script was dependent on the picture space, not vice versa.

190
'Abdallah al-Ansari and his disciples

Manuscript 203 ff. and 49 miniatures
Sultan Husain Baiqara, *Majalis al-'Ushshaq* ("Assemblies of the Lovers")
Shiraz style, c. 1590–1600
London: By permission of the Director of the India Office Library and Records Ethé 1871, f. 48b
Dimensions: leaf 260 x 155 mm; painting 165 x 115 mm
Published: Robinson, *IOL*, 138–44 and no. 474

The theme of this work is typically Sufi: the desire of the soul to be united to God. The "lovers" of the title are therefore principally lovers of God, such as *shaikhs* and Sufis, though some

of the great lovers of secular literature also figure among the biographies, usually 76 in number, which comprise the book. Sultan Husain, a descendant of Timur, ruled Herat during the Indian summer of Timurid civilisation at the close of the fifteenth century.

The eighth biography deals with the Sufi saint 'Abdallah al-Ansari, a native of Herat (1005–1089). He is shown sitting on a *minbar* or pulpit. It is not clear whether he is preaching or praying. The raised hands naturally suggest prayer, but the fact that each person has removed his turban, the open-air setting and the presence of children indicate that some Sufi ritual is being enacted and that this is not an orthodox religious service.

191
Moses and Aaron vanquish the magicians of Pharaoh

Manuscript: 192 ff. and twenty miniatures
Ishaq b. Ibrahim b. Mansural-Nishapuri, *Qisas al-Anbiya* ("History of the Prophets")
Probably Isfahan, c. 1590–1600

190

Inscribed "exercise of Aqa Riza"
Dedication is partially effaced but
  mentions a royal patron, presumably
  Shah 'Abbas I
Paris, Bibliothèque Nationale,
  Supp. pers. 1313, f. 79b
Dimensions: page 290 x 190 mm.
Previously exhibited: Paris 1938
Published: Blochet, *Inventaire*,
  243–5; Blochet, *Peintures 1911*,
  19–20, pls. 30–32; Blochet,
  Enluminures, 116–7, pls. LXVII–
  LXVIII; Blochet, *Peintures*, 298–303,
  pls. 54–55; Blochet, *MP*, pls.
  CXXX – CXXXIII; Blochet,
  Catalogue, no. 365; Arnold, *ONT*,
  22–3, 28 and pls. VI, XI; *Arts de
  l'Iran*, 159–60; Schroeder, *Fogg*,
  122–3; Robinson, *Bodleian*, 159;
  Gray, *PP 1961*, 162–3 (colour plate
  of this miniature); Stchoukine,
  SA, 120, 138, 169, 172, 188, 206–7
  and pls. XXI–XXIII; Welch,
  Artists, 143, 145

In the Islamic as in the Biblical
tradition Moses discomfited the
magicians of Pharaoh by turning his
rod into a serpent (Robinson, *PMP*,
pl. 12). Here Aqa Riza has substituted a
dragon, a familiar set piece in the
repertory of most Persian painters.
The effect of the change is to electrify
the whole episode. Yet this fearsome
apparition in maroon and vermilion,
spitting golden fire against a steel-blue
ground, has a decorative function too.
It shows the same delight in outré
colour schemes as the horse and groom
attributed to this artist (168). But its
draughtsmanship is appreciably
inferior to that drawing; indeed,
Stchoukine suggests that the attribution of these book illustrations to
Aqa Riza is false. Be that as it may,
the slapdash treatment of rocks,
grass, tree and flowers make a sorry
contrast to the splendid colours
employed. They suggest that the artist
was bored by that painstaking
depiction of landscape detail which was
traditional in Persian book painting.
Even his use of outline in the figures is
perfunctory and on occasion arbitrary,
while the leaning pose of the prophets
is pure convention. Thus the prime
distinction of the painting rests in
colour rather than drawing. It may be
relevant to note that Riza made only
very rare forays into book painting;
for one example, see 117.

Moses, as tradition demands, is
given greater prominence than Aaron,
who even lacks a halo. Red *naskh* is
used to distinguish the Qur'anic
quotations from the black *nasta'liq* of
the Persian text.

192
Abraham surrounded by angels
Miniature painting
Jami, *Haft Aurang* ("Seven Thrones")
Provincial school, mid-16th century
Private collection
Dimensions: painting, excluding
  margins, 163 x 100 mm
Published: Maggs Bros Ltd.,

Oriental Miniatures & Illumination,
Bulletin No. 1 (December 1961),
no. 3 (illustrated)

The story tells how Abraham was
tested when a group of angels created
an image of human shape to which he
(and they? cf. Qur'an ii. 32 and xv. 31
among other passages) prayed.
Thereupon his own wisdom failed him
and he heard the name of God.

Only two angels are mentioned by
name in the Qur'an but in the
following centuries, partly through
the influence of Jewish and Christian
beliefs, Islam developed its own
angelology. In the Islamic tradition all
angels worship and obey God; indeed,

miniatures often show them
performing the ritual prayers.

The text of this miniature states that
the angels are uttering pious formulae.
These are *tahlil* (repetition of the
formula "There is no god but God")
and *tasbih* (repetition of the formula
"Glory be to God"). *Tasbih* is held to
be the food of the cherubim in
particular.

Despite this other-worldly element,
the setting is clearly that of a mosque,
complete with a minaret and an upper
gallery, and the figures conform to the
prescribed attitudes of Muslim prayer.

For brief remarks on the style and
dating of the leaves from this
manuscript see **29** and **163**.

POETRY and MYTH

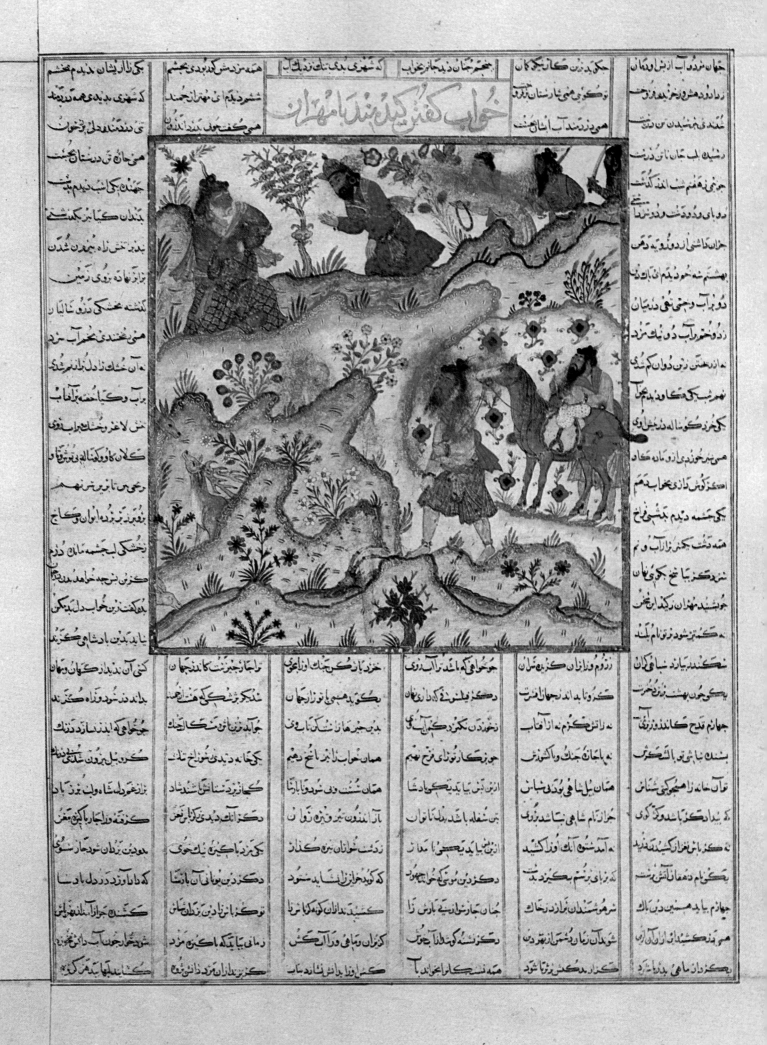

خواب گزاردن هند بامهران

It is no accident that the majority of Persian paintings illustrate poetic texts. Many princes were keen connoisseurs of poetry and the numerous small courts which flourished in Iran during the Mongol and Timurid periods would usually have their quota of poets. Thus the troubled political conditions favoured the wandering poet. The outstanding patrons of the time were without doubt the princes of the house of Timur, who have often been likened to oriental Medici. Shah Rukh was a rarity among them in that he quoted poetry but did not write it. Sultan Ahmad Jala'ir, a key patron of the later 14th century, can perhaps stand as the exemplar of the royal polymath: a painter, an illuminator, a craftsman in marquetry and mosaic, skilled in music – on which he composed treatises – a calligrapher in seven different hands, and a poet in Persian and Turkish. When menaced by the armies of Timur, he composed some defiant verses which he sent to the conqueror, only to be answered in kind by one of Timur's sons. The tradition of the royal poet continued into modern times in the person of Fath 'Ali Shah. In 'Assar's romantic poem *Mihr u Mushtari* (43, 127), the king of Khwarizm prepares various tests to discover whether Mihr is indeed a prince. In one of these tests Mihr displays his prowess as a chancery official by writing in elegant calligraphy a well-turned answer to the message of some foreign monarch. In another he provides some of the entertainment at a banquet by striking up an extempore melody on the harp and accompanying himself in singing an ode which he has composed impromptu.

The royal predilection for poetry, then, is a constant of Persian court life and the paintings in this exhibition, which mainly illustrate poetical works, bear witness to this fact. Nevertheless, the role of poetry in this courtly civilisation can easily be misinterpreted. The commissions of some royal patrons, such as Shah Rukh, laid more emphasis on historical works than on poetry. The demand for scientific works was steady. Above all, manuscripts of religious texts were produced in great numbers throughout the medieval period and the majority of these were not illustrated – although copies of the Qur'an in particular were richly illuminated. Even poetic texts had a wider significance to their readers than might at first sight appear. The *Shahnama*, for example, was valued as a work of history, even though elements of myth and fantasy may seem predominant to modern eyes. Mahmud of Ghazna went to great lengths to gather together extant manuscripts so that a received text of the national history could be established and then serve as the basis for a poetic rendering of this material. It seems very likely that the divisions which a modern reader makes between the "historical" and the "mythical" sections of the epic would have seemed

far less clear to the medieval mind. One further dimension of Persian poetry remains to be considered: the esoteric religious and mystical significance which underlies the exoteric subject-matter of so many poems. Sometimes, as in the case of the *Yusuf u Zulaikha* of Jami, the allegorical meaning of the story is explicitly expounded by the poet; at other times the reader is left to infer that such meanings are intended. In the case of the countless lyrics celebrating wine the controversy as to the

exact meaning intended by the poet still rages.

These remarks are not designed to imply that the fabulous recitals of the *Shahnama* and other texts were taken as the literal truth. The feats of Rustam especially were relished precisely for their hyperbole and became a staple of the iconography of the epic (205, 206). On the other hand belief in fairies and demons, and in their power to affect man's fate, is widespread in Iran to this day.

193
The Demotte Shahnama

Nineteen leaves from the most important illustrated *Shahnama* of the 14th century are exhibited here. Some sixty miniatures from this manuscript are known. In the early years of this century they were still bound together in a single volume: the Demotte *Shahnama*, named after the dealer who broke it up.

No Persian manuscript has given rise to more controversy than this. To an extraordinary degree it seems to come out of the blue and, despite the grand scale and ambition of its pictures, it seems to have left little lasting imprint on Persian painting. In these two respects the parallel with the Rashid al-Din codices is most striking. As in the case of those codices, several painters worked on the manuscript. But while the painters of the earlier manuscript almost all belonged to a single recognisable school, the Demotte artists exhibit several distinct styles. This variety within a single manuscript is yet another reminder that Persian painting was still in a state of flux. Part of the book's originality could be explained by the likelihood that the *Shahnama* had only recently established itself as a text for book illustration. Probably, therefore, the artists had to invent a good many of these scenes. Hence the uncertain, even clumsy, nature of some of the compositions. The awkwardness proclaims that a new, indigenous style is finding its feet.

This same awkwardness greatly complicates the problem of dating. A whole series of solutions has been proposed. Suggested dates have ranged between 1320 and 1400, though a date around 1335 seems to commend general support. Some scholars believe that work on these paintings continued for two generations. A book on the entire manuscript from the pen of Professor Grabar, who has spent many years studying these paintings with his students, is now in press and this may settle once and for all the vexed questions of dating and provenance.

The general characteristics of the Demotte *Shahnama* paintings can quickly be summarised. Their outstanding feature is a penchant for the dramatic. The later styles of Persian painting by and large lost the sense of frightening urgency that animates these pictures. The scenes depicted are of great moment, not simply decorative. They matter. So engrossed are the participants in the action that they turn their backs to us. The artists evoke at will the emotions of tragedy and terror, triumph and pensiveness. Their special affinity for scenes of the supernatural finds no satisfactory parallel in later *Shahnamas*, and the more familiar themes of grief and carnage take on a new portentousness. Bahram Gur slaying the dragon conveys a sense of hulking menace which it seems no 15th century figure can evoke, while the contortions of the dragon cause a premonitory shudder even before we locate its gaping maw. Faces are habitually huge in relation to hands and feet. Warriors or monsters loom in the shadows enclosing the main scene; indeed the colossal size of many of the figures in relation to their surroundings is unparalleled in 14th century painting except where giants are depicted.

Colour, too, is imaginatively employed to bring home the terror of a scene. Colour is in fact used in multifarious ways in the manuscript. The artists have departed decisively from the pale washes and tints of colour favoured by the painters of Rashid al-Din's *Compendium of Histories*. But although their colour range is much wider, they have not returned to the pure, intense, unmodelled colour of the Baghdad school; they prefer to model. In this respect too their lead was not followed by later painters.

Lastly, among many possible features of the style which there is not room to discuss here, emphasis must be laid on the spatial experiments carried out in the Demotte *Shahnama*. The most important innovation sounds quite simple: all the space is used. A powerful sense of design ensures that the compositions seem to fill the area available quite naturally. This sense of space is decidedly not Chinese, for in this manuscript, unlike those of Rashid al-Din, there are few blank spaces to rouse the imagination. The fleshy plants found in so many Mesopotamian paintings are used not simply as a base line but as borders or within the picture. The high horizon which was later to become so beloved a device of Persian painters is already in evidence, but it is only one spatial device among many. A coulisse system of overlapping diagonals leading the eye ever further back into the picture recurs repeatedly; elsewhere the artist displays a rudimentary sense of perspective or forces an understanding of the extent of the picture space by crowding figures into it.

The stature of the Demotte *Shahnama* cannot be denied. Perhaps it was, paradoxically, the very success of the manuscript that disheartened the next generation of painters and caused them to follow a different and altogether safer line of experiment. As it is, the book is a fragment that evokes a heroic age. It offers us a tantalising glimpse of what Persian painting might have become had conditions been different.

The bibliography for the book is vast. This *Shahnama* is mentioned in almost every handbook of Islamic art and some of its leaves have been very frequently exhibited and published. For reasons of space alone this massive massive bibliographical apparatus must be omitted. So too is a detailed analysis of each miniature. It must suffice to analyse only one leaf is depth. For the rest of the leaves the catalogue entry is confined to the subject, its description in the text of Firdausi, the dimensions of the leaf and the number it bears in the check-list drawn up by Doris Brian.

Select bibliography: *BWG*, no. 29; Stchoukine, *PI*, no. XV; de Lorey, *RAA* IX (1935), no. 1; D. Brian, *AI*. VI (1939), 97-112 and figs. 1-30; E. Schroeder, *AI* VI (1939), 113-42 and figs. 1-11; Schroeder, *Fogg*, 35-50 and pls. III-VII; I. Stchoukine in *AA* V (1958), 83-96 and figs. 1-6; R. Ettinghausen, in *KdO* III (1959), 56-65; Gray, *PP 1961*, 28-32; Grube, *MMP*, 13-20 and pls. 10-13; CB *Catalogue* I, no. 111; Robinson, *PMP*, no. 4; J. B. Travis, in *AQ* III/1 (1968), 63-75; O. Grabar in *Paintings from Islamic lands*, ed. R. H. Pinder-Wilson (Oxford, 1969), 32-47; Grube, *Classical Style*, 21-23 and pls. 2-12; O. Grabar in *The Cambridge History of Iran* V, ed. J. A. Boyle (Cambridge 1968), 653-7

193
(a) Rustam avenges his own impending death

Text, tr. Warner, V, 272

London, British Museum no. 1948 12-11 025 (formerly in Eckstein collection)

Dimensions: leaf 415 x 302 mm; painting 149 x 291 mm

Brian, no. 23

The distinctive qualities of the "Demotte" *Shahnama* can perhaps most conveniently be explored by the detailed examination of one miniature. This scene depicts how the dying Rustam, whose beloved horse Rakhsh has been impaled in a pit, shoots the culprit, his own half-brother Shaghad. Perhaps the single most striking feature of the painting is its expressive use of curves – e.g. the death agony of Rakhsh; the curve of the tree, whose concavity embraces Rustam just as its convexity crushes Shaghad, forceing him to the very edge of the picture frame, and the rhythmical undulation of saddle and quiver. There are still echoes of the Rashid al-Din manuscripts (**131** and **170**) in the use of tinted drapery. Thus the buff of the robes is heightened at the edges by red and the multiple small folds of the arm, shoulder and leg are etched in red or dark brown. But a significant change is that landscape has been allotted a more important role than hitherto. The tree plays a major part in the composition

not only by its bulk but by its shape, its size and its internal patterning reminiscent of some Chinese bronze. Indeed, the entire picture frame is invaded by landscape – diminutive flowers, fleshy plants, small trees and clumps of grass. Unlike later artists who repeated this scene, the artist here has the psychological penetration to show Rustam aged. The effort of his shot – another expressive if not realistic detail – has lifted him off the ground. Only the quintessentially heroic nature of the deed – shooting his enemy through a tree-trunk – justifies this. As elsewhere in the manuscript, the artist devotes much attention to the horrific aspects of the illustration – in this case, the scene of the horse and its gasping head. But he is capable of more subtle drama too: one has only to contrast the massive figure of Rustam, charged with tension, with the slack boneless quality of the slumped Shaghad. Finally, it is perhaps worth noting the use of colour – the gentle pastel tones belie the ferocious action.

The painter's response to the inherent drama of his subject did not blind him to his duties as a book illustrator. His picture had to be

193a

legible. He achieves this aim by means of a simple compositional schema – the picture divides quite naturally into four areas, all arranged serially, in the frontal plane – the horse in the pit, Rustam, the tree and Shaghad. This order follows the action of the story.

(b) *The funeral of Rustam and Zavara*
Boston, Museum of Fine Arts, no. 22.393
Dimensions: 296 x 157 mm
Text, tr. Warner, V, 274-5
Brian, No. 24.

(c) *Mihran Sitad selects a Chinese princess for Nushirvan*
Boston, Museum of Fire Arts, no. 22.392
Dimensions: 296 x 460 mm.
Text, tr. Warner, VII, 349-00
Brian, no. 58

(d) *Nushirvan's fifth banquet for the sage Buzurgmihr*
Cleveland Museum of Art, no. 59.330
Dimensions: page 412 x 292 mm; painting 242 x 215 mm
Text, tr. Warner, VII, 304
Brian, no. 54

(e) *Bahram Gur killing a dragon*
Cleveland Museum of Art, no. 43.658
Dimensions: page 407 x 295 mm; painting 197 x 290 mm.
Text, tr. Warner, VII, 42-3
Brian, no. 49.

(f) *Combat between Rustam and Isfandiyar*
The William Rockhill Nelson Gallery of Art, Kansas City, no. 33.60
Dimensions: page 401 x 292 mm; painting 162 x 289 mm
Text, tr. Warner, V, 229
Brian, no. 20

(g) *Afrasiyab killing Nawdar*
The William Rockhill Nelson Gallery of Art, Kansas City, no. 55.103
Dimensions: page 403 x 292 mm; painting 22.7 x 28.9 mm
Text, tr. Warner, I, 363
Brian, no. 13.

(h) *Bahram Gur in a peasant's house*
McGill University, Montreal
Dimensions: page 400 x 286 mm; painting 197 x 204 mm
Text, tr. Warner, VII, 46
Brian, no. 50

(i) *Bahram Gur hunting onagers*
Worcester Art Museum, no. 1935.24
Dimensions: page 593 x 401 mm; painting 219 x 196 mm
Text, tr. Warner, VII, 80-1
Brian, no. 51

(j) *Iskandar and his warriors fight a dragon*
Private collection
Dimensions: page 470 x 310 mm; painting 300 x 290 mm
Text, tr. Warner, VI, 151-00
Brian, no. 34

(k) *Iskandar leaving the land of darkness*
Private collection
Dimensions: page 430 x 310 mm; paintain 195 x 230 mm

Text, tr. Warner, VI, 162
Brian, no. 36

(l) *Ardashir and his dastur*
Private collection
Dimensions: page 440 x 315 mm; painting 220 x 190 mm
Text, tr. Warner, VI, 263
Brian, no. 44

(m) *Faridun leading Zahhak captive*
Chester Beatty Library and Gallery of Oriental Art, Dublin, no. P.111.1
Dimensions: 400 x 290 mm.
Text, tr. Warner, I, 169.
Brian, no. 4

(n) *Faridun, as a dragon, tests his sons*
Chester Beatty Library and Gallery of Oriental Art, Dublin, no. P.111.2
Dimensions: 400 x 290 mm.
Text, tr. Warner, I, 186-7
Brian, no. 5

(o) *Salm and Tur killing Iraj*
Chester Beatty Library and Gallery of Oriental Art, Dublin, no. P.111.3
Dimensions: 400 x 290 mm.
Text, tr. Warner, I, 200-01 (cf. **41**)
Brian, no. 6

(p) *Zal pays homage to Shah Minuchihr*
Chester Beatty Library and Gallery of Oriental Art, Dublin, no. P.111.4
Dimensions: 400 x 290 mm.
Text, tr. Warner, I, 306
Brian, no. 11

(q) *King Kaid of Hind and the sage Mihran*
Chester Beatty Library and Gallery of Oriental Art, Dublin, no. P.111.5
Dimensions: 400 x 290 mm.
Text, tr. Warner, VI, 91-7
Brian, no. 29

(r) *Bahram Bahramiyan enthroned*
Chester Beatty Library and Gallery of Oriental Art, Dublin, no. P.111.6
Dimensions: 400 x 290 mm.
Text, tr. Warner, VI, 313
Brian, no. 45

(s) *Nushirvan writes to the Khaqan of Chin*
Chester Beatty Library and Gallery of Oriental Art, Dublin, no. P.111.7
Dimensions: 400 x 290 mm.
Text, tr. Warner, VII, 349
Brian, no. 57

194
The Berlin Anthology of 823/1420-1
Manuscript: 950 ff. and 29 miniatures
Anthology containing works by Firdausi, Nizami, 'Attar, Khwaju Kirmani and Amir Khusrau Dihlavi
Shiraz, 823/1420-1
Copyist, Mahmud al-Katib al-Husaini
Berlin, Staatliche Museen, Preussischer Kulturbesitz, Museum für Islamische Kunst
Dimensions: leaf 236 x 157 mm; painting, variable
Previously exhibited: London 1931, Rome 1956, London 1976
Published: E. Kühnel, *Die islamische Kunst*, in A. Springer, *Handbuch der Kunstgeschichte* VI (Leipzig 1929), pl. X; E. Kühnel, in *Jahrbuch der Preussischen Kunstsammlungen* 52 (1931), 133-52, figs. 1-4 and pls.

6-16; *London 1931*, no. 467; *BWG*, 54, no. 45 and pls. XXXVII A-B; Kühnel in *SPA*, 1847 and pls. 862-4, 941A and 943A; Stchoukine, *MT*, 12, 16, 42-3, 45, 93, 99, 114 and 145; *Islamische Kunst aus den Berliner Museen* (Berlin, 1954) no. 329; *Mostra d'Arte Iranica* (Rome, 1956), no. 501 and pl. LXXXIII; B.W. Robinson in *AO* II (1957), 384; Robinson, *Bodleian* 95; Kühnel, *PM*, 12, 58 and pl. 16 (colour); J. Zick-Nissen, *Islamische Kunst. Ausstellung des Museums für Islamische Kunst* (Berlin, 1967; no. 273 and pl. 43; E. Kühnel, *Islamic Arts*, tr. K. Watson (London, 1970;, 48 and pl. IV; V. Enderlein, *Die Miniaturen der Berliner Baisonqur-Handschrift* (Frankfurt-am-Main, 1970); Kirketerp-Moller, *Bogmaleri*, 110 and 113; Hayward Gallery Catalogue, no. 555 a-b

Iskandar Sultan, a grandson of the great Timur, and briefly governor of Shiraz, was perhaps the major patron of book painting in the first two decades of the fifteenth century. The production of illustrated anthologies was something of a speciality of his atelier. Such a book was therefore a natural gift for his successor and cousin, Ibrahim Sultan, to send to his own bibliophile brother Baisunghur, the ruler of Herat.

This manuscript inaugurates a style which flourished in Shiraz for a generation. It marks the parting of the ways with the metropolitan style which had also been practised at Shiraz under Iskandar Sultan and which now removed to Herat. This new style is not fully formed in the Berlin *Anthology*. Moreover, at least two artists worked on the manuscript. The miniatures exhibited here include some of the best work in the book; many of the other paintings have ample vigour but are somewhat bare. Even the leaves on display attest a marked stylistic range and it is not inconceivable that they represent the work of more than one master.

The styles of the artists approximate most closely to each other in the depictions of battle. Such scenes were to characterise this Shiraz school. Mailed and helmeted soldiers, packed together in carefully arranged groups, peer out at the action from behind a rocky horizon. Frequently the central subject of the picture is the decisive moment in a single combat. The style is essentially masculine. Towering heroes perform remarkable feats of arms. These exploits are given maximum prominence not only by the size of the central tableau but also by the omission of extraneous detail. This starkness underlines the archaic quality of these miniatures – indeed, close parallels exist in late 14th century work. In some of the scenes the artist concentrates on the troops rather than the generals, and charging masses of cavalry roll remorselessly across the page. In these episodes, too, there is no room for pretty landscapes. The special quality of these battle scenes derives from the painter's awareness of where his true abilities lie. He is quite ready to jettison the decorative aspects of his art in order to create a striking illustration. Thus his clarity of purpose moulds his style.

Although battle scenes form the largest single group in the paintings of the manuscript, they do not predominate. An altogether more delicate treatment is reserved for most of the interior scenes, with their small figures and patches of jewelled colour. Occasionally the artist shows that he can command a monumental style, with impressive dignified figures against a choicely decorated landscape or interior setting. Both types of back-cloth display a remarkable zest for variety. In the more ambitious landscapes the only feature which recurs from one painting to the next is the general scheme of overlapping rounded hillocks. All the richer landscapes have a gold rather than a blue sky. But even in the more sumptuous miniatures the painter did not try to rival the achievement of the contemporary school of Herat. For him the attraction of simple, direct story-telling outweighs the desire for meticulous execution.

A constant variation in the size and shape of the painting from one page to the next testifies to the resourcefulness of the painter in dovetailing text and illustration. The text itself is arranged with such diversity that it too contributes to the aesthetic impact of page. It is transcribed in the newly fashioned *nasta'liq* ductus. Sometimes the calligraphy is tight and upright, with short ligatures; elsewhere, the scribe has room for manoeuvre, executes bold flourishes and increases the slant of the line. Headings and captions are given whole panels to themselves with thick gold margins, and their script is not in black but in red or gold, within a lightly ornamented setting. The central text, reserved for lengthy epics, is written within the disciplined format of four columns. The marginal verses, which are shorter lyrics, have no such divisions. They are punctuated by triangular end-pieces filled with floral sprays for which vermilion and blue are the favoured colours.

(a) *Khusrau before his father, Hurmuzd* (*cf.* **100**)

(b)|*Khusrau espies Shirin bathing* (*cf.* **23**)

(c) *Khusrau and Shirin hunting* (*cf.* **25**)

(d) *Khusrau and Bahram fighting*

(e) *Humay sees a picture of Humayun* (*cf.* **200**)

195
A Khamsa of Nizami dated 945/1538-9
Manuscript; 14 miniatures of which 6 are separately mounted
Nizami, *Khamsa*

Shiraz school, 945/1538-9
Signed Shaikhi Mudhahhib on (c) and (d) (information provided by B.W. Robinson
Private collection; formerly in Paul R. Loewi collection
Dimensions: leaf 312 x 200 mm
Previously exhibited: London 1951; Zürich and the Hague 1962; London 1967
Published: Robinson, *VAM 1951*, no. 43; Robinson, *VAM 1952*, 7 and pl. 19; Robinson, *PM*, pl. XVI (in colour; ; Stchoukine, *MS*, no. 105; B.W. Robinson, "Persian Painting", in *The Concise Encyclopaedia of Antiques* V, ed. L. G. G. Ramsay (London, 1961), 77 and pl. 55; *Kunstschaze atus Iran*, no. 995;

Robinson, *PD*, 140 and pl. 88; Robinson, *PMP*, no. 140

These paintings are typical of the best work produced by Shiraz painters in the second quarter of the 16th century. With pictures of this quality it becomes less easy to maintain the distinction between provincial and metropolitan work. Perhaps the decisive factor is a slight stiffness of drawing or, more likely, the firmly traditional handling of each scene. Clearly Shaikhi Mudhahhib is chary of innovation. Thus the sense of humour and caricature, or even the unexpected revealing detail, which marks contemporary Tabriz work is missing. Instead, the painter yields himself wholeheartedly to rendering textures. His carpets are gardens, his gardens carpeted with flowers. The emphasis on greenery is a Turkoman heritage. While the variety of the landscape cannot rival that in the best Turkoman work of c. 1500, its effect is almost equally rich. Like the Turkoman painters this artist relies on the accumulation of little details rather than on large expanse of colour.

Both interior and exterior scenes observe quite strict formulae. Interiors are blocked out in geometrical fashion by architectural features and by the text itself. The main action takes place within an arch whose apex is flanked and crowned by text panels with a further body of text acting as the base. Long narrow niches close off the sides of the composition; at least one of these niches has people watching the central scene from the window and the doorway. Every inch of the wall surface is covered with delicate patterning. The formula is a little less rigid for exterior scenes. Skies are usually ultramarine and have a gold Chinese cloud with a trailing wisp; sometimes these colours are reversed. The same flower-strewn meadow recurs constantly in the same colours, relieved by distinctive trees like golden Chinese lanterns. Neatly spaced spectators always punctuate the horizon.

This Nizami manuscript therefore exemplifies the degree to which a single artist could observe strict conventions and yet maintain a remarkably high standard of execution.

(a) *An old woman demands justice from Sultan Sanjar*
Dimensions: |307 x 203 mm.

(b) *Alexander and his seven sages in council* (*cf.* **78**)
Dimensions: 307 x 203 mm.

(c) *Bahram Gur in the blue pavilion* (*cf.* **18**)
Dimensions: 307 x 203 mm.

(d) *Shirin visits Farhad* (*cf.* **27**)
Dimensions: 307 x 203 mm.

(e) *Khusrav and Shirin playing polo*
Dimensions: 307 x 203 mm.

(f) *Bahram Gur hunting, watched by Fitna* (*cf.* **58**)
Dimensions: 307 x 203 mm.

(g) *Khusrau espies Shirin bathing* (*cf.* **23**)
Dimensions: 307 x 203 mm.

196
Isfandiyar slays the dragon
Miniature painting
Firdausi, Shahnama (text, tr. Warner)
Tabriz school, c. 1330
Boston, Museum of Fine Arts, no. 22.393
Dimensions: 162 x 125 mm

The stepped format recurs in many other "small Shahnama" painting (e.g. **134**), many of which have the same sense of explosive action as this leaf. The bold juxtaposition of gold and dark blue, however, lends this painting unusual distinction.

197
Mahan plagued by demons in the wilderness
Miniature painting; parent manuscript has 440 ff. and 38 miniatures
Anthology; this leaf illustrates the *Haft Paikar* from the *Khamsa* of Nizami (text, tr. Wilson, 196-7)
Probably Shiraz, 813/1410-11
Copyists, Mahmud b. Murtaza b. Ahmad al-Hafiz al-Husaini and Hasan al-Hafiz
Dedicated to Iskandar Sultan
Lisbon, Calouste Gulbenkian Foundation Museum L.A. 161, f. 72
Dimensions: 273 x 180 mm
Previously exhibited:
Published: for a general bibliography of this manuscript, see **45**

For the general context of the *Haft Paikar*, see **18**. On the fifth day, Wednesday, Bahram Gur is entertained by the Moorish princess in the blue pavilion. She tells the story of Mahan, an unfortunate who is beguiled by demons (see **198**) in the desert. He is befriended by a stranger in the night who gives him a horse, but to his horror this turns into a seven-headed dragon. Only when he calls on God for help does the prophet Khidr appear to restore him to his home.

The artist has allowed himself a certain licence in depicting the "dragon", and in adding trees to the desert landscape he has entered with gusto into the spirit of the text. The plight of Mahan, encompassed by *divs* and *ghuls,* is vividly rendered. These creatures are still popularly held to infest deserts. In the sharp, groping branches of the contorted trees harshly outlined against the sky the painter has found an apt symbol for the dangers that beset Mahan. They hem him in from above and below, evoking the greedy clutching hands of the *divs*. A

similar use of trees and other natural features is found in the Rashid al-Din manuscripts and in the Demotte *Shahnama* but this device was to lose favour in the course of the 15th century. Like other leaves from the manuscript, this painting divides the action into basically three superposed tiers. In this case it is a most effective technique, for every detail combines to focus on the diminutive forlorn figure of Mahan.

198
Sa'd fights demons
Miniature painting
Maulana Muhammad b. Husam al-Din, *Khavar Nama*, f. 104
Perhaps Shiraz, 881/1476–7
Signed: "the least of the slaves, Farhad. 881."/1476–7
Dublin, Chester Beatty Library and Gallery of Oriental Art, Pers. MS. 293, no.·1
Dimensions: page 400 x 280 mm
Published: for the parent manuscript and its dispersed leaves, see **16**. For this leaf, see CB *Catalogue III*, 61.

As in other leaves from this manuscript (**16, 101, 181, 187**) Farhad here demonstrates his gift for constantly evolving new colour harmonies. The

Islamic general Sa'd is shown dealing death to the *divs,* demons of ogreish appearance. These creatures, formerly prominent in the Zoroastrian religion, retained much of their importance in orthodox Islamic belief and played a major role in folklore. Thus it is told of 'Ali – a crucial figure in the *Khavar Nama* – that he subdued the strongholds of the *divs* and even converted them to Islam. The frequency with which these ogres appear in the *Khavar Nama* has indeed caused it to be placed in the category of "books for children".

The outward mark of the *div* is a bizarre animal head (cows' heads predominate) set on a blotchy human body. Perhaps primitive customs such as wearing animal skins and zoomorphic masks account for these peculiarities. At all events, while the *divs* shown here afford ample scope for colour experiments, they are not creatures of the artist's fantasy. Numerous illustrated *Shahnamas,* and even monumental paintings, provided ready parallels for such scenes. Perhaps, too, Rustam's horse Rakhsh inspired the detail of Sa'd's horse attacking a *div*. The crocodile on the other hand, whose

body seems encased in hexagonal tilework, deserves special praise as an original creation.

199
The prince at the court of the fairy queen
Manuscript; 220 ff., one double page and 13 single miniatures
Nizami, *Khamsa, Haft Paikar*: text, tr. Wilson, Rabi'I 823/April 1420
Shiraz or Yazd, end of
Copyist, Ja'far al-Hafiz (later known as Baisunghuri)
London, British Library, Or. 12087, ff. 153b – 154a (formerly in French collection)
Dimensions: open book 245 x 375 mm; each page 212 x 147 mm
Previously exhibited: London 1951
Published: Robinson, *V AM 1951*, no. 30; Robinson, *V AM 1952*, 7 and p. 2 ; Meredith-Owens, *Handlist*, 75; Titley, *Catalogue*, no. 322

For the text in general see **18**.
In the black pavilion of Saturn, the planet of disaster in Muslim astrology, the Indian princess tells Bahram Gur a story whose esoteric import is that man in his undisciplined state cannot hope to reach God. A prince, curious to know why the men of a certain country wear black, is shown how to reach an enchanted land. Here he falls violently in love with the queen of the fairies, who is rather unpropitiously entitled "Charming Turkish Predatory Raid". She leads him on but at the same time urges him to control his ardour for a brief period. This unsatisfactory situation continues for a month until the frustrated lover can no longer restrain himself, and seizes her. At once the idyll dissolves and he finds himself back where he began. Nothing remains for him but to don black attire too.

Despite the quantity of text on this double page, the composition is so well organised that the entire scene can be reconstituted in the mind's eye as if the text were not there. This is partly due to the unusual feature of leaving the illustration unconfined by any margin other than the page itself. The artist also responds to the demands of the page in making the figures in the narrow margin at the extreme right taller than any others in the picture. He has pictured the court of the fairies as a transfigured earthly court, as was customary (cf. f. 159b. of the *Anthology* in the British Library, Add. 27261, produced at Shiraz in 813-14/1410-12, but his choice of layout and his saturated colours are his own. The romantic paradisal setting is heightened by the star-spangled sky and a background carpet of vegetation. This latter detail foreshadows the Turkoman style whose earliest works are found, also in Shiraz, in the following generation.

This picture has suffered less from overpainting than the other miniatures of the manuscript, but even so it is far removed from its original splendour. The kneeling fairy offering refreshment

198

gives something of the flavour of the painting in its pristine state.

200
Humayun in the palace of the fairies

Manuscript; 67 ff. and 3 miniatures
Khwaju Kirmani, *Humay va Humayun*
Herat, 831/1427–8
Copyist, Muhammad b. Husam,
    called Shams al-Din al-Baisunghuri

Vienna, Nationalbibliothek, Cod.
N.F. 382, f. 10v
Dimensions: page 242 x 146 mm;
    painting 213 x 115 mm
Previously exhibited: Vienna 1901,
1935, 1953; London 1976
Published: Flugel, *Handschriften* I,
544, no. 561; *Katalog* 1901, no. 208;
Schulz, *PIM*, 95; *Ausstellung*,
E. Wellesz, *Wiener Beiträge zur Kunst –
und Kullurgeschichte Asiens* X (1936),
3–20 and figs. 1–3, 7–11; Holter, *Les
principaux manuscrits*, 95–7, no. 4;
Kühnel, in *SPA*, 1853; no. 16, fig. VII;
Schroeder, *Fogg*, 56, 70; *Buchkunst*,
no. 96; Stchoukine, *MT*, no. XXXII,
53, 99, 115, 146 and pl. LV;
B.W. Robinson *AO*, II (1957), 383–4,
390; Robinson, *Bodleian*, 62–3;
Robinson, *PD*, 132 and pl. 13
(colour plate of the opening exhibited
here); P. P. Sovcek in *Iranian Studies*
VII 11–2 (1974), 77–8; Hayward
Gallery, Catalogue, no. 557

Few miniatures could sum up more comprehensively than this the achievement of the early Herat school.

The painting depicts how Humay, while visiting the palace of the fairies, sees the portrait of Humayun, the daughter of the King of China, and is moved to tears. It has plausibly been suggested that the prince is a portrait of Baisunghur himself.

The format of the picture – almost twice as high as it is broad – recurs frequently in early Timurid painting and was especially favoured for interiors (c.f. for example the Khwaju Kirmani in the British Library, the Nizami in the Freer Gallery, the Rustam and Tahmina leaf in the Fogg Museum and the Gulbenkian *Anthology;*. Such interior scenes demanded ambitious architectural settings crowded with figures on several levels. Here the artist exploits empty spaces so deftly that a sense of clutter is avoided. Similarly, the exquisitely finished detail is subordinate to the stately overall design.

The portrait of the beloved, which is normally represented as being on paper, is here executed on a large-scale wall-hanging, presumably of silk. Not only is this peculiarly appropriate to Humay's Chinese descent; it also accords with a marked taste for paintings on silk at the Timurid court before c. 1450 (e.g **98**).

201
Scene from a fairy tale

Miniature painting
Unidentified text
Shiraz school, c. 1440

Private collection
Dimensions: leaf 265 x 175 mm;
    painting 105 x 45 mm

Previously exhibited: Oxford 1966
The miniature depicts fairies (*paris*) issuing from their castle to offer gifts to a ruler and his attendants, while two demons (*divs*) at the top of the wall glower at the scene. According to orthodox Muslim belief, God created other intelligent beings besides man. These were the tribe of *jinn*, created from fire; like man, they could be saved or damned. The *paris* (or *peris*), as benign *jinns*, still play an important role in Muslim folklore. The equivalent being in pre-Islamic belief in Persia was the *pairika*, "enchantress", and this sense lingered, for those who saw *paris* were apt to turn crazed with love. But they were considered well-disposed to mankind and their help was implored in time of trouble.

In its format the leaf recalls the slender anthologies of early 15th century Shiraz; its size suggests that, like the *Iskandar Nama* of c. 1405 in the British Museum, the parent manuscript was intended to be carried in a pocket. Similar books were still being produced in Shiraz in the early 19th century (cf. Robinson, *PMP*, no. 97, with further examples of this type of book). Even on this tiny scale certain Shirazi characteristics assert themselves, notably the rich deep colours and the faces of the courtiers stacked one above the other.

202
Angels in combat and amidst animals

Miniature painting
Firdausi, *Shahnama*
Herat school, c. 1450

Lisbon, Calouste Gulbenkian
    Foundation Museum, no. M. 66a
Dimensions: leaf 263 x 175 mm
Previously exhibited: Lisbon 1963
Published: Martin, *MP*, 100 and fig.
    241; R. Ettinghausen, *SPA*, 1966;
    Gray, *AOI* no. 121 (illustrated)

Manuscript illumination in Iran
reached its high-water mark in the
15th century and this leaf is worthy of
that great age. A good deal of ornament
is accommodated in the lateral
inscription panel but such is the
finesse of execution that the design
feels spacious rather than crowded,
while the inscription itself stands out
by virtue of its intense purity of colour.
In the rest of the margin the scale is
grander and thus the scrolls describe
their slow rhythms even more
casually. But the underlying discipline
is clear in the way that secondary
rhythms, which develop with equal
ease, are never permitted to disturb
primary ones. The eye is enticed to
enter this seemingly tangled thicket but
it cannot lose itself for long. The
companion leaf (M. 66b) depicts no
living beings and has much denser
ornament, but it lacks the hypnotic
rhythm that pervades this leaf.

As decoration for a *Shahnama* these
marginal scenes are highly unusual in
their format alone. The presence of
angels, and of heads both human and
animal, is even more unprecedented.
The daring poses – especially that of
the angel to the upper left – seem
stylistically out of tune with what is
known of metropolitan work around
1450. It also bears no relation to the
text. To parallel the playful fantasy of
these paintings one must turn to the
West, perhaps most conveniently in
the first instance to Armenian manuscript illumination. But such
ornament would not be wholly out of
place in 15th century Burgundian
illuminated prayer books. The concept
of a continuous scroll containing
creatures or masks ("the inhabited
scroll"), which underlies this leaf, is
also of western – in this case Roman –
origin. It is quite conceivable that
western manuscripts should have
reached the court of Herat, especially
since diplomatic ties had been
established with Europe in the
Ilkhanid period. For a similar scene
datable in the early 16th century and
attributed to Shah Quli, cf. E.
Preetorius, *Persische Miniaturen*
(Munich, 1958), 45 and pl. 4. At a later
stage an illustrated medieval western
manuscript is recorded in the library
of Shah 'Abbas.

203
Alexander and the sea-maidens
Miniature painting; parent manuscript

has 440 ff. and 38 miniatures
Anthology; this leaf illustrates the
    Iqbal Nama from the *Khamsa* of
    Nizami (see the translation by
    S. Robinson of W. Bacher's
    paraphrase and translation, in
    Persian Poetry (Glasgow 1883),
    222–3)
Probably Shiraz, 813/1410–11
Copyists, Mahmud b. Murtaza b.
    Ahmad al-Hafiz al-Husaini and
    Hasan al-Hafiz
Dedicated to Iskandar Sultan

Lisbon, Calouste Gulbenkian
    Foundation Museum, no. A. 161,
    f. 215
Dimensions: 231 x 144 mm
Previously exhibited: Lisbon 1963
Published: for a general bibliography
    of the manuscript, see **45**; for this
    leaf, see Gray, *PP 1961*, 70 and 76
    (colour plate;

In the second half of Nizami's version
of the Alexander legend an angel visits
the king and acquaints him with his
prophetic mission. He is commanded
to travel throughout the world
converting the nations to his faith and
civilising them. In the course of this

journey he chances on a sea-shore not
far from China where
"Every night, radiant as sun and moon,
The ocean-brides emerge from the bay,
Make on the shore their place of repose,
Warble their songs and frolic in their
    sports;
And every one whose ear their melody
    reacheth,
Loseth his reason in the sweetness of
    their voices."
Accompanied only by a sailor (who
here seems to glance at Alexander in
sly amusement) the king saw how
"Their ringlets lay scattered on their
    fair bosoms,
Like black musk on a plate of virgin-
    silver"
and at their song "his heart was set on
fire". The fable may ultimately derive
from the legend of the sirens.

The frank decorative bias of Persian
painting, and its prime function as book
illustration, find classic expression
here. The star-spangled night sky,
the extravagant rearing rocks and the
silver sea are not merely visual
hyperbole. They are the appropriate
setting within which to re-enact this
glamorous fantasy. A very similar

composition is repeated in at least three other manuscripts of the early 15th century: the British Library *Anthology*, Add. 27261; the so-called "Cartier Nizami"; and a Nizami in Leningrad, Hermitage MS. YP1000.

It is difficult to imagine the scintillating aspect of the painting in its original form, when the untarnished silver sheen of the ocean was the foil for all the other colours. In its diagonal bands of colour the painting recalls other Shiraz work executed a decade previously (**159**), while the mountains prefigure the bizarre crags of the Juki *Shahnama* (**28**). As in many other paintings in the manuscript, the scene is divided into horizontal tiers, but the artist has responded to his carefree subject so that no trace of rigid grouping remains. In fact the elegant gestures of the upper trio of maidens are used to focus attention on the centre of the picture. The light, insubstantial bodies evoke the fragile charm of these fairies and convey, by by means hard to analyse, the evanescent quality of this vision.

For other leaves from this manuscript, see **45, 65, 95, 174** and **197**.

204
A prince and page riding a fantsatic elephant composed of people, animals and fish

Tinted drawing in ink
Perhaps Bukhara, c. 1580–90; the trees and flowers in the foreground are later additions

London, British Museum, no. 1937 7–10 0328; formerly in Shannon collection
Dimensions: leaf 430 x 303 mm; painting 255 x 185 mm
Previously exhibited: London 1949, 1959

The concept of a creature composed entirely of other creatures is itself alien and disturbing to the Western eye, but the image itself exerts a repulsive fascination. The choice of creatures which make up the elephant's body seems to be arbitrary, and it is hard to detect a symbolic meaning for them – unless, indeed, they are intended to represent all creation of which the ruler is lord. Other drawings of this type, however, allow no such interpretation (cf. Grube, *MMP*, no. 70, and J. Strzygowski *Asiatische Miniatur-malerei* (Klagenfurt, 1933), Taf. 104). The idea may well have come from India; it was at any rate a popular manner both there and at Bukhara. Nonetheless, stirrings of similar concepts may be seen in the animated rocks of Turkoman painting (**110**) and in the evanescent figures of "The Court of Gayumarth" in the Houghton *Shahnama*, tentatively identified by Welch (*RPM*, 38) as earth spirits.

The medium of the tinted drawing is especially typical of late 16th century work. Here the touches of colour are few but varied. Most noticeable is the gold used for the trappings of the elephant-anklets, bells, howdah, straps and even the ankus of the mahout.

The youth serving the prince recalls the accounts of European visitors to the Safavid court, who noted that the Shah was served by boys trained to remain kneeling immobile, eyes downcast, as they offered him his food.

205
Rustam kicks away the rock rolled by Bahman

Miniature painting
Firdausi, *Shahnama* (text, tr. Warner, V. 184–5)
Shiraz, c. 1440
Private collection
Dimensions: leaf 165 x 110 mm

Isfandiyar was commanded by his father, King Gushtasp, to place Rustam in fetters, and he sent his son Bahman to Rustam to announce his intentions. Bahman, peering over a mountain crag, caught sight of Rustam and, fearful of his strength, rolled down a boulder to kill him. Rustam ignored the warning shouts of his brother and, addressing himself to his meal, nonchalantly kicked the boulder aside.

The miniature keeps closely to the text, though the artist has omitted the figure of Bahman who often peeps out from behind the rocks. Landscape and facial types accord with provincial Shiraz work of c. 1440; cf. **142**. Some of the miniatures in this latter manuscript share the rather muddy colours of this scene. Faces are drawn with much more care than any other element in the painting.

206
Rustam avenges his own impending death

Miniature painting
Firdausi, *Shahnama* (text, tr. Warner, V, 272)
Probably Shiraz, Shawwal 887/October 1482
Copyist, Murshid b. 'Izz al-Din Warzan
New York, The Metropolitan Museum of Art, no. 40, 38.2 (Samuel D. Lee fund, 1940)

Dimensions: page 324 x 214; painting
62 x 93 mm
Previously exhibited: Venice ,1962
Published: H. McAllister, *MMAB*
N.S. II (1943), 126–132 with
illustration on p. 127; Grube,
MMP, no. 50

Rustam had a half-brother, Shaghad,
who, envious of his success, plotted
with his father-in-law, the King of
Kabul, to compass his death.
Accordingly he dug a pit in Rustam's
favourite hunting grounds and
planted it with sharp weapons.
Rustam, mounted on his faithful
Rakhsh, plunged in and both were
fatally impaled. The hero begged a
bow from his treacherous half-brother
to protect himself from lions, and then
with his dying strength transfixed
Shaghad through the tree behind
which he had prudently sought refuge.

Like other favoured themes of the
Shahnama, the iconography of this
episode had by this time become fixed
almost beyond hope of renewal. The
sense of pathos with which Mongol
artists had imbued the scene (**193a**)
had been rejected, as had the dramatic
participation of nature. Instead, a
streamlined iconography had evolved.
The artist could now be sure that the
viewer would recognise the scene
instantly. He could therefore
concentrate his powers on embellishing
the scene with refinements of colour
and landscape. An example is the
treatment of the pit. In 14th century
painting this was habitually depicted
as a shallow depression of neutral
colour. Here it is a dramatic black gulf.

This image became the norm in
Safavid painting for scenes depicting
caverns, depths and the like. The most
pathetic figure here, paradoxically
enough, is Rakhsh, his legs buckling
under him in his death agony.

207
Shah Kai Ka us attempts to fly to heaven
Firdausi, *Shahnama* (text, tr., Warner, II, 102–4)
Copied for the Inju vizier al-Hasan
Qiwam al-Daula wa'l-Din, 741/
1340–1

Geneva, collection of Prince
Sadruddin Aga Khan, no. Ir. M. 6/B
Dimensions: 286 x 248 mm
Bibliography: Welch, *Collection* I, 68
and pl. on 72

The subject is a cautionary tale.
The mythical warrior king Kai
Ka'us had subjugated the demons
of Mazandaran and in revenge
one of them encouraged him to
believe that the sky itself should be his
domain. The king accordingly
devised "a distorted scheme devoid of
sense", harnessing four eagles to his
throne and setting meat skewered on
poles must beyond their reach.
Straining towards the meat they flew
up to the heavens, but their strength
failed at last and they came down in a
forest. There the humiliated king

lingered, begging forgiveness for his
hubris. Thus although the visual image
calls to mind the theme of apotheosis,
the king – like Lucifer, Icarus and even
Alexander – is reproved for his
blasphemous ambition. That the
source of this image is Sasanian – if not
ultimately Babylonian – has been
shown convincingly by H. P. L'Orange
in his book *Studies on the iconography of
cosmic kingship in the ancient world*
(Oslo, 1953).

The artist has freely interpreted the
text. The layout of the page has
persuaded him to show the birds
flying horizontally rather than
upwards; the meat is not shown; and
the birds have as much in common
with the ubiquitous Chinese phoenix
of Ilkhanid art as with eagles. The
canopied wicker-work contraption in
which the king sits is certainly no
throne. Lastly, the artist has preferred
not to show the king holding a goblet;
instead, he raises a pointing hand aloft,
perhaps as a humorous gesture of
encouragement to the birds. Their
haloes recur in other Ilkhanid versions
of this scene.

208
Bahram Gur wins the crown
Miniature painting
Firdausi, *Shahnama* (text, tr. Warner, VI, 409–10)
Possibly Tabriz, early 14th century

Kansas, William Rockhill Nelson
Gallery of Art, no. 46–41
Dimensions: leaf with borders,
155 x 121 mm; painting 57 x 119 mm

Previously exhibited: Syracuse 1967
Bahram Gur, the great hunter, found
his way to the throne barred because
the nobles of Iran, smarting under the
memory of his father's misrule,
distrusted his ability to govern wisely.
When Bahram arrived from exile they
had already sworn allegiance to a
certain Khusrau. Bahram thereupon
proposed that the crown of the realm
should be set on the imperial throne,
that two savage lions should be
chained to the throne, and that whoever
seized the crown from between them
should become Shah. The heart of
Khusrau failed him but Bahram duly
clubbed the lions with his ox-headed
mace and ascended the throne.

The hero, dressed in a robe of
flowered silk, dominates the frontal
plane, along with the leaping 'lions',
here depicted as tigers. The old man
wearing a similar robe, his hands falling
limply in a gesture of astonishment, may
be Khusrau or the high priest put in
charge of the throne and crown. Most
of the courtiers strung irregularly
along the rear plane seem indifferent to
the drama being unfolded. It is typical
of the simplifying trend of the artist
that the throne should scarcely be
recognisable as such; human and
foliate forms are apt to be rendered in
equally summary fashion. Such details
mark this as a reduced and speedily
executed reflection of one of the

metropolitan styles of Tabriz. For
other leaves from this manuscript see
133 and **135**.

209
Bahram Gur wins the crown from between the lions
Miniature painting
Firdausi, *Shahnama* (text,tr. Warner, VI, 409–10)
Provincial Persian, perhaps western
Indian, c. 1450
Private collection

Dimensions: leaf 265 x 180 mm;
painting 160 x 160 mm.
Previously exhibited: London 1967
Published: Robinson, *PMP*,
no. 113(c)

For the subject matter, see **208**; for
comments on style and provenance,
see **144, 145**. Shirazi features in this leaf
include the massed banks of spectators,
so arranged that they seem to peer
down at the action as if on a stage; and
the grassy background. Perhaps some
vestigial memory of the Samson
theme and of related lion-strangling
images – motifs that were especially
popular in early medieval textiles in the
Near East – can account for this
unusual interpretation of Firdausi's
text. Bahram Gur, bereft of his
ox-headed mace, rides one of the lions
bareback, while the ivory throne of
the King of Kings has shrunk to a
tarnished stool.

210
Bahram Gur and the dragon
Manuscript; 368 ff. and 8 miniatures
Nizami: *Khamsa* (*Haft Paikar*,
tr. Wilson, 52–4)
Shiraz style, 839/1435–6
Copyist, 'Abd al-Rahman al-katib
London, British Library, Or. 12856,
f. 177a
Dimensions: page 201 x 325;
painting 155 x 140 mm
Previously exhibited: London 1967
Published: B. Gray in *East and West*
XIV (1963), 220–23; Robinson,
PMP, no. 119; Meredith-Owens,
Handlist, 75; Titley, *Catalogue*, no. 324

This is one of the most imaginative
uses of nature in the whole canon of
Persian painting. The entire landscape
burns with the fury of the dragon.
His convulsive rage is well symbolised
by his claws which clamp themselves
on to rocks or clutch tree stumps. He
uncoils across the page, filling the
entire centre and lower part of the
picture. But his baleful glare and the
switchback position of his head draw
attention to Bahram Gur himself.
Narrow-waisted, his long flat face
encased in an ear-flapped helmet, he
conforms precisely, in his physical
type, his armour and his jerky movements, to the Shiraz style of Ibrahim
Sultan. Comparable conventions for
landscape characterise the Juki
Shahnama (**28**) and also occur in a
Jami' al-Tawarikh in Paris datable
c. 1415 (Stchoukine, *MT*, pl. L). A very
similar dragon-slaying occurs in a

manuscript formerly in the Martin collection and also dated 1436 – Martin, *PM*, pl. 53). It is easy to understand how the technique of rendering rocks by large spots should eventually have suggested to some artist that they contained faces (110), especially as similar modes are found in Islamic epigraphy.

211

Khusrau and the lion

Miniature painting
Nizami, *Khusrau u Shirin*
Probably Isfahan, 1091/1680 (for 1041/1631)
Copyist, 'Abd al-Jabbar
Signed Riza-yi 'Abbasi

London, Victoria and Albert
   Museum, no. L. 1613–1964
Dimensions: 245 x 140 mm
Previously exhibited: London 1967
Published: Robinson, *PD*, 136–7 and
   pl. 58; *VAM Bulletin* (April 1955), 57
   and fig. 3; Robinson, *PMP*, no.
   71 (b) and pl. 30

Khusrau and Shirin were disturbed in their tent one night by the roaring of a lion. The king at once rushed out and felled the lion with a blow of his fist. In this miniature detached from 117, Riza-yi 'Abbasi slightly varies the traditional composition. No reference to night-time is made. Khusrau is in night attire (his splendid hat apart) but there is no sign of Shirin and the tent. Instead, two ephebes watch impassively beside a carefully delineated architectural setting. As elsewhere in the manuscript, large areas of blank, unmodelled and rather violent colour compete. The 19th century illuminated border, though fine in itself, adds another jarring element to the colour scheme.

212

The simurgh swoops

Manuscript; 756 ff. and 148 miniatures
Firdausi, *Shahnama* (text, tr. Warner,
   V, 131–4)
Isfahan style; completed at Mashhad
   Rabi' II 1058/April-May 1648
Copyist, Muhammad Hakim al-Husaini
Artists: double-page frontispiece
   (ff. 5b, 6a) signed by Malik Husain
   al-Isfahani; f. 320b signed by
   Muhammad Yusuf. Robinson
   attributes 43 of the paintings
   (including f. 439a) to Muhammad
   Qasim
Patron: Khan 'Ali Shan Qarajaghay
   Khan, Governor of Mashhad and
   supervisor of the Mashhad shrine

By Gracious Permission of Her Majesty
   Queen Elizabeth II, MS A/6, f. 439a
Dimensions: Written surface
   265 x 150 mm
Previously exhibited: London 1951,
   1967
Published: Holmes, *Specimens*, no. 151;
   Robinson *VAM 1951*, no. 120, B. W.
   Robinson, *The Connoisseur*
   CXXVIII (1951), 180–1 and pls.
   X–XI; Robinson, *VAM 1952*, 7 and
   pl. 1; Robinson, *VAM 1965* and

pl. 35; Robinson *PD*, 137 and pl. 62; Robinson, *PMP*, no. 78; B. W. Robinson, *BM CX* (1968), 133–8 and figs. 24–35

The parallel between the Seven Stages (adventures) of Isfandiyar and those of Rustam has often been noted.

Isfandiyar repeatedly outshines the deeds of Rustam. The rivalry thus implied, which has its origins in the poem, is openly expressed when Isfandiyar undertakes to kill the Simurgh, the benefactor of Rustam and his father Zal (see 2). He approaches its lair in a chariot bristling with swords and when the simurgh has fairly impaled itself he emerges somewhat unheroically to complete the slaughter. But Firdausi, with fine poetic licence, resurrects the bird so that by its advice Rustam is finally able to kill Isfandiyar.

Although this is one of the most splendid manuscripts in its period, it was produced for a nobleman rather than for the King himself. In 1839 it

was presented to Queen Victoria by the principal wife of Kamran Shah, Prince of Herat.

The audacious colour harmonies of these luscious landscapes are not easy to parallel. In them a tradition of nature painting some three centuries old hovers on the brink of dissolution. The uniformly sharp focus of every plant and rock obeys ancient conventions, but elsewhere these are flouted. Careful modelling co-exists uneasily with the notion that the colour of an object is determined not by nature but by its fitness in the overall colour harmony (hence the blue horse).

The pages of this manuscript will be turned in the course of the exhibition and the following subjects will be shown:

(a) ff. 5b, 6a: Sulaiman and Bilqis (Solomon and the Queen of Sheba).
(b) f. 69b: Rustam kills the mad elephant.
(c) f. 520b: Haftawad and his son Shahvi hanged by Ardashir.

212

LIST OF LENDERS

Her Majesty the Queen	87, 150, 212
Anonymous	2, 11, 13, 17, 27, 29, 39, 46, 61, 62, 86, 97, 127, 150, 163, 182, 186, 192, 193j, 193k, 193l, 195, 201, 205, 209
The Aga Khan	16, 57, 71, 81, 132, 189, 207
Ashmolean Museum, Oxford	41
Berlin, Museum für Islamische Kunst	194
Bodleian Library, Oxford	19, 111, 112, 139
Boston, Museum of Fine Arts	51, 74, 75, 94, 98, 114, 156, 167, 188, 193b, 193c, 196
British Library, London	3, 12, 23, 37, 40, 48, 54, 79, 82, 83, 84 110, 119, 125, 128, 147, 149, 159, 161, 199, 210
British Museum, London	30, 56, 64, 70, 72, 76, 80, 85, 90, 91, 92, 99, 105, 107, 115, 123, 133, 135, 143, 151, 157, 158, 162, 168, 193a 204
Cambridge University Library	36, 177
Chester Beatty Library, Dublin	38, 100, 101, 108, 109, 120, 124, 125, 181, 193m, 193n, 193o, 193p, 193q, 193r, 193s, 198
Cincinnati Art Museum	22, 134, 173
Cleveland Museum of Art	5, 26, 96, 102, 136, 193d, 193e
Copenhagen, Royal Library	60
Edinburgh University Library	129, 130, 131, 180
Eton College, Windsor	178, 183
Fitzwilliam Museum, Cambridge	15, 18, 32, 35, 78, 113, 169
Fogg Art Museum, Cambridge, Mass.	7, 33, 67, 69, 116, 144
India Office Library, London	10, 24, 25, 47, 50, 89, 103, 121, 154, 165, 190
King's College Library, Cambridge	8, 9, 55
Lisbon, Calouste Gulbenkian Foundation Museum	20, 42, 45, 65, 95, 160, 174, 185, 186 197, 202, 203
McGill University, Montreal	122, 193h
Metropolitan Museum of Art, New York	93, 145, 172, 187, 206
Montreal Museum of Fine Art	137, 141
Paris, Bibliothèque Nationale	142, 191
Pierpont Morgan Library, New York	49, 106, 153
Princeton University Library	21, 63, 118, 171
Royal Asiatic Society, London	28, 34, 43, 77, 88, 104, 152, 164, 170
Royal Scottish Museum, Edinburgh	148
St. John's College Library, Cambridge	166
Selly Oak Colleges Library, Birmingham	31, 44, 52
Uppsala University Library	6, 14
Victoria and Albert Museum, London	58, 117, 140, 176, 211
Vienna, Nationalbibliothek	73, 175, 200
Walters Art Gallery, Baltimore	1, 53, 66, 138
William Rockhill Nelson Gallery of Art, Kansas City	68, 179, 193f, 193g, 208
Worcester Art Museum	193

BIBLIOGRAPHY

The bibliographies preceding the individual catalogue entries are not intended to be exhaustive. The better-known manuscripts are mentioned in most general histories of Islamic art, and in these cases the bibliographies are confined to a selection of the major publications.

For the sake of brevity, articles in journals are cited not by the title but by the volume number, date and page references. Articles in *Fetschriften* are also not given by title. Books and journals which are referred to more than once are cited throughout in abbreviated form.

The following abbreviations are used: *aarp Art and Archaeology Research Papers AA Arts Asiatiques*

Ackermann, *Guide*	P. Ackerman, *Guide to the Exhibitions of Persian Art* (New York, 1940)
Arnold, *PI*	Sir T.W. Arnold, *Painting in Islam* (Oxford, 1928) reprinted, New York, 1965)
Arnold, *ONT*	Sir T.W. Arnold, *The Old and New Testaments in Muslim Religious Art* (London, 1932)
Arnold and Grohmann, *IB*	Sir T.W. Arnold and A. Grohmann. *The Islamic Book* (Paris, 1929)
AI	*Ars Islamica*
AO	*Ars Orientalis*
Barrett, *PP*	D. Barrett, *Persian Painting of the Fourteenth Century* (London, 1952)
BDM	*Buchkunst des Morgenlandes. Katalog der Ausstellung im Prunksaal. Juni-Oktober 1953* (Vienna, 1953)
Blochet, *Inventaire*	E. Blochet, *Inventaire des manuscrits orientaux de la Bibliotheque Nationale* (Paris, 1900)
Blochet, *Peintures 1911*	E. Blochet, *Les peintures des manuscrits arabes, persanes et turcs de la Bibliotheque Nationale* (Paris, 1911)
Blochet, *Peintures*	E. Blochet, *Peintures de manuscrits arabes et turcs de la Bibliotheque Nationale. Societe francaise de reproduction de manuscrits a peintures* (Paris 1914-1920)
Blochet, *Enluminures*	E. Blochet, *Les Enluminures des Manuscrits orientaux de la Bibliotheque Nationale* (Paris, 1926)
Blochet, *MP*	E. Blochet, *Musulman Painting*, tr. C. M. Binyon (London, 1929)
Blochet, *Catalogue*	E. Blochet, *Catalogue des manuscrits persans, Bibliotheque Nationale*, III and IV (Paris, 1928 and 1934)
BMQ	*The British Museum Quarterly*
BM	*The Burlington Magazine*
BMMA	*Bulletin of the Metropolitan Museum of Art*
Brown, *LHP*	E. G. Browne, *A Literary History of Persia* (4 vols., London and Cambridge, 1908-1924)
BWG	L. Binyon, J.V. S.Wilkinson and B. Gray, *Persian Miniature Painting* (London 1933)
CB Catalogue	A. J. Arberry, E. Blochet, M. Minovi, J.V. S. Wilkinson, B.W. Robinson, *The Chester Beatty Library. A Catalogue of the Persian Manuscripts and Miniatures* (3 vols., Dublin, 1959-62)

Clarke	H. W. Clarke, *The Bustan* (London, 1879), Sa'di
Clarke	H. W. Clarke, *The Sikandar Nama e Bara* (London, 1881). Translation of part of the *Iskandar Nama* of Nizami
Cleveland Bulletin	*Cleveland Museum of Art Bulletin*
Cleveland Handbook	*The Cleveland Museum of Art Handbook* (Cleveland, 1958)
Codrington	O. Codrington, "Catalogue of the Arabic, Persian, Hindustani, and Turkish MSS in the Library of the Royal Asiatic Society (*JRAS* 1892, 501-69)
Connoisseur	*The Connoisseur*
Coomaraswamy, *Goloubew*	A. K. Coomaraswamy, *Les Miniatures orientales de la Collection Goloubew* (*Ars Asiatica* XIII, Paris and Brussels, 1929)
Darab	G. H. Darab, *Makhzanol Asrar. The Treasury of Mysteries of Nizami of Ganjeh* (London, 1945). Translation of the first book of the *Khamsa* of Nizami
Dimand, *Guide*	M. S. Dimand, *Guide to an Exhibition of Islamic Miniature Painting* (New York, 1933)
Dimand, *Handbook*	M. S. Dimand, *A Handbook of Muhammadan Art* (New York, 1958)
Ethé, *Catalogue*	H. Ethé, *Catalogue of Persian Manuscripts in the Library of the India Office* (2 vols., Oxford, 1903-37)
Flügel, *Handschriften*	G. Flügel, *Die arabischen, perischen und turkischen Handschriften der K. K. Hofbibliothek zu Wien* (3 vols., Vienna, 1865)
Gelpke, Mattin and Hill	R. Gelpke, E. Mattin and G. Hill, *Nizami. The Story of Layla & Majnun* (London, 1966)
Gladwin	F. Gladwin, *The Gulistan or Rose Garden* (London, 1808). Sa'di
Gray, *AOI*	B. Gray *et al., Arte do Oriente Islamico. Coleccao da Fundacao Calouste Gulbenkian* (Lisbon, 1963)
Gray, *PP 1930*	B. Gray, *Persian Painting* (London, 1930)
Gray, *PP 1961*	B. Gray, *Persian Painting* (Geneva, 1961)
Griffith	R. T. H. Griffith, *Yusuf and Zulaikha. A Poem by Jami* (London, 1882)
Grube, *MMP*	E. J. Grube, *Muslim Miniature Paintings from the XIII to XIX Century from Collections in the United States and Canada* (Venice, 1962; also in Italian)
Grube, *WI*	*The World of Islam* (Landmarks of the World's Art) (London, 1967)
Grube, *Classical Style*	E. J. Grube, *The Classical Style in Islamic Painting. The early school of Herat and its impact on Islamic painting of the later 15th, the 16th, and 17th centuries* (Edizioni Oriens, 1968)
Grube, *Kraus*	E. J. Grube, *Islamic Paintings in the Collection of H. P. Kraus* (New York, 1972)
Grube, *MI*	E. J. Grube, *Miniature islamiche* (Padua, 1976)

Guest, *SP*   G. D. Guest, *Shiraz Painting in the Six-*
                                           teenth Century (Washington, 1949)

Hayward Gallery Catalogue   *The Arts of Islam, Catalogue of the*
                                           Exhibition held at the Hayward Gallery
                                           8 April-4 July 1976 (ed. D. Jones and
                                           G. Michell, London, 1976)

Holmes, *Specimens*   Sir R. R. Holmes, *Specimens of royal,*
                                           fine, and historical Bookbinding
                                           selected from the Royal Library,
                                           Windsor Castle (London, 1893)

Holter, *Les principaux manuscrits*   K. Holter, *Les principaux manuscrits*
                                           a peintures de la Bibliotheque Nationale
                                           de Vienne. 2me partie. Section des
                                           manuscrits orientaux. Bulletin de la
                                           Societe francaise de reproduction des
                                           manuscrits a peintures XX (Paris,
                                           1937), 85-150, pls. XVII-XXXI

Holter, *PM*   K. Holter, *Persische Miniaturen*
                                           (Vienna, 1951)

Huart, *Calligraphes*   C. Huart, *Les Calligraphes et les*
                                           Miniaturistes de l'Orient musulman
                                           (Paris, 1908)

IAMMA   R. Ettinghausen (ed.), *Islamic art at the*
                                           Metropolitan Museum of Art (New
                                           York, 1972)

Ipsiroglu, *PCM*   M. S. Ipsiroglu, *Painting and culture of*
                                           the Mongols, tr. E. D. Phillips
                                           (London, 1967)

JRAS   *Journal of the Royal Asiatic Society*
KdO   *Kunst des Orients*
Katalog 1901   *Katalog der Miniaturen-Ausstellung*
                                           (Vienna, 1901)

Kühnel, *MIO*   E. Kühnel, *Miniaturmalerei im*
                                           islamischen Orient (Berlin, 1922)

Kühnel, *PM*   E. Kühnel, *Persische Miniaturmalerei*
                                           (Berlin, 1959)

Lillys, *OM*   W. Lillys, R. Reiff, E. Esin, *Oriental*
                                           Miniatures (London, 1965)

London, 1931   *Catalogue of the International Exhibi-*
                                           tion of Persian Art (Burlington
                                           House, London, 1931)

Marteau and Vever, *MP*   G. Marteau and H. Vever, *Miniatures*
                                           persanes exposees au Musee des Arts
                                           Decoratifs (2 vols., Paris, 1913)

Martin, *MP*   F. R. Martin, *The Miniature Painting*
                                           and Painters of Persia, India and
                                           Turkey (London, 1912; reprinted
                                           1968)

Martin, *MB*   F. R. Martin, *Les Miniatures de Behzad*
                                           dans un Manuscrit persan date 1485
                                           (Munich, 1912)

Martin, *MPT*   F. R. Martin, *Miniatures from the*
                                           Period of Timur in a MS of the
                                           Poems of Sultan Ahmad Jalair
                                           (Viennam, 1926)

Martin, *NM*   F. R. Martin and Sir T.W. Arnold, *The*
                                           Nizami MS in the British Museum
                                           (Or. 6810) (Vienna, 1926)

Meisterwerke   F. Sarre and F. R. Martin, *Die*
                                           Ausstellung von Meisterwerken
                                           muhammedanischer Kunst in
                                           Munchen 1910 (3 vols. and vol of
                                           photographs, Munich, 1912)

Meredith-Owens, *Handlist*   G. M. Meredith-Owens, *Handlist of*
                                           Persian Manuscripts 1895-1966
                                           (London, 1968)

Meredith-Owens, *PIM* — G. M. Meredith-Owens, *Persian Illustrated Manuscripts* (London, 1965)

Moghadam and Armajani, *Catalogue* — M. E. Moghadam and Y. Armajani, under the supervision of P. K. Hitti, *Descriptive Catalogue of the Garret Collection of Persian, Turkish and Indian Manuscripts, including some Miniatures, in the Princeton University Library* (Princeton, 1939)

Morley, *Catalogue* — W. H. Morley, *A descriptive catalogue of the historical manuscripts in the Arabic and Persian languages preserved in the library of The Royal Asiatic Society of Great Britain and Ireland* (London, 1854)

Mustafa, *Behzad* — Mustafa, *Persian Miniatures of Behzad and his School in Cairo Collections* (London, 1960)

Nott — C. S. Nott, "The Conference of The Birds by Farid ud-Din Attar" (from the French translation of *Garcin de Tassy*) (London, repr. 1974)

OA — *Oriental Art*

Pinder-Wilson, *Muslim Courts* — R. H. Pinder-Wilson, *Paintings from the Muslim Courts of India* (London, 1976)

Pinder-Wilson, *PP* — R. H. Pinder-Wilson, *Persian Painting of the Fifteenth Century* (London, 1958)

RAA — *Revue des Arts Asiatiques*

Rice, *IP* — D. T. Rice, Islamic Painting. A Survey (Edinburgh, 1971)

Rieu, *Catalogue* — C. Rieu, *Catalogue of the Persian Manuscripts in the British Museum* (3 vols. and Supplement, London, 1879-1895)

Riefstahl, *Catalogue* — R. M. Riefstahl, *Catalogue of an Exhibition of Persian and Indian Miniatures from the Collection of Demotte* (New York, 1934)

Robinson, *VAM 1951* — B. W. Robinson, *Catalogue of a Loan Exhibition of Persian Miniature Painting from British Collections* (London, 1951)

Robinson, *MMAM* — B. W. Robinson, *Persian Painting. Metropolitan Museum of Art Miniatures* (New York, 1953)

Robinson, *Bodleian* — B. W. Robinson, *A Descriptive Catalogue of the Persian Paintings in the Bodleian Library* (Oxford, 1958)

Robinson, *PD* — B. W. Robinson, *Persian Drawings* (New York, 1965)

Robinson, *PM* — B. W. Robinson, *Persian Miniatures* (Oxford, 1957)

Robinson, *VAM 1952* — B. W. Robinson, *Persian Paintings* (London, 1952)

Robinson, *VAM 1965* — B. W. Robinson, *Persian Paintings* (London, 1965)

Robinson, *PMP* — B. W. Robinson, *Persian Miniature Paintings from Collections in the British Isles* (London, 1967)

Robinson and Gray, *PAB* — B. W. Robinson and B. Gray, *The Persian Art of the Book* (Oxford, 1972)

Robinson, *Keir* — B. W. Robinson *et al.*, *Islamic Painting and the Arts of the Book* (London, 1976)

Robinson, *PMA* — B. W. Robinson *et al.*, *Persian and Mughal Art* (London, 1976)

Robinson, *IOL*   B. W. Robinson, *Persian Paintings in the India Office Library* (London, 1976)

Rome, 1956   *Mostra d' Arte Iranica. Exhibition of Iranian Art*. Istituto Italiano per il Medio ed Estremo Oriente (Rome, Palazzo Brancaccio, 1956)

Ross   J. Ross, *Sadi: Gulistan or Flower-garden: Translated, with an Essay, by James Ross* (London, n.d.)

Royal Persia   *Royal Persia*. British Museum (London, 1971)

Schroeder, *Fogg*   E. Schroeder, *Persian Miniatures in the Fogg Museum of Art* (Cambridge, Mass., 1942)

Schulz, *PIM*   P. W. Schulz, *Die persisch-islamische Miniaturmalerei* (2 vols., Leipzig, 1914)

Sotheby   Sotheby and Co., New Bond Street, London Sale Catalogues

Souvenir   *Persian Art: an Illustrated Souvenir of the Exhibition of Persian Art at Burlington House* (London, 1931)

Stchoukine, *MS*   I. Stchoukine, *Les Peintures des Manuscrits Safavis de 1502 à 1587* (Paris, 1959)

Stchoukine, *MT*   I. Stchoukine, *Les Peintures des Manuscrits Timurides* (Paris, 1954)

Stchoukine, *PI*   I. Stchoukine, *La Peinture iranienne sous les derniers 'Abbasides et les Il-Khans* (Bruges, 1936)

Stchoukine, *SA*   I. Stchoukine, *Les Peintures des Manuscrits de Shah 'Abbas Ier à la fin des Safavis* (Paris, 1964)

Stockholm, *OM*   Oriental Miniatures, National Museum (Stockholm, 1957)

SPA   A. V. Pope and P. Ackerman (eds.), *A Survey of Persian Art from Prehistoric Times to the Present* (London and New York, 1939)

Titley, *Catalogue*   N. M. Titley, *Miniatures from Persian Manuscripts. A Catalogue and Subject Index of Paintings from Persia, India and Turkey in the British Library and the British Museum* (London, 1977)

Tornberg, *Catalogue*   C. J. Tornberg, *Codices arabici, persici et turcici Bibliothecae Regiae Universitah's Upsaliensis* (Uppsala, 1849)

Warner   A. G. and E. Warner, *The Shah Namah of Firdausi* (9 vols., London, 1909-25)

Welch, *Collection*   A. Welch, *Collection of Islamic Art* (2 vols., Geneva, 1972)

Welch, *Isfahan*   A. Welch, *Shah 'Abbas and the arts of Isfahan* (New York, 1973)

Welch, *Artists*   A. Welch, *Artists for the Shah* (Yale, 1976)

Welch, *KBK*   S. C. Welch, *A King's Book of Kings. The Shah-Nameh of Shah Tahmasp* (London, 1972)

Welch, *RPM*   S. C. Welch, *Royal Persian Manuscripts* (London, 1976)

Wiet, *Exposition*   G. Wiet, *Exposition d'art Persan, janvier-fevrier 1935* (Cairo, 1935)

Wilson   C. E. Wilson, *The Haft Paikar* (2 vols., London, 1924). Translation of the fourth book of the *Khamsa* of Nizami

Zurich and the Hague, 1962   *Kunstschatze aus Iran* (Zürich, 1962)

CONCORDANCE

PREVIOUS EXHIBITIONS

List of exhibitions referred to in catalogue

Vienna 1901	*Miniaturenausstellung der K.K. Hofbibliothek*
Munich 1910	*Meisterwerke Muhammadanischer Kunst*
Paris 1912	*Exposition d'art persan*; Musée des Arts Decoratifs
Vienna 1916	*Buchkunst-Ausstellung der K.K. Hofbobliothek*
Philadelphia 1926	*International Exhibition of Persian Art*; Pennsylvania Museum. October-December 1926
Gothenburg 1928 } Copenhagen 1929 }	*Det danske Kunstindustrimuseum och Rohsska Kontslojdmuseet, Goteborg. Orientaliska miniatyrer och manuskript*
London 1931	*International Exhibition of Persian Art*, Burlington House. January-February 1931
London, BM 1931	British Museum. January 1931
New York 1933	*Islamic Miniature Painting and Book I Illumination*. Metropolitan Museum of Art. October 1933-January 1934
New York 1934	*Exhibition of Indian and Persian Paintings*. Demotte Inc.
Detroit 1935	*Institute of Arts*
Cairo 1935	*Exposition d'Art persan*. January-February 1935
Vienna 1935	
London 1936	British Museum
San Francisco 1937	*Exhibition of Islamic Art*. M. H. De Young Memorial Museum
Buffalo 1938	
Paris 1938	*Les Arts de l'Iran L'Ancienne Perse et Baghdad*. Bibliothèque Nationale.
London 1939	British Museum, March 1939
New York 1940	*Exhibition of Persian Art* The Iranian Institute
Baltimore 1941	
Cleveland 1944	*Exhibition of Islamic Art*. Cleveland Museum of Art
London 1949	British Museum. June 1949
London 1951	*Loan Exhibition of Persian Miniature Paintings*, Victoria and Albert Museum
Vienna 1953	*Buchkunst des Morgenlandes* Osterreichische Nationalbibliothek. June-October 1953
London 1954	British Museum

New York 1955	*Islamic and Indian Miniature Paintings.* Metropolitan Museum of Art. December 1955-February 1956
London 1955	British Museum
Rome 1956	*Mostra d'Arte Iranica.* Istituto Italiana per il Medio ed Estremo Oriente. May-September 1956
Ann Arbor 1959	*Persian Art before and after the Mongol Conquest.* The University of Michigan Museum of Art. April-May 1959
London 1959	British Museum. November 1959
Paris 1961	*Sept mille ans d'art en Iran.* Le Petit Palais. October-November 1961
Zürich and the Hague 1962	*Kunstschatze aus Iran*
London 1963	British Museum
Venice 1962	*Muslim Miniature Paintings from Collections in the United States.* Fondazione Giorgio Cini, San Giorgio Maggiore. September-October 1962. Shown thereafter at The Asia Society, New York. December 1962-February 1963
Lisbon 1963	*Exposicao de Arte do Oriente Islamico.* Museu Nacional de Arte Antiga
Oxford 1966	Ashmolean Museum
Syracuse 1967	Syracuse University, Syracuse, New York. April 1967
London 1967	*Persian Miniature Painting from Collections in the British Isles,* Victoria and Albert Museum. June 1967
New York 1968	*The Classical Style in Islamic Painting,* Pierpont Morgan Library
New York 1968	Metropolitan Museum of Art
New York 1970	*Masterpieces of Asian Art in American Collections.* Asia House Gallery
London 1971	*Royal Persia;* British Museum. October 1971
Oxford 1972	Bodleian Library. September 1972
London 1973	*Oriental Manuscripts,* British Museum
New York 1973 Cambridge, Mass., 1974 }	*Shah' Abbas & the Arts of Isfahan* Asia House Gallery, October-December 1973; Fogg Art Museum. January-February 1974
Abu Dhabi 1976	*Exhibition of falconry*
London 1976	*The World of Islam,* Hayward Gallery. April-July 1976
London BM 1976	*Paintings from the Muslim Courts of India,* British Museum. April-July 1976
London 1977	British Library, exhibition of oriental illumination

ERRATA

Owing to shortage of time, the text contains a fair number of mistakes and omissions. Errors and inconsistencies of punctuation are too numerous and too minor to be listed here, though they may disturb the attentive reader. Islamic specialists will note, for example, that the signs for *'ain* and *hamza* are occasionally transposed. The erratic punctuation occurs especially in the individual bibliographies. The separate headings of the catalogue information are also run together on occasions. These occasions, plus certain errors which occur repeatedly, such as the use of a semi-colon in place of a closing bracket, or the various misspelling of the name Kühnel, are not listed individually.

p.5
line 12 for *Humurzd* read *Hurmuzd*
line 21 for *Sebuktian* read *Sebuktigin*

p.7
the last two sentences should read: How much the work owes to my wife she knows better than anyone. My gratitude for her painstaking criticism of the text, and even more for the countless ways in which she has lightened my load over the past year, is heartfelt.

p.8
column 1, last line, should read: taste tended to favour poems above histories.
column 3: transpose lines 33-34

p.9
column 1, 8 lines from end: for *perenially read perennially*
column 2, 10 lines from end: for *surpringly read surprisingly*

p.16
no. 11, line 2: for Hilai read Hilali

p.17
no. 11, line 29: for *examplar* read *exemplar*

p.18
no. 14, line 21: for Lamm, *read* C. J. Lamm
no. 16, line 5: for Herat area, *read* Shiraz
no. 16, line 10: for *Mardun*, read *Mardum*

p.20
no. 21, line 19: for *Catalog*, read *Catalogue*

p.21
no. 24, line 6: add: , f. 124a
no. 24, line 42: for this *read* his
no. 24, line 64: for Khausrau read Khusrau

p.22
no. 27, line 9: for *v.i read* vi.

p.25
no. 34, line 4 should read: Wilson, I, 91)
no. 34, line 43: for inconography *read* iconography
no. 35, title: for cow *read* ox
no. 35, line 7 should read: Wilson, I, 91)
no. 36, line 9: for Brown *read* Browne
no. 37, line 2: for *Yusu* read *Yusuf*
no. 37, line 12: for, Stochoukine *read* ; Stchoukine
no. 38, line 1: for manuscript *read* manuscript is an

p.26
no. 39, line 3 should read VI, 52-6
no. 39: *delete* lines 7-8

p.27
no. 40, line 1 should read: Manuscript; 219ff. and 7 miniatures
no. 40, line 2: for *Mibr* read *Mihr*
no. 40, line 8: for Morley *read* Codrington

p.28
no. 45, line 7 should read: Probably Shiraz, 813/1410-11
no. 45, line 9: for al-Hasaini *read* al-Husaini
no. 45, line 12: for 1617f. *read* 161, f.7
no. 45, line 28: for Moller *read* Moller

p.30
no. 46, line 27: for Ali *read* 'Ali
no. 47, line 7: add, f. 372a
no. 47, line 29: for similarity *read* similarly
no. 48, line 20: for Pinder Wilson *read* Pinder-Wilson

p.32
no. 51, line 13: for *1951* read *1961*

p.33
no. 55: delete first line of bibliography

p.35
section title should read: The Court and its Ceremonies
no. 60, line 13: for *Refiae* read *Regiae*
no. 61, line 2 should read Firdausi, *Shahnama* (text, tr. Warner, III, 301-5)

p.36
no 62, line 2 should read Firdausi, *Shahnama* (text, tr. Warner, III, 337)
no. 63, line 10: for *Catalog* read *Catalogue*

p.37
no. 67, line 2: for Hafiz i Arbru *read* Hafiz-i Abru
no. 67, lines 18-19: for and (131

170) *read* mss. (131 and 170)

p.38
no. 70, in title: for **Guyuk** *read* **Güyük**
no. 70, line 29: for fig. g; *read* fig. 19;

p.39
no. 70, penultimate line: delete second "the"
no. 72, title: for **Hulegu** read **Hülegü**
no. 72, line 17: for *Hulegu* read *Hulagu*

p.40
no. 73, line 44: for 'mams *read* Imams
no. 74, line 8: for c. *read* C.

p.41
no. 76, line 4: for formerly Anet *read* formerly in Anet
no. 77, line 11: for Morley *read* Codrington

p.42
no. 80, line 1 should read: Miniature painting; c.1680

p.43
no. 82: delete line 15
p. 44 no. 86, line 7: for Kunstschatze *read* Kunstschätze
no. 87, title: for **Ali** read **'Ali**

p.46
no. 93: place line 31 after line 25

p.47
no. 94, line 9: for 1963 *read* 1962
no. 94, lines 14-15 should read: I. Stchoukine, *La peinture turque d'après les manuscrits illustrés* I
no. 94, line 36: for *Karagoz* read *Karagoz*
no. 95, line 7: for Mahamud *read* Mahmud
no. 95, line 22: for curiousity *read* curiosity

p.49
no. 99, line 7 should read: painting 180 x 115mm.

p.50
no. 102, line 14 should read: no. 82 and pl. LXXXIA; Dimand,
no. 102, lines 22-23 should read: no. 723; *Sept mille ans d'art en Iran* (Paris, 1961), no. 1080;

p.51
no. 104, line 1: for oo *read* 92
no. 104, line 11: for Morley *read* Codrington

p.53
no. 108, line 1: for present *read* parent
no. 109, line 2 should read: manuscript has 445 ff.

p.54
no. 111, line 5: for Din al *read* al-Din al-

p.55
no. 114, line 12 should read: Previously exhibited: Cleveland 1944
no. 115, line 5 should read: 10-10013

p.57
no. 119, line 19: for *Bogmaleir* read *Bogmaleri*
no. 120, line 2 should read: has 597 ff. and 131 miniatures

p.58
no. 122, line 7 should read: Montreal, McGill University, McGill
no. 122, line 10 should read: painting 105 x 243 mm.

p.59
no. 126, line 2: for ooff. *read* 230 ff.

p.60
no. 129, line 23: for Birnuni *read* Biruni

p.61
no. 131, line 16: for Ipsiroglu *read* Ipsiroğlu
no. 131, line 26: for 000-00 *read* 108-43
no. 131, line 69: for accoutements *read* accoutrements

p.62
no. 133, line 14 should read: L (1949), 89, fig. 1; Barrett, *PP*, 16
no. 133, line 16: delete
no. 135, line 5: add: , no. 1948 12-11 021; formerly in Eckstein collection

p.63
no. 139, line 4 for ruffian *read* cavalier

p.65
no. 143, line 13: for to *read* 16 no. 144, line 4: delete Art
no. 144, lines 55-6: for convention *read* conventions

p.66
no. 147, line 11: for Rich *read* Rieu

p.68
no. 152, line 1: for ff. *read* 269 ff.
no. 155, line 30: *Kunstschutze* read *Kunstschätze*
no. 155: delete lines 37-41

p.69
no. 158, line 10: add, 1931, 1949
no. 158, line 12: *delete* 1931, 1949

p.70
no. 159, line 30: *add* 44

p.71
no. 161, line 3: for *Yusufu* read *Yusufu*

p.72
no. 164, line 1: delete ff. and
no. 164, line 28: *add* a

p.74
no. 168, delete

p.75
column 3, line 37: for Sufim *read* Sufism

no. 170, line 63: for *PP* read *PP 1961*
no. 171, line 10: for *Catalog* read *Catalogue*

p.76
no. 172, line 18: for Suralo *read* Sura 10
no. 173, delete line 7
no. 173, line 51: delete e.g.

p.77
no. 175, line 11: for *manuscrit*, read *manuscrits,*

p.78
no. 176, line 28: for Qu'ran *read* Qur'an
no. 176, line 37: for *jinn* read *jinns*
no. 177, line 2 should read: Zakariya Qazvini, *'Aja'ib al-Makhluqat*
no. 177, line 3: delete *'Aja'ib*
no. 177, line 21: for frontispiece *read* frontispieces

p.80
no. 188, line 11: for Coomaraswanny *read* Coomaraswamy
no. 189, line 5: *add* II, 221
no. 189, line 37: for perhaps by *read* perhaps
no. 191, line 3: for Mansural *read* Mansur al-

p.85
column 2, 11 lines from end: for commend *read* command

p.86
column 1, line 39: *delete* massive
column 1, line 42: for is *read* in
column 1, line 61: for III/I *read* XXXI
column 2, line 18: for forceing *read* forcing

p.87
column 1, line 19 should read: Text, tr. Warner, VII, 349-53
column 1, 6 lines from end should read: Text, tr. Warner VI, 151-2
column 1, last line: for paintain *read* painting
column 2, 9 lines from end: for painting *read* paintings
column 3, line 14: for fur *read* für
column 3, line 20: for Moller *read* Moller

p.88
column 1, line 42: for fashioned *read* fashionable
column 2, last line should read: 55; *Kunstschätze aus Iran*, no. 995;

p.89
column 1, line 9: for expanse *read* expanses
no. 196 line 2 should read: Firdausi, Shahnama (text, tr. Warner, V, 127)
no. 197: *delete* line 14

p.90
no. 199, lines 4-5 should read: tr. Wilson, I, 126-42. Shiraz or Yazd, Rabi'I 823/April 1420
no. 199, line 16: for p. 2 *read* pl. 2

p.91
no. 200, line 12: for Flugel *read* Flügel
no. 200, line 14: delete *Ausstellung,*
no. 200, line 16: for Kullurgeschichte read *Kulturgeschichte*
no. 200, line 27: for Sovcek *read* Soucek

p.93
no. 203, 5 lines from end: *delete* by
no. 204, title: for **fantsatic** read **fantastic**

p.94
no. 207, title: for **Ka us** *read* **Ka'us**

p.95
no. 212, line 38: *add* early part of

p.96
last line: for 193 *read* 1931

p.97
line 6: for *Fetschriften* read *Festschriften*
line 11: for *Exhibitions* read *Exhibition*
lines 29, 33, 35, 41 and 45: for *Bibliotheque* read *Bibliothèque*
line 36 should read: *Nationale Société française de*
line 37: for *a* read *à*
line 50: for *Brown* read *Browne*

p.98
line 33: for *perischen* read *persischen*
line 34: for *turkischen* read *turkischen*

p.99
line 12 should read: *à peintures de la Bibliothèque Nationale*
line 15 should read: *Société française de reproduction des*
line 16: for *a* read *à*
line 26: for Ipsiroglu *read* Ipsiroğlu
line 43 should read: *persanes exposées au Musée des Arts*
line 50: for *date* read *daté*
line 55: for *Viennam* read *Vienna*
line 62 should read: *Munchen 1910* (3 vols. and vol. of

p.100
line 6: for *Garret* read *Garrett*
line 17: for Mustafa *read* M. Mustafa

p.101
line 46: for *Universitah's* read *Universitatis*
line 62: for *Persan* read *persan*
last line: for *Kunstschatze* read *Kunstschätze*

p.104
line 7: for *Hofbobliothek* read *Hofbibliothek*
line 18: delete *I*